CONTENTS

Just as our bread, mixed and baked, packaged and sold without benefit of human accident or frailty, is uniformly good and uniformly tasteless, so will our speech become one speech.

—*John Steinbeck,* Travels with Charley

INTRODUCTION

This is a book about American rock climbing. It's a celebration of the rich diversity in American climbing experiences, and it's an attempt to stand in the way of the insidious homogenization that is erasing the regional distinctiveness in every facet of American culture, rock climbing included.

Climbing, to me, isn't just climbing. It's experiencing places and people, and it's relishing their variety. When I began to travel as a climber, almost thirty years ago, the climbing areas seemed like different planets to me. And I liked this. Yet now, with rock gyms sprouting everywhere, and with a national climbing press chronicling the achievements and trends in the sport, climbers have been swept into a national group instead of being renegade members of odd local bands.

I fear, sometimes, that in the frenzied quest for high-end difficulty ratings, we risk seeing our places as simple means to an end. I hear people describe a route as "a 5.11" instead of "a beautiful crack." If this is the tendency for some climbers, then they are missing something important. If they don't know the wonder of the natural world, seasoned with the legends and myths of human endeavor—in other words, essences more abstract but every bit as vital as the handhold in front of their face—then their pursuit is sadly distilled to plain gymnastics. If their vocabulary doesn't include Camp 4, the Gendarme, the *Naked Edge,* or the Hex, or if they have to ask Yvon who?, then their experience is thin and bland and incomplete.

If you are new to rock climbing, or even contemplating giving it a try at the local indoor rock gym, *American Rock* will give you some grounding in the evolution of the sport, a description of the natural and human histories of America's climbing places, and a feel for what it might be like to experience the wide diversity of American rock climbing for yourself. If you are a climbing veteran, then you need no convincing. You already understand, and I hope you enjoy the tour. Use this book to reminisce—or, better, to inspire you to get back on the road.

My own first climbing trip was right after college, when a friend and I drove my 1967 Chevy Malibu across the Plains from his home on Long Island to Rocky Mountain National Park. The year was 1975, and the country was still nervously conserving gasoline two years after the Arab oil embargo given to us as punishment for our siding with the Israelis during the Yom Kippur War. The gas shortage (coupled with the fact that whenever my car exceeded fifty miles per hour, motor oil would spurt out from who knows where deep under the hood and coat the windshield with brown sludge) kept Mike and me poking our way cross-country at forty-eight miles per hour. After a brief breakdown on the Pennsylvania Turnpike followed by more than forty hours of straight driving, we crossed the state line into Colorado, where we picked up our first six-pack of Colorado's legendary Coors beer. Those were the days before Coors had gone national, and ceremoniously cracking open a sixteen-ounce beer brewed "naturally from Rocky Mountain spring water" meant we had made it. I somehow forgot that the mountains were still far off, and with six empties in the backseat, I was sound asleep as Mike drove into Denver.

You've got to do the drive to appreciate the size of America. Hopping a plane on one edge of the continent and stepping out at the other just won't do. The flat stretch between the eastern cities and the abrupt rise of the western mountains is a vastness that description can't capture. On and on it goes (especially at 48 mph). Rows and rows of corn flicker by your side windows like the lights of an old movie reel, while coffee overload and all-night talk radio team up to get you through that surreal stretch between two in the morning and the wondrous first pink of morning in the eastern sky. Stop at Denny's or Stuckey's or, better yet, find one of those four-calendar diners that William Least Heat-Moon describes in his classic *Blue*

Highways. Get out, stretch, and let the other guy take over the wheel and with it the all-important decisions of interior car temperature and choice of radio station. Eyes glaze over, hair gets greasy, and when you finally arrive in the mountains, your body feels as if it hasn't exercised in a month.

That 1975 trip and the many that would follow called up for me the magic of childhood trips with my family: the small victory felt when we passed another state line, the thrilling authenticity of places far away. And when I'd return, my own region took on sharper lines of relief to me, its culture more distinct, its flavors more local. Having been away, I now knew my home even more intimately as it became a caricature of itself in my mind.

VISITORS TO MY HOME AREA, New York's Adirondacks, enjoy the *place* every bit as much as the climbs. They appreciate its regional feel. To climbers around the country, the Adirondacks mean something. They hear the word and they think of nasty weather and moss-covered rock, cocky traditional climbers who take sadistic pride in creating routes that no one else will be able to do, routes that will lichen over in a few years anyway and so it won't matter. They think of heavy snows and beards, of stick furniture and blackflies, of unclimbed ice right off the road and a culture of climbers deeply resentful of any magazine that spills such news. In other words, when people hear "Adirondacks," they feel the sense of place on both conscious and less-than-conscious levels. They visit not just to do the climbs, but to immerse themselves in something bigger.

The Adirondacks isn't alone in its regional distinctiveness. Every climbing area has its own culture, its own feel. It offers its own unique experience to the traveler. I doubt that there's any country in the world where the climbing is so varied. Mention French rock climbing, for example, and people will generally conjure up the same singular image: gorgeous bolted sport climbing on white walls of limestone. But go to France and mention American climbing, and French climbers will construct a variety of images. Some will see the familiar lineup of the Teton Range, the most photographed mountains in America. Others will envision the odd volcanic plug of Devil's Tower jutting above the Wyoming plains, its fluted sides lined with vertical cracks, each a climbing route. Still others will think of the huge gray walls of Yosemite's El Capitan and Half Dome, vertical crack climbing so daunting to European pocket pullers. Mention American rock climbing and some will see the stark red towers of Utah's canyon country, its eerie silences echoing even in the imagination; still others will think of the northeastern hardwood forests exploding into color beneath historic crags like the Gunks or Cathedral Ledge.

On the most obvious level, each of these places offers a physical environment unlike the rest, with climbing as distinct as the views all around. To succeed at such a place requires adapting your technique to its unique demands. In Yosemite, it's repetitive jamming, patient grunting up cracks, and an immunity to acrophobia. Devil's Tower demands that you can stem like a gymnast. Southern sandstone rewards the climber with fingers of steel and lats like a flying squirrel. And Utah's canyon climbing wants a soft touch, for on some routes you can scratch your initials into the rock with your fingernails, and the insides of cracks are scarred with the double-tracked lines where well-placed Friends have ripped out in a fall.

Just as the physical qualities of a region are unique, so is its culture. And just as we need to widen our eyes to the peculiarities of a certain kind of rock and adjust our techniques accordingly, so too should we see the eccentricities of a place and experience it on its own terms. Just last evening I listened to a climber who had recently done the *Case Route* on Wallface Mountain here in the Adirondacks. It's not a climb you ought to have heard of; it's a tree-covered, zigzagging line typical of the climbing around here. He was a first-year climber, but he was astute enough to say, "As a climbing route, it was awful, but that's not why we did it. It was such a cool place, and to think of John Case finding his way up there back in 1933!" This climber understood that if he were to evaluate the *Case Route* according to standards fixed at other places and exposed in magazine images, then the climb would fall way short. The route was simply what it was, and for that it was a worthy adventure. By the same token, if you complain about the crowds at the Gunks, you are missing the essential truth about what the Gunks is. Mark Twain said that some people are such pessimists that they complain about a load of coal because it has too many prehistoric toads. There is probably a little of this in all of us, and unless we consciously resist it, we won't have as much fun when we travel.

THERE WAS A TIME not too long ago when rock climbing was the pursuit of a fringe element in just a few isolated pockets. Climbers learned locally and developed their methods in response to the demands of a specific rock type. There were so few climbers that everyone in a particular place knew each other, and a culture emerged unfettered by standards imposed from without. Seen through a Darwinian lens, each area was its own Galapagos, an isolated gene pool developing by itself, replete with its own language, its own grading system, its own shared goals and expectations. There were few travelers to seed gene pools elsewhere and few publications to rub smooth the hard edges of local quirkiness. As stories seeped out from the provinces, climbers learned not only where the places were, but, more important, what they meant.

They knew that the Gunks of southern New York, for example, was the site of a revolution where Vulgarians broke free of the Appalachian Mountain Club, treading on its rules and pissing on its members from the roof of a New Paltz bar. They knew about those North Carolina boys, running it out so far without protection on bald granite that a half bottle of Rebel Yell bourbon would hardly take the edge off after a day on the rock. They knew that Granite Mountain in Arizona had grades so stiff that El Cap veterans might be stymied there by a 5.7 crack. They knew where the gods lived: Boulder, Colorado, the land of Layton Kor; Camp 4 in Yosemite, where hands blackened by endless pitches of nailing passed a bottle around a picnic table and important stories were told.

Today there are so many climbers and so many climbs at so many climbing areas, it's impossible for us to know what each is all about. It's hard even for local climbers to know for sure who they are and what makes their own place different from the rest. Climbing is everywhere. The gene pools have mixed and merged. A national media has fixed in our minds an image of what climbing is and ought to be, an image by which we judge the quality of our climbing experiences.

Without doubt, the biggest change in the sport in the last decade or two has been the proliferation of sport climbs. Not only has the top-down approach opened up terrain considered unclimbable before, but it's also led to an explosion of new routes. Some cliffs get grid-bolted and only later do climbers connect the dots and establish the routes. This isn't necessarily bad, but it certainly doesn't seed the same romantic legends as in the days when the climbers set out from the ground, their route unclear and its outcome uncertain. A Colorado climber told me that he could easily recollect the name of his partner for every traditional route he had done over a thirty-year career but that he'd have a hard time naming many of his belayers for his sport routes.

This climber began like most climbers of old, as a hiker. Rock climbing was just a step in his development in becoming a complete mountaineer. Rock climbers of old were good with a compass, could read the clouds, knew the names of the trees and the wildflowers. Their eyes were wide open to the place, and they saw climbing as only one of many ways to experience it. The newcomer today comes from a climbing gym or instructional service, entryways to the sport in which the focus too often shifts from the wilderness experience to the numerical difficulty of the moves. Many new climbers are strong and skilled, but they tend to have gaps, both in their understanding of outdoor living and in their appreciation for the depth of climbing's heritage. A friend of mine visiting Smith Rock watched a teen lead a 5.12. Impressive for one so young. But unlike routes at the gym, this one had closed rings on the chains, not carabiners, and the kid was befuddled by the challenge of getting the rope through the rings to lower off until my friend (who wouldn't have been strong enough to do the route himself) patiently talked him through the process. A ranger at Hueco Tanks in Texas told me that he finally understood the widening gap between climbers and their world when he had to show two of them how to set up their own tent. I read of another on Mount Rainier who spoke with disgust about a cell phone message he had received from a climber high on a hard route, actually expecting this ranger to call back with directions.

This is not intended to be a shot aimed at the new generation of rock climbers. To the contrary, *American Rock* is intended to welcome them further into the rich and varied world of American rock climbing. It's a pursuit that simply does not exist in a vacuum. A route is more than just a route—it's an encounter with the physical world, and it's an association with climbers of past generations, climbers who set standards that we need to know and respect, regardless of whether we strictly adhere to their model.

ON ITS MOST BASIC LEVEL, *American Rock* celebrates the diversity of American rock climbing. It tosses a net over geographic regions or particular kinds of climbing, looks at the places and the people, and offers an idea of what it might be like to go there. On a more important level, the book encourages you to look with renewed freshness at your own place and reinvigorate your appreciation of it. Two friends of mine, having come back from Tahoe's Cave Rock (with its paved floor, stone belay benches, and dangling perma-draws), talked excitedly about all the new-route possibilities on the Adirondacks' Moss Cliff, potential lines they thought we had neglected in our staunch refusal to bolt. Later that week, a writer from *Climbing* magazine walked with me under the same cliff and, looking up at an unclimbed arête, said, "Wow. If this were in Colorado it would be a line of bolts. You guys have something special here."

The book is arranged according to categories, mainly geographic groupings, but also cultural and geologic ones as well. The groups distinguish themselves for a variety of reasons. At some, you want to immerse yourself in the legends and lore, the idiosyncrasies of the locals, the shared tales of human endeavor. At other places, the games men and women have played there seem insignificant relative to the grandeur of the place itself.

The discussion begins in the Northeast, the region physically closest to American climbing's European ancestry and the first to develop a sophisticated climbing culture. Yes, experiments in mountaineering were ongoing elsewhere, but not on the scale of New England. In fact, it was Harvard professor Robert Underhill who brought modern belay techniques west and became the catalyst for technical advances in the Tetons, the Sawtooths, and, most significantly, the Sierra. New England's climbing heritage is old and proud, and even now it's hard to find too many well-bolted sport routes up there. Geographically (if not chronologically), it is logical to move next to the Southeast. More than anywhere else in the country, the climbers there are aware of where they are from. Their traditions are deep, and it's impossible to climb on the big granite domes or the winding sandstone canyons without being aware that you are in Dixie.

The Northeast and the Southeast are entities based on cultural homogeneity. Further west, the exposed geology is so overwhelming that places are defined more by the rock than the people who have explored it. The Colorado River drainage, covered in chapter 6, "Canyon Country," is one such place. Here the West's mightiest river carves its way through soft red sandstone, stranding slender fingers of rock as islands in the sky and exposing sheer walls splintered by long, parallel-sided jam cracks. A visitor to canyon country is less prone to think about the peculiarities of Utah as a culture than to reflect upon the earth, so soft and so readily examined in layers of stone.

Same for the granite of California's Sierra. Just as one contemplates the softness of the canyon-country rock, so does one think about the apparent permanence of white granite on these, the country's biggest and blankest sheets of rock. If sandstone reminds one of the temporary earth, granite becomes the symbol of its perpetuity. Sure, Utah's canyons and California's granite have climbing stories as rich as those anywhere, but at places like these, the efforts of men seem puny in relation to the scale of the grand geological drama.

Still, climbing is a game played by people, and when they congregate, the shared experience becomes a facet of the pursuit as vital as the rock itself. As climbing evolved from the reckless antics of daredevils more toward a real sport with its own gear and language, outposts of activity emerged as well. Boulder, Yosemite, the Gunks—these were climbing's first hotbeds. Knowing this original holy trinity is still an important part of understanding the modern games. Chapter 5, "Tales from Three Cities," examines today's three largest and most vital hub cities of American climbing—Salt Lake City, Las Vegas, and, still, Boulder—drawing the relevant comparisons but, more important, enjoying the fun of their differences.

At the other end of the spectrum, chapter 10, "High and Wild," selects the best of American alpine rock climbing. Here the individual gymnastic moves are irrelevant next to the isolation, the effort, and the commitment of taking the game to high places like the Tetons or the Cascades. Many climbers see all the rest as merely practice for real climbing, alpine climbing. This last regional chapter completes the continuum from small-cliff cragging through big-wall climbing to real mountaineering.

Finally, *American Rock* closes with a discussion of the qualities that bring the regions together and a plea for climbers to unite in their defense. Though it is important to see the differences between the places, it's crucial to be able to step back as well and see their commonality. The future of rock climbing demands a confederacy of the outposts against forces much more ominous than homogenization.

THERE'S A FRIGHTENING PARADOX inherent in such a book as this: to celebrate the wonder of a place is to invite people to crowd it and jeopardize everything worth celebrating. Perhaps. But I feel strongly that it isn't the numbers of people using a place that matter as much as their sensitivity toward it. Some people grumble when they see others on a mountain trail that the wilderness is being spoiled. Not me. In those numbers I see a growing population of sensible voters, a strengthening voice in important decisions. Look at current access issues and imagine where we'd be without the power of our numbers. It isn't the two climbers ahead of you on the route who are the problem. It's the bonehead who doesn't know the place intimately enough to understand the impact of his campfire, his litter, his graffiti, his chisel, or his short-sighted failure to rally as an environmental activist. If such a person were to step back from the wall, perhaps even turn around to see the view, then we'd have little to worry about from his decisions.

Neither *American Rock* nor any other book can fully capture the essence of places and experiences in American climbing. Photos might show how a place looks. Words might describe its history. But nothing can supplant the spice smell of wildflowers on a high Colorado plateau, the cold gray touch of granite when you awaken on a Yosemite wall, the blue fear that pools in your chest as the weather turns worse and you're high on a Wind River ridge, or the desert sun resting like a malevolent weight on your shoulders and head. These you experience in your soul and in your gut, and these you must experience for yourself.

Appreciate what little travel you can squeeze into a hectic life. Look with fresh eyes at your own local climbing area, and know that though it might not match Yosemite for size or Boulder for history, it holds its own unique wonders. Appreciate them. And when you do find the chance to get on the road, know that it's the place, not just the climb, that will change the way you see your world.

Smith Rock, Oregon

1 AMERICAN ROCK CLIMBING

It is easy to interpret the games played out on local rock around the world as reflections of the larger culture. From the humble cliffs of Great Britain, where scruffy and irreverent working-class Brits act out life-or-death dramas on unbolted, unprotected 40-foot gritstone edges; to the fun-in-the-sun French Calanque, limestone crags that soar above busy Mediterranean beaches, with bolts everywhere and colorful arrows painted on the wall to show the way; from the famed Elbsandstein, sandstone towers near Dresden, Germany, where 5.10s were first climbed in the early 1900s, barefoot and protected with little more than knotted slings wedged into cracks in the soft rock; to the tent sites beneath Australia's Arapiles Mountains and the unruly locals who welcome visitors from the States by tossing aerosol cans unseen into their campfires. The richness of international culture is infused into an equally rich subculture of rock climbers.

So it is in America, a land blessed with all kinds of rock and all kinds of rock climbing experiences. Here, myriad climbing cultures emerged separate and distinct from one another, each a reaction to the particular challenges of a rock type of the region and a reflection of the people who lived there. To the European visitor, the American climbing scenes appear inconsistent, disjointed. At one place it's OK to drill anchor bolts while hanging on a rappel rope. Nearby, such behavior would ruin the integrity of the ascent, and so one is instead expected to fiddle with clean protection to protect the rock and the purity of the endeavor. At one place the handholds might be shaped mysteriously like the business end of a power drill. Somewhere else, modifying the rock would be like drawing a mustache on the Mona Lisa. And when change seeps into climbing scenes in Europe and elsewhere, it crashes like a giant wave over America's climbing scenes.

Even in the vastness and diversity of American rock climbing, however, themes universal to American climbing have emerged, mirroring in many ways the experience of the country itself. These are:

- The rapid development of tools and the associated questions about whether technology helps or interferes with our experience
- The struggle between structure and freedom. Even among climbers, once thought to be eccentrics rebelling against

social order, there's a paradoxical desire to impose rules and definitions to preserve this freedom.
- The people who push the boundaries and set the trends and the increasingly sophisticated media chronicling and interpreting their actions

Before getting to the individual regions, it is helpful to have an overview of American rock climbing; the local eccentricities stand out more clearly when you know how the tools, the techniques, and the interpretations have emerged universally.

Simple Beginnings

Hard to say where and when climbing began in America. Was it when the first Native scout scaled a high place to look for game or enemies? Was it Darby Field's ascent of New Hampshire's Mount Washington in 1642? Or later when prospectors Robert Clarke and Alexander Ralph ventured out onto more dangerous terrain in their 1850 ascent of Mount Colden's *Trap Dike Route* in New York's Adirondacks? What about the scramblings of the survey crew of Josiah Whitney, William Brewer, and Charles Hoffman, who began climbing peaks in California's Sierra in the 1860s? Or the Owen, Spaulding, Shive, Peterson ascent of Wyoming's Grand Teton in 1898? All were probes into steeper ground, each a significant step toward technical climbing as we define it today. Rock climbing, however, for the purposes of such a discussion and in the minds of the public, is probably best defined by its tools, the clever technology that allows passage over steeper and more perilous terrain as mountain hiking blends into technical rock climbing.

In the beginning, it would usually take two kinds of people to create a so-called technical rock climb: someone to declare it impossible and someone to envision a method by which to prove him wrong. Members of the 1860s' survey team that explored and documented California's Sierra climbed to the top of several major peaks, but they found one mountain simply out of the question. They described Half Dome in Yosemite Valley as "perfectly inaccessible, being probably the only one of all the prominent points about the Yosemite which has never been, and never will be, trodden by human foot." Such a claim

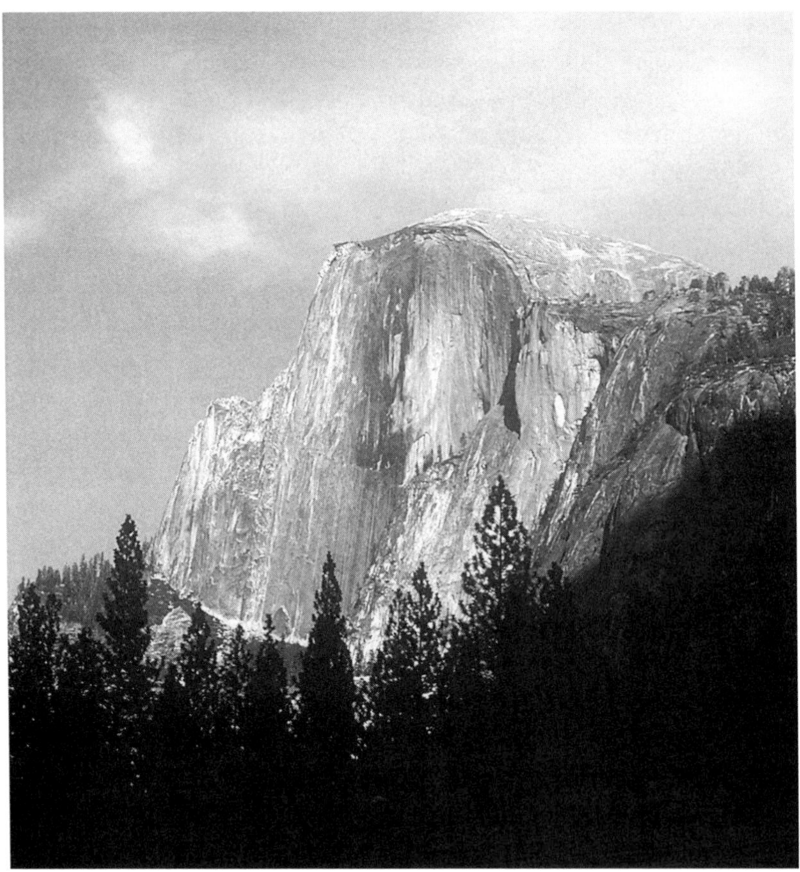

Half Dome

was bound to be challenged, first in 1871 when John Conway and company headed up with metal spikes they planned to hammer into cracks on the mountain's north flank, an abortive project picked up in 1875 by Scottish trail builder George Anderson. Using Conway's ropes to ascend the lower slopes, Anderson tackled the steeper upper section by arduously drilling eyebolts into the smooth stone, each a body-length apart, and standing perilously on one while drilling the next one higher. An outrageous accomplishment and America's first artificial climb.

Half Dome would go on to play a symbolic part in the changing role of technology in mountain climbing in this country. Near Anderson's route, a series of handrails and foot rests would later be installed, affording access to thousands annually drawn to this "perfectly inaccessible" summit but lacking the skills or equipment to get there. Today, the unsightly line of posts and cables seems inconsistent with the preservation of a park in tribute to a beauty John Muir called "a temple lit from above." Purists complain that the cables route on Half Dome should be removed. Temples like Half Dome ought not be desecrated.

In 1973, out to the right of the cables on the dead-vertical 2,000-foot *Northwest Face,* three climbers made such a statement—not with words, but with an ascent of the wall using radical "clean" gear, wedges of aluminum slotted into constrictions in the cracks instead of traditional pitons, steel spikes hammered into place but detrimental to the rock. By the early 1970s the crack scarring was getting serious, and popular routes were becoming lines of shallow holes where climbers were hammering in and then hammering back out progressively wider pitons. *National Geographic* ran a cover story about Galen Rowell, Dennis Henneck, and Doug Robinson and their successful leave-no-trace climb of the *Northwest Face.* Its influence was huge. By 1975 wedges, also called chocks or nuts, were commercially available, and the pinging sound of iron driven into rock so familiar to a generation of climbers was silenced. An era of rock conservation had begun.

In a flat corner of northeastern Wyoming stands another "inaccessible" summit, Devil's Tower, a volcanic plug rising 900 feet above the plains. It is one of America's oddest features, like the giant stump of an ancient tree, flat on top but sheer and vertical on all sides. Even if mortals would never set foot on its top, it was a place that needed, at least in legend, a first ascent and an explanation of its unique design. It seems that many years ago, seven Indian maidens were fleeing a great bear. They jumped upon a low rock and prayed that it would grow above their pursuer's reach. With the great bear's claws embedded in the stone, the rock steadily rose, leaving marks that stand today as proof of the event. The seven maidens rose to the heavens to become the constellation Pleiades.

For a while, divine intervention was the only way to the top of Devil's Tower. This was true until the down-home ingenuity of two local ranchers led to another strange technological triumph over the impossible. Willard Ripley and William Rogers toiled away for several weeks, pounding wooden stakes into a vertical crack on the south face of the column to fashion a crude and airy ladder to the otherwise inaccessible summit. On July 4, 1893, quite a crowd gathered at the base of Devil's Tower to watch the raising of the Stars and Stripes from its top. The flag was unfurled, shouts echoed from the Tower, cheers erupted from below, backs were slapped, and the party that had begun the night before went on with new fervor.

In the following years, the stake ladder grew increasingly rickety. After about two hundred ascents, the National Park Service removed the lower stakes, rendering the ladder useless and ensuring, the rangers supposed, that no one would ever again set foot on this odd piece of elevated prairie. Wrong. Renowned German climber Fritz Wiessner made the first conventional rock climbing ascent of the Tower in 1937 with Lawrence Coveny and Bill House, following a series of strenuous wide cracks to the left of the stake ladder. The crux this time wasn't the climb itself but the two years of bureaucratic haggling with park officials over permission for the climb.

The Tower was quiet again until October 1, 1941, when George Hopkins landed atop the Tower by parachute. Hopkins was a well-known skydiver, having established records for height, length of free fall, and number of jumps. This time he planned to collect on a fifty-dollar bet by lowering himself off the Tower on a thousand-foot rope dropped from a plane. Hopkins would toss the rope over the side to a group of assistants and pull up a sledgehammer, pulley, and iron spike. He'd pound the spike into a crack in the rocks on top, attach the rope, and let himself down. Simple. But rangers, fearing a public relations disaster compounded by tragedy, refused the party permission to send up the tools. None of this mattered anyway, since the rope dropped from above lay tangled on a ledge below the stranded parachutist. By this time, headlines about the stranded jumper shared American front pages with news of fighting on the European front of World War II.

When a series of attempts to rescue Hopkins was unsuccessful, Jack Durrance, who had made the Tower's second ascent only a few years earlier, cabled from New Hampshire, offering his help. By the time he arrived on the scene—after bad-weather flights and all-night train rides—the weather had worsened and ice coated the rock. Nonetheless, Durrance led a group of eight to the top, where he introduced himself to a remarkably calm George Hopkins, who began a series of rappels to the ground. He was greeted by more than three thousand spectators.

Trick ascents would fade in the years to come and technical rock climbing would gain some legitimacy, symbolized by the rope and its deft use to safeguard climbers. The rope was first employed for such a purpose in Europe in the 1800s, arriving on the North American scene around the turn of the twentieth century with European guides in the Canadian Rockies, such as Edward Feuz Jr. and Conrad Kain. Both were very accomplished climbers for their time, but they had little influence on the burgeoning activity in the United States. Here, there were some unschooled, seat-of-the-pants employments of the rope by climbers ignorant of current belay techniques, who were simply figuring out what to do with the rope as they went along. In 1910, for example, George Flagg, Mayo Tollman, Paul Bradley, and a partner they called Mr. Dennis climbed the Pinnacle in New Hampshire's Huntington Ravine. Flagg was a cartoonist who later sketched the event with scenes of two men hauling a less able companion up a steep section and of one man holding his partner roped on the edge of a platform, heaving boulders into the abyss. (These sketches were discovered and reprinted many years later by Guy and Laura Waterman when they were researching *Yankee Rock and Ice,* their history of northeastern climbing.) About the same time in Colorado, the Rocky Mountain Climbers Club was making ascents of the 1,300-foot *East Face* of the Third Flatiron above Boulder, but generally adhering to the idea that using a rope was cheating.

In 1916 John Case, who would later become president of the American Alpine Club, returned to his summer home in the Adirondacks of New York from a season of climbing in the Alps, bringing with him the latest in roped climbing techniques. Shortly before his death at age ninety-three, Case would explain his explorations on the cliffs around Keene Valley, New York, as simply "sparkin' a young lady," a girl brave enough to accompany him on some of the country's earliest technical climbs, later to become Mrs. Case. In 1919 Willard Helburn, another climber schooled by alpine guides in Europe, led a roped party up the *Chimney Route* on Maine's high and remote Katahdin. Either way, whether it was simply an intuitive method to save one's skin or a direct transplant from the experienced guides in the Alps, the rope soon became a regular part of mountaineering in America.

A New Attitude Emerges

Two events changed the course of rope work in American climbing. First was the systematic importation of European methods by Harvard professor Robert Underhill, with his paper *On the Use and Management of Rope in Rock Work,* and second was the introduction of nylon to make that rope virtually unbreakable. Underhill had already impressed the climbing world by adding a second route on the Grand Teton. The *Underhill Ridge* ascent was so unlikely, the story goes, that his camp cook threatened to carry a six-shooter to town because he knew people would call him a liar. Underhill's 1931 visit to the Sierra Nevada Range of California forever changed American rock climbing. Not only did he succeed in easily knocking off the unclimbed *East Face* of Mount Whitney, but he also held "Underhill camp," where he taught up-to-date rope skills to the Sierra climbers.

The essence of that rope work was the belay, a nautical term adopted by climbers to describe protecting a partner by wrapping the rope around one's hip, ready to hold tight to arrest a fall. Soon after Underhill's visit, the Californians devised the *dynamic belay,* in which one gradually arrested a fall by letting some rope slip deliberately through one's hands. With the fall stopped more gently, the hemp rope was more likely to survive the impact, and it even became conceivable to stop a falling leader. Up to this point, the hemp rope was only expected to hold a sliding fall on a snowfield or the body weight of a second climber slipping below a well-positioned leader belaying from above. But the huge forces that accumulate with a falling body would likely sever the rope. Climbers all knew the story of the 1865 first ascent of the Matterhorn and its tragic outcome. The lead climber, Edward Whymper, and two others braced themselves when a lower climber slipped. The hemp rope connecting the team broke, sending four others 4,000 feet down the mountain to their deaths.

Leaders, thus, simply didn't fall. They couldn't take the risk. The game of rock climbing was mainly based on one skilled climber ascending to a ledge where he could brace himself and offer rope

Wyoming's Teton Range

assistance to a weaker climber below. Each section was called a *pitch*, and though modern pitches might be as long as 200 feet, early pitches were defined by the distance to the nearest secure ledge. New Hampshire's classic *Whitney-Gilman Ridge* route, for example, was initially climbed in seventeen pitches in 1929. Today, the 600-foot route is often done in five. To be a leader in those days was to be so sure of oneself that a fall wasn't even possible. John Case, for example, never fell even as second on the rope in all his years of climbing. To do so, he said, would expose a weakness, and he pledged to quit climbing for good if it ever happened to him.

This was the way and thinking of all climbers until World War II and the development of a synthetic fiber they would call nylon. Its first commercial application was for bristles in toothbrushes, and later it replaced silk in ladies' stockings; but for the climber, here was a rope strong enough to hold any fall, and elastic enough to absorb any shock. Mountain troops were first to use the new ropes, but after the war, nylon quickly replaced hemp on the crags.

Nylon changed attitudes. At Tahquitz Rock in southern California a group of rebellious upstarts, including Don Wilson and

Royal Robbins, began challenging the limits found by the old guard of the Rock Climbing Section of the Los Angeles chapter of the Sierra Club. In 1952 Wilson and Robbins took a look at the *Open Book,* a route that had been climbed only by standing in slings attached to pitons in the crack to pass sections thought impossible to climb unaided. Robbins knew that a free ascent of the *Open Book* would be a coup, yet such an ascent would require a shift in attitude: accepting the risk of a leader fall. Robbins placed a solid piton below the crux, trusted that his nylon rope could hold a fall from above this protection, and decided that he could "probably" make it. The "probably" is where climbing leapt from old to new. He didn't fall, and his newly freed route was the hardest yet done in America, the first to receive a 5.9 grade in the decimal rating system.

The American difficulty rating system is mistakenly called YDS, or Yosemite Decimal System, when in fact it originated at Tahquitz Rock. It refines an older system that rated climbs as first class through sixth class—first class being little more than a steep trail; fifth class being the hardest level of *free climbing,* where ropes and other gear are used only to stop a fall; and sixth class being artificial climbing, or *aid climbing,* where the climber ascends by standing in stirrup ladders attached usually to pitons driven into cracks. The fifth-class designation included what we generally refer to as rock climbing today. The YDS broke this down decimally, calling the easiest fifth-class category 5.0 and the ultimate attainable 5.9. Inevitably, harder routes than the *Open Book* were climbed, and despite initial reluctance to embrace the mathematically illogical 5.10, 5.11, and so on, the system is now open-ended, with climbers now edging into the 5.15 range. Routes graded 5.10 and up are further delineated by the letter grades of *a* through *d,* with 5.12a, for example, being much easier than 5.12d. Grades are subjective, of course. Some regions or areas are soft, handing out high grades freely; older areas in particular adhere to more conservative grading.

Today, climbers fall. A lot. Gone are the days when falling meant failing, when hanging on a rope for repeated ascents was disparaged as shameful *hangdogging.* Today's hardest routes require many attempts, and with solid bolts, steep rock, and skilled belayers, leaders can take to the air with impunity. There are times when the protection is sketchy or the terrain so low-angled and blocky that a leader can't afford to take the risk of falling; but in the modern bolt-protected sport-climbing venues, falling and hanging on the rope are essential to progress, and anyone with John Case's conservative reluctance to fly is doomed to mediocrity.

Innovations in climbing equipment are usually followed by surges in new and more difficult routes. And typically, any time a new piece of gear is introduced by one climber, another is quick to dismiss it as cheating and stealing away the essential meanings of climbing itself. Crampons and pitons, gymnastic chalk and expansion bolts, sticky rubber and camming units called Friends—each was scoffed at by doomsayers who believed the new technology marked the death of climbing, but each gradually gained admission and the sport remains healthy.

Yosemite National Park, where George Anderson first drilled his bolt line up the shoulder of Half Dome, would be the scene of many of these innovations that would push the sport of rock climbing forward. First in a series was the introduction of the hard steel piton by eccentric Swiss ironworker John Salathé in response to the thin and endless cracks on Yosemite's big walls. European pitons had till then been made of softer iron that would deform to fit the crooked crack as it was hammered in. The soft iron pitons would generally remain fixed in place for future ascents. Finding the parallel-sided and hairline cracks of Yosemite distinctly unsuited to such malleable pitons, and knowing that walls the size of Yosemite's would require repeated use of the same pitons, Salathé got to work forging his own design out of harder carbon steel, some say from the axle of a Model-A Ford. These tough new pitons would penetrate a dead-end seam, and even when driven to the hilt could be removed by hammering them back and forth (unfortunately leaving a rounded scar behind). With his new pitons and his unusual fortitude, Salathé completed several historic, multiday ascents, including the *Lost Arrow Chimney,* Sentinel Rock, and the *Southwest Face* of Half Dome. Big-wall climbing was born.

Like all challenges once deemed impossible, the 3,000-foot face of El Capitan, the country's largest and highest expanse of sheer vertical rock, drew glances from an increasingly audacious group of climbers dwelling in Yosemite's Camp 4, the exclusive climbers' camp. Again, not only would it take a visionary to even read the linkage of cracks and corners up the smooth face, but it would require some new gadgets as well. Warren Harding was a maverick of the 1950s' climbing scene, often engaged in verbal sparring matches with the cerebral Robbins, who was articulating in articles and interviews a higher meaning to climbing than simply getting to the top. Harding, it seemed, was indeed interested in simply getting to the top, and he was willing to bend some rules to do so.

First, he acknowledged that such an ascent would require siege techniques, fixing ropes higher and higher on the face and rappelling down for rest and supplies. Keeping a lifeline back to the ground was considered poor form by many climbers because it demonstrated a lack of commitment to the adventure. Even so, the 1958 climb of El Cap's *Nose* route was a monumental effort. In order to facilitate the hauling of supplies, Harding's partner Bill Feuerer designed a wheeled contraption that could be pulled more easily up the rope than a simple hauled bag. The *dolt cart* took on Feuerer's self-deprecating nickname. A third of the way up, Harding's team encountered a series of long vertical cracks too wide for any of the pitons of the day. Harding scrounged old angle-iron legs from discarded stoves to solve the problem; today, the stoveleg cracks are among the *Nose* route's most classic passages.

Blank sections on the route required either pendulum swings to link climbable cracks or lines of expansion bolts drilled laboriously into the hard granite. Harding burned out a few partners, but finally, with Wayne Merry and George Whitmore, he topped out after an all-night drilling session to install the final twenty-eight bolts up the blank headwall. After forty-five days over eighteen months, America's highest cliff had been climbed.

Big-wall siege tactics like those employed on Harding's ascents of El Cap and Half Dome would be played out with some controversy the world over, but none was so maligned as Cesare Maestri's 1970 *Compressor Route* on Patagonia's Cerro Torre, during which more than 350 bolts were drilled using a 160-pound gas-powered air compressor. Obviously, given the time and the tools, any steep piece of stone could be climbed, and fear of assured success galvanized American climbers to adhere to a higher standard, to impose limits, and to accept the style of ascent as more vital than the result of the effort.

Throughout the 1970s climbers sought clean, ecologically pure ways to climb, leaving the hammer behind and relying on skill and commitment. Advocates of purity preached to America's climbers that it was better to raise themselves to meet the challenges of a climb than to lower the climb to accommodate their own weaknesses. It was an era of idealism, of long hair and drugs, of wildly flowered shirts. More than ever, climbers took to the road, cross-pollinating the isolated climbing scenes. Volkswagen vans with license plates from all over clustered at campsites, and legends grew. In the East, Henry Barber and John Stannard were systematically free-climbing the aid routes and trumpeting the virtues of clean climbing. In Colorado, Steve Wunsch and Jim Erickson were doing the same. In persuasive and often elegant prose, leaders such as Royal Robbins and Doug Robinson in California and Pat Ament in Colorado were describing climbing as so much more than simple raw athleticism; it was a far more spiritual thing. It elevated and enlightened. And it was worth doing right. The rock-friendly gear grew more sophisticated as Tom Frost introduced the six-sided Hexentric nut, and in the late 1970s Ray Jardine took the Hex's camming principle a giant step further when he marketed the first spring-loaded camming device, the Friend. This single piece of gear solved once and for all the frustrating problem of the parallel-sided crack, typical of Yosemite and so hard to climb without a hammer.

With their burgeoning climbing heroes and their walls bigger and more sheer than those in Europe, American climbers believed that they had achieved a level of accomplishment unmatched anywhere else. Henry Barber toured Germany, England, and Australia and dazzled locals wherever he went. *Mountain* magazine of Great Britain, the English-speaking world's leading climbing voice, pictured Barber on its cover, calling him Hot Henry. As they entered the decade of the 1980s, American climbers were smug about their position in climbing, declaring one route after another to be the world's hardest. *Supercrack* (5.12) at New York's Shawangunks reigned for a while after its first ascent by Steve Wunsch in 1974. In Yosemite, Jardine climbed *Phoenix* in 1977, unveiling his clever new Friends on the world's first 5.13. In 1979, Tony Yaniro free-climbed Tahoe's *Fracture Roof,* saying this was harder than the rest and renaming the climb *Grand Illusion.* America was king and its kingdom was cracks.

But American supremacy was a grand illusion indeed. In 1985, four visitors from four different countries arrived, and these same hardest routes fell, one after the other. German Wolfgang Gullich and Australian Kim Carrigan climbed *Grand Illusion.* British climber Jerry Moffatt climbed *Phoenix* first try, no falls. Perhaps most impressive of all was the visit of Le Blond, French climbing star Patrick Edlinger. After a string of successes during his 1985 visit, he came back in 1988 to dominate the country's first big commercial sport-climbing competition on the 110-foot Cliff Lodge at Snowbird, Utah. His performance was dazzling: after pulling through a hard section by jamming a single ring finger in a hole, he stood in perfect balance and calmly put *both* hands behind him at the same time to chalk up. The women's division was taken by another French climber, Catherine Destivelle.

There was some irony to the French sweep at Snowbird because for a while the French hadn't been given much respect in the climbing world. In the 1970s two of Britain's top climbers, Ron Fawcett and Pete Livesey, had visited the thousand-foot limestone walls of the Gorge of the Verdon in south-central France. Not only did they repeat the hard routes, but they also gave a lesson in cleanliness to the French, who had adopted a "pound and pull" approach to climbing. Rather than trying to free a hard move, they'd just whack in a piton and aid-climb through it. It was a vestige of alpine mountaineering, where getting to the top in one piece was more important than doing it stylishly. Grabbing slings to get through hard moves became known disparagingly as French-free. Speed climbers on El Capitan would French-free sections instead of standing in stirrup ladders, or *etriers,* on aid routes. That was OK. In the realm of free climbing, however, the term implied that the French weren't up to American standards. But while American climbers were concentrating on style more than difficulty, their counterparts across the Atlantic were turning their fingers into steel on steep pocketed limestone, safely protected by bolts installed on rappel. For the first time the boundaries of raw physical achievement, unencumbered by stylistic constraints, could be probed and expanded.

The Great Shift of the Late 1980s

In 1987 three of America's top climbers, Scott Franklin, Christian Griffith, and Dale Goddard, traveled to France, climbed extensively, and confirmed that climbers on French limestone had come a long way since their lessons from the British and that they had indeed surpassed the Americans. Griffith later wrote a funny, self-deprecating confession called "Learning to Crawl" for *Climbing* magazine. He described his humbling struggle in France, including a vain effort to lose weight by forgoing water and even sculpting his fingertips with files and sandpaper to fit the tiny pockets on *Chouca,* a route he finally grabbed toward the end of his visit. Goddard followed it with "Where We Stand," admitting that the United States had fallen behind in the past few years but predicting that we could close the "Euro-American gap" if we changed our attitudes.

Yet critics dismissed so-called Eurotactics—practicing moves and bolting on rappel—as a specific response to crackless limestone and insisted that such methods had no place on American rock. When such practices reared up at traditional areas like the Gunks or Yosemite, they met militant resistance. Yet in unknown places that had earlier been dismissed as either unclimbable, unprotectable, or simply unappealing, where there was no deep tradition of clean climbing, no cadre of judgmental locals, climbers began experimenting with Eurotactics. Within a span of five years, sport climbing—hard gymnastic rock climbing on routes with closely spaced protection bolts installed on rappel—would explode across the land. New areas nudged the traditional bastions from the headlines. Out West it was American Fork and later Logan Canyon in Utah, Virgin River Gorge in Arizona, and Mount Charleston near Las Vegas. In the East, it was the overhanging sandstone of the Cumberland Plateau, home to Kentucky's Red River Gorge, West Virginia's New River Gorge, and a host of lesser-known gashes in the rolling hills of the South. One after another these crags would be pictured in the national magazines, and one after another each would reign as hot spot of the moment.

The real birthplace of American sport climbing, however, was an isolated outcrop near Bend, Oregon, called Smith Rock. Here the first shots of the revolution were fired. It was here that Alan Watts and others abandoned the traditional start-from-the-bottom method and began to establish routes by cleaning and bolting on rappel. At first these practices met almost universal scorn. But when a few of the world's best climbers arrived from overseas and proclaimed Smith Rock to be the best area in America, sport climbing was given a stamp of legitimacy. Bolted routes multiplied, while in places like Yosemite it seemed that more energy was expended in bitter wrangling than in climbing itself.

TO BOLT OR NOT TO BE

When the story of the emergence of sport climbing is told many years from now, Smith Rock will be at the center of the tale. It's a place today that exudes history, albeit a short and recent one, but one that in time will surely stand out as embodying one of the most important shifts in climbing practice and philosophy that this country has seen. Walk along the Dihedrals and look up at *Watts Totts,* or marvel at the overhanging profile of *Chain Reaction,* or finger the ground-level pockets of *To Bolt or Not to Be,* the country's first 5.14 and the aptly named symbol of the French Revolution, climbed by J. B. Tribout during his historic 1988 visit. To be at the base of these routes is akin to being in a museum, for each was embedded in the Great Debate, and each is a familiar name to a generation of climbers, whether they visited Smith in the flesh or watched the evolution vicariously through articles and letters to the editors in *Mountain, Climbing,* and *Rock & Ice.*

Even old-school visitors to Smith Rock agree that the place simply wouldn't be much of a climbing area without the new tactics. The rock is soft, and cracks are few. But it's hard to nudge aside a clean climbing tradition rooted in the beliefs of mountaineers like Geoffrey Winthrop Young, who said, "Getting to the top is nothing. How you do it is everything." These values were shared by most American climbers, and in the early days of sport climbing, anyone who chose to employ dirty tactics at established climbing areas would meet blistering opposition, including verbal attacks, written diatribes in the climbing media, vandalism to cars and property, and even fistfights. The heavies of the sport were simply not going to allow the sacred values to be violated. To do so would "rob future generations" of good climbing projects and would be an affront to the bold pioneers who had gone before.

But central Oregon wasn't part of any such scene. It was home to a very small band of explorers and saw very few climbing visitors. It was free from any deeply rooted culture. (Two of the pioneers at Smith

Rock, in fact, were Jack Watts and Jim Ramsey, whose sons Alan and Bill were leaders of the new-tactic revolution. There isn't much animosity when it's all in the family like this.) And it isn't as though climbers like Watts didn't try to follow the rules established at places like Yosemite Valley. It was just that such methods didn't seem to apply to the soft rock, called welded tuff. Watts would later write in his *Climber's Guide to Smith Rock* that he had spent "two years climbing increasingly disgusting cracks [but] the crack climbing era was dead-ending quickly, so I turned to the blank faces of the Dihedrals out of desperation for something new." In retrospect, the move was logical. To continue in a traditional style that grew from drastically different rock types would have led only to dangerous and dirty routes. To Watts, the adoption of Eurotactics wasn't simply a cheap way to get harder routes; it was the only sensible way to proceed.

Within a few short years, Alan Watts had become one of the country's best climbers, and his *East Face of Monkey Face* route was reputed to be the hardest route in America. Climbers elsewhere, especially those who hadn't been to Smith, derided his tactics, took cheap shots in the magazines, and even harassed Watts when he traveled to other places. When he climbed Yosemite's hardest thin crack, *The Stigma,* in good style from the ground up with very few falls, locals who hadn't even witnessed the achievement claimed that he had cheated his way up the route. He must have. He's a hangdog. They shouted obscenities from afar and left nasty notes on his car.

But confrontation wasn't Watts's style. Instead, he just bore down on Smith and the list of 5.12s and 5.13s grew to surpass the number of hard routes at every other area in the nation. But the isolation of Smith Rock was about to change. It wouldn't be long before the top European climbers who had sampled Watts's routes were effusive in their praise of Smith Rock and its enlightenment. International climbers began skipping Yosemite when they toured America. The scene there was just too stagnant, the ethics debate too fruitless. British climber Jerry Moffatt described Yosemite as one of the most apathetic places he'd ever seen. And when Australian climber Kim Carrigan plucked a line right on the popular Cookie Cliff in Yosemite, he rubbed salt into the wound of our recent loss in yachting by calling the route *America's Cup* and challenging locals to come back and get it when they were good enough.

It's also ironic that such a charge as Moffatt's would come from a Brit. For most of its history American climbing was modeled after British climbing. We knew the Brits of lore to be made of steely stuff, that they had elevated boldness over all other attributes in climbing. This value, boldness, had crept unquestioned into the jargon of American climbing. That it was a good thing was axiomatic. Unprotected routes were more esteemed than well-protected ones. Climbers who could run it out far from their last piece of gear were better than those who couldn't. From the British legends like Joe Brown and Don Whillans, who would sling a pebble stuffed in a crack and consider it protection, to the writings of Robbins, Robinson, and Chouinard, who thought the British practice was the highest form of expression, to the young Americans like Barber in the Northeast, Erickson in Colorado, and John Bachar in California—the leading voices in American climbing stated in word and deed that risk was essential to the game.

As sport routes proliferated, the axiom of risk and its place in climbing persisted for a while. At Smith Rock, the earliest sport climbs were indeed sporty: hard moves were made way out from the last bolt, and an aspirant for a given route must be willing to take a whipper if he erred. As sport climbing became more popular and a new generation of climbers took to the crags without having been schooled by their traditional elders, the interdependence of risk and climbing melted away. One newcomer to the sport asked incredulously, "Why is it that of all sports publications, the climbing magazines are the only ones with an obituary column?"

Though early bumper stickers used to claim that "sport climbing is neither," most sport climbs are established with safety in mind, concentrating instead on pure gymnastic difficulty. Most sport-climbers think it foolish to deliberately add risk by spacing bolts too far apart. For a while, the traditional value of risk would inhibit a climber from placing too much fixed protection on a new route. But over time, it became obvious that unprotected routes remained unpopular routes. Some climbers, after having summoned the nerve to establish a hard, committing line, would even return later to add a few bolts simply to increase traffic on the route. Perhaps it was public service; perhaps the need for affirmation by others in the climbing community leads the first-ascent climber to go back and retro-bolt.

In any event, risk, that essence so lauded in yester-climbs, isn't necessarily a key ingredient today.

No question—the late 1980s will be seen in mountaineering history as a revolutionary period of American rock climbing, a time when climbers tossed the rule book aside and embraced methods brought to these shores from abroad. It all happened so fast. In the early 1980s, the United States was a fortress of traditional climbing. But by 1990, all that had changed. Today, bolt-protected sport climbing coexists with traditional climbing on clean gear. In many areas, lines of bolts have sprouted between the older natural routes, and despite the woeful prognostications of traditionalists, neither has the sky fallen nor has every crack been bolted. A war fought with missionary zeal has since settled into a solid cease-fire, if not a lasting peace.

But what a battle it was, one played out in similar fashion at hundreds of cliffs around the country. One climber would add a dirty route, and hordes would scream "foul," attacking not only the methods but also the character of the villain. Reminiscing about a decade past, climbers in almost every area in America tell the same story about the Great Bolt War, about the first transgressions and the vehement response, about the bitterness, the accusations, even the acts of vandalism. But in almost every area, they now look back on the revolt through a different lens, believing that the threats to the sport no longer hide within the climbing community itself, but lurk outside in the guise of state and federal regulation. As Californian guidebook author and veteran climber Bob Gaines describes things, "It isn't whether or not the bolts are placed on the lead that matters now; it's whether bolting, or even climbing, will be able to exist." Most climbing in this country is done on public lands, and land managers have stepped in all over to impose restrictions on fixed anchors. In response, most climbers have put away their mutual animosities and joined together to face the new and very real threat to rock climbing on public lands.

The New Challenge

In the beginning of the battle for access, climbers were an unorganized lot. In fact, climbers as a subculture in America were not too keen on organization. The venerable American Alpine Club was considered by younger climbers to be on the stodgy side, conjuring up images of old rich men in black ties and tails reminiscing about safaris or guided climbs on the Matterhorn. Such a view was unfair; in fact, years back, the Alpine Club was a vital mountaineering organization whose ranks included most of the alpine luminaries in the country. But along with the cynicism of the '70s came a disenchantment with organizations in general, and by the 1980s the Alpine Club meant very little to the average rock climber.

The cynicism was ironic in that, during its infancy, American climbing was a decidedly organizational thing. Groups like the Sierra Club, the Appalachian Mountain Club, and the Mountaineers in the Northwest dominated the scenes. In the East, it was the college outing clubs—Dartmouth, Harvard, Yale, MIT—that led the way. Yet there was still something fringe about climbing, something that attracted oddballs and eccentrics, rebels against social order. Climbing moved from the Ivy League to a more blue-collar position in American society, and it adopted an attitude that mirrored the nation's skepticism of conformity. The best-known revolution against the imposition of order occurred at the Shawangunk Mountains in southern New York. There, the self-described Vulgarian Mountain Club rejected the certification process imposed by the Appalachian Mountain Club's Safety Committee and ventured without authorization into the 5.8, 5.9, 5.10 level and beyond. By day they were irreverently climbing impossible and dangerous routes. By night they were pushing other boundaries—civil, sexual, and bacchanalian—and building themselves into the Jack Kerouacs and James Deans of the vertical. When the '50s merged into the '60s, and the country was splitting down the middle over civil rights at home and war in Southeast Asia, climbers inevitably rejected the establishment, siding instead with advocates of either peace or anarchy. Theirs was a more meaningful pursuit, a struggle more introspective and honest to the bone than they saw in the shallow culture at large. Climbing wasn't just a recreation; it was a lifestyle and a badge. In a tongue-in-cheek letter to his friend Don Lauria that was reprinted in *Climbing,* Yosemite legend T. M. Herbert captured the dilemma:

"Can you come to the Valley over Easter vacation? Or are your kids gonna play jacks . . . And your wife is probably entering a local knitting contest . . . Are you a man or a mouse? Order those dip-shits into the car and tell them to head for the Valley, where your wife and I have special hideaways while you stay home and spray the aphids and pull crabgrass . . ." Good satire. But for many of the voices of the times, climbing wasn't as much an escape from the status quo as it was a statement against it.

With the Great Bolt War of the 1980s over, and with climbing access on public lands in jeopardy, the need for organization was obvious. No longer could climbers operate solely as individuals. Without the power of numbers, their rights to use public lands might well disappear. Leading the cause this time was the Access Fund, born in the American Alpine Club and splintering off independently in 1990. Today, it has broad support from all ends of the ideological spectrum, supported generously by gear manufacturers and individual memberships. Unlike earlier climbing organizations, the Access Fund isn't so much a social entity as it is a sophisticated public advocacy group.

The Interpreters

American climbing has always been an endeavor infused with meaning. It has been a culture bonded by some common understandings. Its symbols—the carabiner on the backpack, the corded chock dangling uselessly but ceremoniously from the rear-view mirror, the bumper sticker of the Gendarme or La Sportiva—are ritual emblems of entry into its proudly select community. Underlying the symbols is a reading list that disseminates information and voices the judgments of a subculture in transition.

Case in point: In 1998, the two national magazines *Climbing* and *Rock & Ice* each ran an article about the placement of ice screws for winter climbers. Contrary to the conventional wisdom that said screws ought to be tilted slightly uphill against the downward force of a fall, much like the way campers drive in tent pegs against the anticipated force, the tests cited in the articles proved the opposite, that tilting the screw slightly downward actually increased its holding power. Within the next month, almost every empty screw hole found on routes across America and Canada was tilted a few degrees downhill, demonstrating more convincingly than any polling data just how powerful and widespread was the word handed down by the magazines.

Climbing and *Rock & Ice* dominate climbing periodicals. Out on the crags, it is safe to assume that the parties to the left and right are familiar with the same gear review, the same news about Chris Sharma's latest boulder problem, or Hans Florine's most recent attempt to shave a few seconds off an El Cap speed record. Having read the same news and editorials, climbers across the country share the same information, if not the same values. *Climbing* came onto the scene in May 1970, joining a market that included *Off Belay* and *Summit,* along with the annual publications *Ascent* and *The American Alpine Journal.* The most influential of all, however, was *Mountain* of Great Britain. For quite a while, the American climbing press would emulate *Mountain*'s layout and reporting style, mimicking its understated British humor. *Mountain* reported on the developments in American climbing through a British lens, implicitly and explicitly evaluating American achievements according to British standards. Yet by the 1980s, *Climbing* had eclipsed the other domestic publications to become the main voice of American climbing.

In 1984, upstart *Rock & Ice* hit the shelves, intent on resurrecting the old irreverence and distinguishing itself from the more conservative *Climbing.* The magazine ran a photo of a group of nude climbers standing atop the Mexican Hat formation in southern Colorado ("clear Lycra," they called it), and published a satirical section called "Schlock and Vice." *Rock & Ice* drew a few protest letters, mainly from readers moralizing about nudity and profanity, but a majority of climbers were amused. What did rile climbers about *Rock & Ice,* however, was a feature called Beta-Max, which ran series of cartoon characters demonstrating the crux sequences of some of the country's hardest and most sacred routes. Now they'd gone too far, fumed many traditionalists. It's one thing to show a little flesh, but quite another to spill the hard-earned secret of how to climb *Supercrack* or *Astroman.* The furor wore off, mainly along with the big shift in thinking of the late 1980s. As it became increasingly acceptable to rehearse a route while hanging on a rope, so it was OK to publicize the route maps. The shift in focus from exploration to gymnastics was nearly complete.

On the instructional side, there was the comprehensive *Mountaineering: The Freedom of the Hills,* published by the Mountaineers in Seattle, and the shorter, more artistic pamphlets *Basic Rockcraft* and *Advanced Rockcraft* by Royal Robbins. In his books, Robbins not only explained techniques, he also espoused values: Don't let the gear come between you and the experience. Be good to the rock. Concurrently, another pamphlet was published, this one ironically by the nation's leading maker of pitons, Chouinard Equipment. It was more than just a catalog; it was a treatise on clean climbing, espousing a more spiritual approach to the physical game of climbing.

The catalog, as much as any publication in the history of the sport, signaled the transition from the brutal hammering of the iron age to the more spiritual era of clean climbing techniques. Included was a photograph of old John Salathé and young Yvon Chouinard, presumably passing the torch from one master piton maker to the next. Then there were photos of British rock climbing, land of legend, where men in knickers would pocket machine nuts found on the rail tracks on the way to the climb, ready to be slung and stuffed into a crack for protection. British climbing, it implied, was the highest form of expression, something to emulate.

Most vital of all was Doug Robinson's *The Whole Natural Art of Protection:*

> *There's a word for it, and the word is clean. Climbing with only nuts and runners for protection is clean climbing. Clean because the rock is left unaltered by the passing climber. Clean because nothing is hammered into the rock and then hammered back out, leaving the rock scarred and the next climber's experience less natural. Clean because the climber's protection leaves little track of his ascension. Clean is climbing the rock without changing it; a step closer to organic climbing for the natural man.*

Other books told of places and what they meant to the world of climbing. Most influential across the broad spectrum of American climbing was *Fifty Classic Climbs of North America,* by Steve Roper and Allen Steck. This large, inspirational book anointed fifty routes as the best on the continent, and many climbers used it as a tick list for their own climbing careers. As a result the routes are known disparagingly as "fifty crowded climbs." Certain regions also saw big photo-essay books elevating routes and climbers to mythic status. In Colorado, it was *CLIMB!,* the story of Colorado rock climbing, told by Bob Godfrey and Dudley Shelton. Its California counterpart was *The Vertical World of Yosemite,* a series of essays collected by Galen Rowell that, like *CLIMB!,* elevated a region's climbers to hero status. Another book, *Shawangunk Rock Climbing,* by Richard DuMais, did the same for this rich eastern climbing scene.

With the selective chronicling of rock climbing history and with certain deeds given importance by the chroniclers, the centers of American climbing were undisputed and held sway over climbers for a generation. The Shawangunks in southern New York state, Yosemite National Park in California, and Boulder, Colorado, had dominion over a tripolar world. Taking the image further, one could pinpoint three epicenters: the Uberfall, under the bulletin board at the Gunks where the trail from the top of the cliff drops down to meet the Carriage Road; Eldorado Canyon, the symbolic gateway to the Rocky Mountains, a sandstone cleft framed on one side by the towering Bastille and on the other side across the river by the Redgarden Wall; and Camp 4, known by Yosemite park officials as Sunnyside Walk-In Campground, but understood by the world's climbers to be the home of gods.

A bulletin board and wire rescue litter under a white conglomerate overhang just seventy miles north of New York City, a dusty dirt road running between tight red Colorado sandstone walls, and a collection of campsites in the boulders and the pines in California—these were the places to hang out, to smoke, to boulder and to boast, to listen and watch and wonder what great things were happening, what famous people might be right there in your midst. To be at such a place at the end of a day was to finger the pulse of American rock climbing. Yes, there were hard routes and colorful characters elsewhere in American rock climbing in the '60s, and '70s. But the holy trinity of the Gunks, Boulder, and Yosemite had the aura and the myths, the collective confidence that they mattered, where newcomers entered as tight-lipped observers in search of giants, listening for famous names, gazing furtively at self-assured locals, knowing that all around, important things were under way.

The earth doesn't spin on a fixed axle riveted solidly into the firmament. No, it oscillates, wobbles a bit in space, and as a result, the north and south poles wander. Iron minerals locked into a magnetic orientation in ancient igneous rocks tell us so. From these paleomagnetic fossils we know that a world that seems solid and timeless under our feet is actually an unsteady ball. Antarctica was once in the tropics. The equator ran for a time through Utah's canyon country. So too do the centers of American climbing shift as certain elements—big-wall climbing, limestone sport climbing, bouldering, for examples—slide into the national focus. For a time, one particular climbing region will take on almost mythic dimensions. It will seem like the center of a universe. The magazines will focus on its local heroes, whose names and accomplishments will float bigger than life across the nation and into conversations around campfires. Climbers will pack their vans and make the pilgrimages. Jaded by hometown crags that seem mere practice areas for trips to the real climbing they perceive elsewhere, climbers will make the journey to the new Meccas, obligatory destinations in the shifting sands, anointed with credibility by *Rock & Ice* and *Climbing* magazines. But the earth's axis remains unsteady, and the poles continue to wander. Rock climbing has emerged from the squalid campsites into the light of big heartland cities. Rock gyms have sprouted all over the country. Good short crags have been discovered and worked over in the most unlikely places. Single climbing areas have lost control of the culture as American rock climbing has grown so far beyond the original big three.

The Basics Remain

Despite the proliferation of both bolted routes and artificial climbing walls, the sport of rock climbing remains intensely natural. Rather than moving toward technologies, climbers have moved away from them. Witness the popularity of bouldering. Instead of being just a training exercise for real climbing, bouldering has emerged as one of the most vital elements of climbing. Climbers now travel to the Sierra not to climb big walls but to work 20-foot problems in the Buttermilks near Bishop. They walk the carriage road under the cliffs at the Gunks, working short unroped routes and ignoring the three-pitch routes above. Places like Hueco Tanks in Texas and even Lincoln Woods in humble Rhode Island have become destination attractions for climbers who'd rather invest in a big crash pad than a rack of fancy cams. The Phoenix Bouldering Contest draws the biggest assemblages of climbers of any annual event in the nation. Clearly, the dazzling new tools have not stood between the climber and his experience.

Surely the indoor wall has a huge impact. Now climbers in every major city and at most colleges can learn the essentials of safe climbing and at the same time become incredibly strong. When they try climbing on real rock for the first time, their footwork might be sloppy, but their grip strength allows them to do moves that generations of earlier climbers viewed as impossible. Still, indoor climbing isn't rock climbing. It trains and it entertains, and many climbers will be perfectly happy pushing their limits on plastic. Most, however, will venture out—or at least dream of venturing out—into a world with a deep history and a dynamic culture. Their initial visits to real rock will be eye-opening. This is good. After all, keeping eyes open wide to the big world of rock climbing is what this book is about: knowing the rock and the people, the values and the controversies, the essence of the sport that unites diverse personalities into a single rich culture of climbers.

Outside Moab, Utah

2 KNOWING THE ROCK

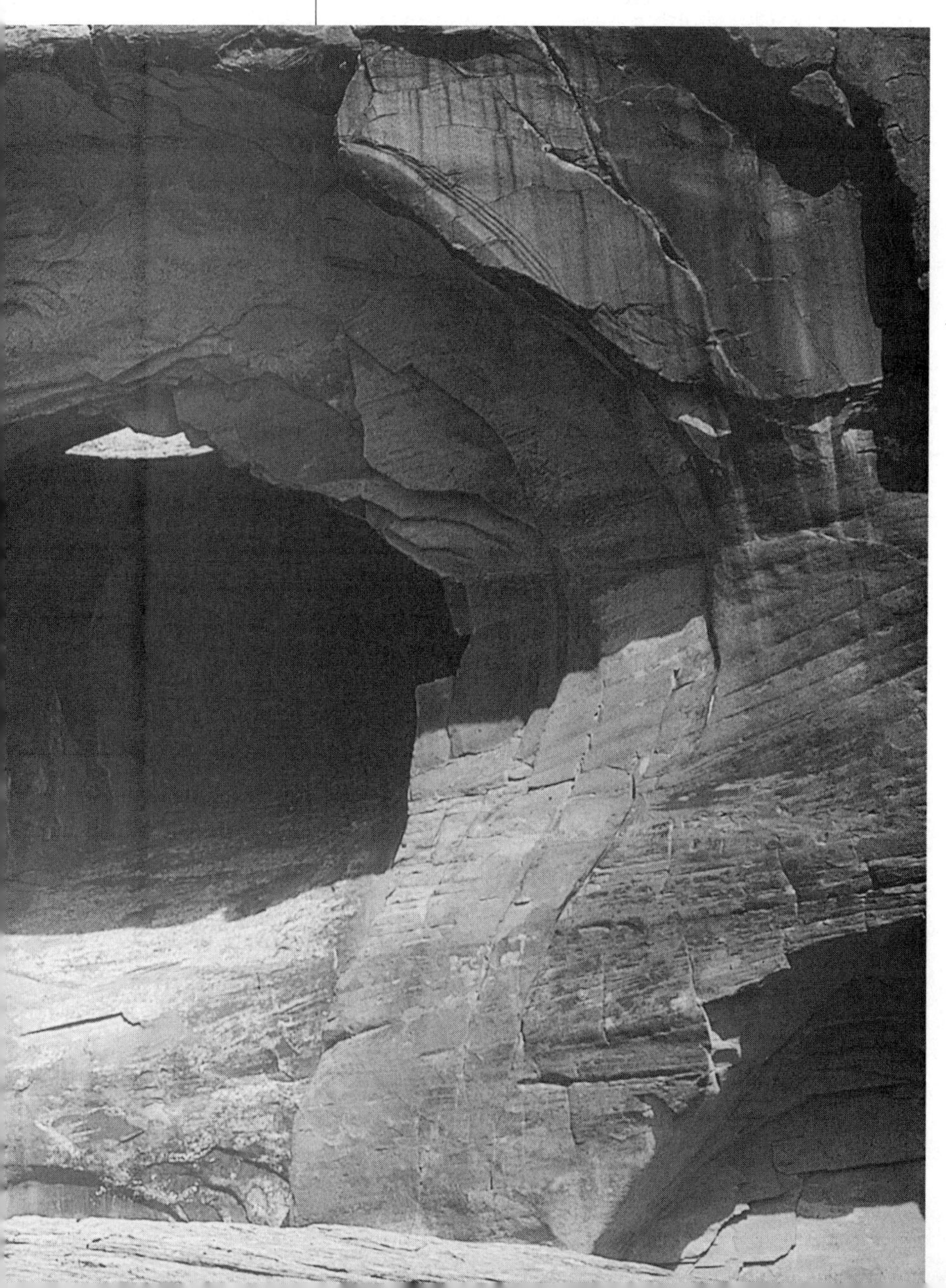

If you are new to the sport, seasoned climbers probably sound like expert geologists. Listen to them talk of the welded tuff of Smith Rock and the feared pegmatite in the Black Canyon of the Gunnison, the quartzite band in Eldorado and the Navajo sandstone in Zion National Park. Such technical language is intimidating, and you wonder whether a degree in geology will be necessary to move forward in a sport that seemed so simple in the gym. No, you don't have to be a geologist to enjoy climbing, but when your eyes are opened to some basic geological concepts, the sport takes on a new pleasure, both from the expanded appreciation of the rock environment and from a new understanding of how to adjust your techniques to the terrain. This chapter is a short course in the formation of rock.

TIME

The first and most important concept is that of time, geologic time. How does one grasp the meaning of 4.5 billion years, the estimated age of the earth? Such an expanse of time is too abstract to comprehend without some kind of concrete model. One simple demonstration of what 4.5 billion means is to start counting, nonstop, at the rate of one number per second. You'll be done in 150 years.

Or if you're in a hurry, condense in your imagination the 4.5 billion years of earth history into a single year. The first two months of this imaginary year won't leave any direct evidence. Rock from those earliest days has been either so deeply buried or so thoroughly reprocessed that it just doesn't show up in its original form on the surface of the earth. The oldest surface rock was formed in March. Life emerged in early May, though with no atmosphere to support terrestrial life, the first crawly things stayed in the sea for almost half the earth's history. It wouldn't be until November that air as we know it would be sufficiently developed for plants and animals to take to the land. All the while, the continental plates kept shifting and grinding, with mountains being pushed up from their collisions and seas invading the lowlands.

Most of the rock-climbing landscape we see today is new, having emerged only in the winter of our imaginary year. By mid-December, the sand dunes that would make up the Wingate layer in Utah were deposited, dinosaurs ruled for about two weeks, and, just in time for

Christmas, molten rock welled into great underground pools in California, bubbles that wouldn't rise to the surface as the Sierra Nevada until New Year's Eve. On the morning of December 30, there was a great explosion of ash in Oregon that would harden and later be called Smith Rock. Humanlike creatures didn't walk erect until late New Year's Eve, and about a minute before midnight glaciers receded from the northern states, leaving behind naked granite walls in New England, across the northern Rockies, and down the jagged spine of California's Sierra. For five seconds Rome ruled the world, and in the blink of an eye remaining, Coronado failed to find El Dorado in the American Southwest, Shakespeare wrote *King Lear,* world wars erupted twice, and Lynn Hill free-climbed *The Nose* of El Capitan.

A better understanding of time and erosion affects both our experience and our behavior. We come to know and appreciate the rock on which we climb, and we put into clearer perspective the meaning of leaving our imprints on the landscape. Seen in the geologic short term, the proliferation of bolts and chipped holds is changing the face of rock faster and more effectively than the processes of the ages. But in the bigger picture, neither the bolt, nor the drilled finger pocket, nor the colossal dam, nor the nuclear power plant, nor the existence of humans themselves will much matter.

Planet earth is a dynamic place. We look out over a mountain landscape, and things seem quiet and still. Mountains are so massive and solid to us that they serve as our metaphor for timelessness. Yet the alpine world seems stable only because our life is so short and our vision so limited. In fact, mountains are growing, as always, and erosion is wearing them back to the sea. Once upon a time, Man understood the landforms to be the result of great cataclysms in an age when the earth was all a-rumble in formation. There was no other way to describe something like the Grand Canyon. Surely a great flood, probably Noah's, gouged out the rock on its angry way to the sea. Just as surely, the Tetons must have been thrust abruptly upward from the Wyoming plains, and the bottom of Yosemite Valley dropped out from below to create the great cliffs of El Capitan and Cathedral Rocks. It is easy to imagine such a thunderous landscape, shaken by earthquakes and spewing smoke and lava from volcanoes all around. It must have been a terrible time, Man thought as he gazed around at the apparent stillness of his own time and thanked his Maker that the creation of the earth was finished business and that all the violence was done.

This view changed in the late eighteenth century when James Hutton published *Theory of the Earth,* introducing the idea of Uniformitarianism. He postulated that today's landscape was not the result of great catastrophes but of quieter processes that are still at work, uniformly shaping the land at a continuous rate. To understand the events of the past, Hutton wrote, we need only to examine the processes at work today. It's an idea to which we have grown accustomed and that helps us understand the geology of the earth.

The rock climber, more than most others, has an easier time grasping the idea of uniformitarianism, because he sees up close the fragility and changing nature of the physical world. Routes like Henry Barber's *Whaleback Crack* in New Hampshire or *Mickey's Beach Crack* in California have simply fallen away, not in exception to the solidity of mountains but as testament to the contrary. The sharp-edged slabs that hang precariously over Alabama's Little River Canyon seem unlikely to stay the day. A look at the fresh rubble fields below most cliffs is proof this is so. Vermont climber Tim Beaman was hanging on a rope one day on an undeveloped cliff in upstate New York when a van-sized block just peeled from the crest above. It fell for about 150 feet before exploding on the big traverse ledge about 100 feet above the forest, and as it did, it blew out a V-shaped notch many times bigger than the original block. Beaman, the quintessential New Englander, watched the show only 200 feet to his left, and then got back to work wriggling pebbles and dirt from the new 5.11 he would climb the next day, even while sand still funneled down the V as through an hourglass. The longer you climb, the more evidence you see that the mountains are falling apart.

Not a bad thing, because climbing is possible only as a result of this steady breaking down of the rock. The solution pockets in limestone at Mount Charleston or the bathtub-sized hollows at Red River Gorge are just the eroding of a temporary surface of stone. The flakes and edges characteristic of good Yosemite granite are nothing but the skin shedding to expose a more solid surface beneath. The harsh friction of Vedauwoo is merely the remnant surface of hard crystals standing out in stubborn relief after the softer minerals have worn away. The splitter cracks down at Indian Creek in Utah are just the fresh edges of blocks poised to tumble down-slope, turn to dust, and scatter in the desert wind, perhaps one day to become cliffs anew. Nearby to the north, Fisher Towers look like giant castles of mud dribbled though a child's hand at the beach; it's rock that will wash away in a relatively few rains, geologically speaking. The seasoned climber doesn't ask *if* the slab will peel from the cliff, or the pillar topple, or the roof collapse. He wonders when.

All of which makes it feel sometimes that the disintegration of the mountains is a one-way process and that someday the world will be flat as a pool table. Gravity, to be sure, would like it that way. But gravity isn't alone in the shaping of the earth's topography. Just as the earth's surface is being smoothed by weather and gravity, it's being uplifted by forces deep within. The main process behind the uplift is called plate tectonics, the shifting of thin crustal plates on a hot, mushy earth's interior. The process has also been called continental drift: Look at a map of the Atlantic Ocean and it's easy to see how the puzzle pieces of North and South America on one side and Europe and Africa on the other fit neatly together. In this case the two huge crustal plates are moving apart, spreading from a seam deep in the middle of the ocean. This line, called the mid-Atlantic rift valley, is a seismically active place, quaking from the movements of the plates and spewing molten rock from the crack to form undersea volcanoes.

The heat of the inner earth is responsible for the convection currents that move the plates; plate boundaries are the sites of most of the mountain-building activity. Where two plates collide, mountains are pushed upward and beds of rock are compressed and buckled, much like a rug kicked up by an errant foot. The Appalachian Mountains are one such range resulting from continental collision: the flat beds of sandstone of the Shawangunks in southern New York State have been tilted up on end, while the range bends around in West Virginia to form the amazing blade of Seneca Rocks.

Often at the site of the collision, one plate slides underneath another and the solid rock is melted as it dives below. The overlying plate then cracks with vents that ooze lava onto the surface. This is the model of the volcanic Northwest as a Pacific plate is submerging under the North American plate. Resulting landforms include the line of volcanoes from California's Mount Shasta on through Rainier and into Canada, and the vast volcanic flows that make up so much of Washington, Oregon, and Idaho. Trace the perimeter of the Pacific Ocean to the north, up past the Aleutian Islands and down to Japan, and you are following what geologists call the Ring of Fire, plate boundaries of seismic hyperactivity.

Given that gravity and weather conspire to smooth out all landforms while at the same time the plates are crinkling up mountain ranges and spewing out volcanoes, the current state of the earth's surface is the result of a budget between uplift and erosion. The steady building up and simultaneous wearing away of mountains also means that the material in rock undergoes continual transmutation. First it might be solid granite. Then it's worn into sediment that is carried into a sea and buried. The heat and pressure might cement the grains back together into a sandstone. Or it might dive down at a plate boundary and be remelted back into a granite deep within the earth or a volcanic rock that flows flaming hot onto the surface. Along with time and uniformitarianism, then, comes the unending process of breakdown and renewal called the rock cycle, the next concept in understanding the rock medium on which we climb. The three basic forms of rock, the three stages in the rock cycle, are basic to any discussion of rock. Geologist or not, any climber who has ventured out from the gym for at least a day knows those three forms to be igneous, sedimentary, and metamorphic.

IGNEOUS ROCK

Igneous rock, as its name implies, is born of fire. It's the cooled and hardened rock that was once molten and fluid. Typically, temperatures necessary to melt rock are found only at depths of over fifty kilometers, and so any igneous rock visible as cliffs must have previously been transported from deep below. This happens two ways. Either the material oozes hot and viscous onto the surface, or it wells into giant underground lakes, where it cools and hardens much more slowly and is exposed on the surface only after the whole mass is pushed upward or the overlying material is eroded away. These two processes of igneous rock formation—the extrusive fiery surface flow or the deep intrusive pooling of molten rock—create very different rock and a very different climbing experience.

Most climbers think of granite when they think of igneous rock.

Granite forms from a melt deep down, welling into vast underground pools called batholiths and cooling over long periods of time before being thrust upward and exposed on the surface. The granite of New Hampshire's White Mountains, of North Carolina's famed friction domes, of Idaho's Sawtooth Mountains, and the Sierra Nevada of California are all huge granite batholiths. (Note that geologists use the term *granite* to describe rock with a particular percentage of minerals, but climbers use the term to denote any light-colored igneous rock containing quartz and feldspars. Specifically, many of the so-called "granite" cliffs are actually quartz monzonite or granodiorite or syenitic porphyry. To avoid any confusion, and the wrath of geologists, one can refer to the whole series as granitic or granitelike rock.)

Two factors work in concert to determine the outcome of intrusive igneous rock production: the rate at which the material cools, and components of the melt themselves. Slow cooling in a deep, extensive batholith gives the crystals a chance to grow. A quicker cooling, the kind that occurs if the molten pool is small or if the material has spewed out onto the surface, results in undeveloped crystal formation and a finer-grained surface texture. Igneous climbing experiences are often defined by the size, and commensurate nastiness, of the crystals. In South Dakota, the bizarre Needles are known for the huge crystals: The rough surface offers lots of things to grab and pinch, but a sliding fall would be too bloody to imagine. Climbers in the Needles either work the steeper faces or they just don't fall.

It isn't just the size of the crystals that determines the coarseness of the rock. Newly splintered or recently glaciated granite is smoother than long-exposed rock where eons of weathering have broken down the softer material, leaving the sharp crystals in jagged relief. Classic white granite found in Utah's Little Cottonwood Canyon, North Carolina's Stone Mountain, and much of California's Sierra Range is very climbable and friendly because the crystals are small and the exposures fresh. Other rock, particularly that which escaped glacial polish, such as Vedauwoo in Wyoming and sections of Joshua Tree National Park, is coarsely crystalline, and climbers come away from such places with sliced fingertips and bloody knees.

Sometimes fragments of rock adjacent to the molten intrusion get

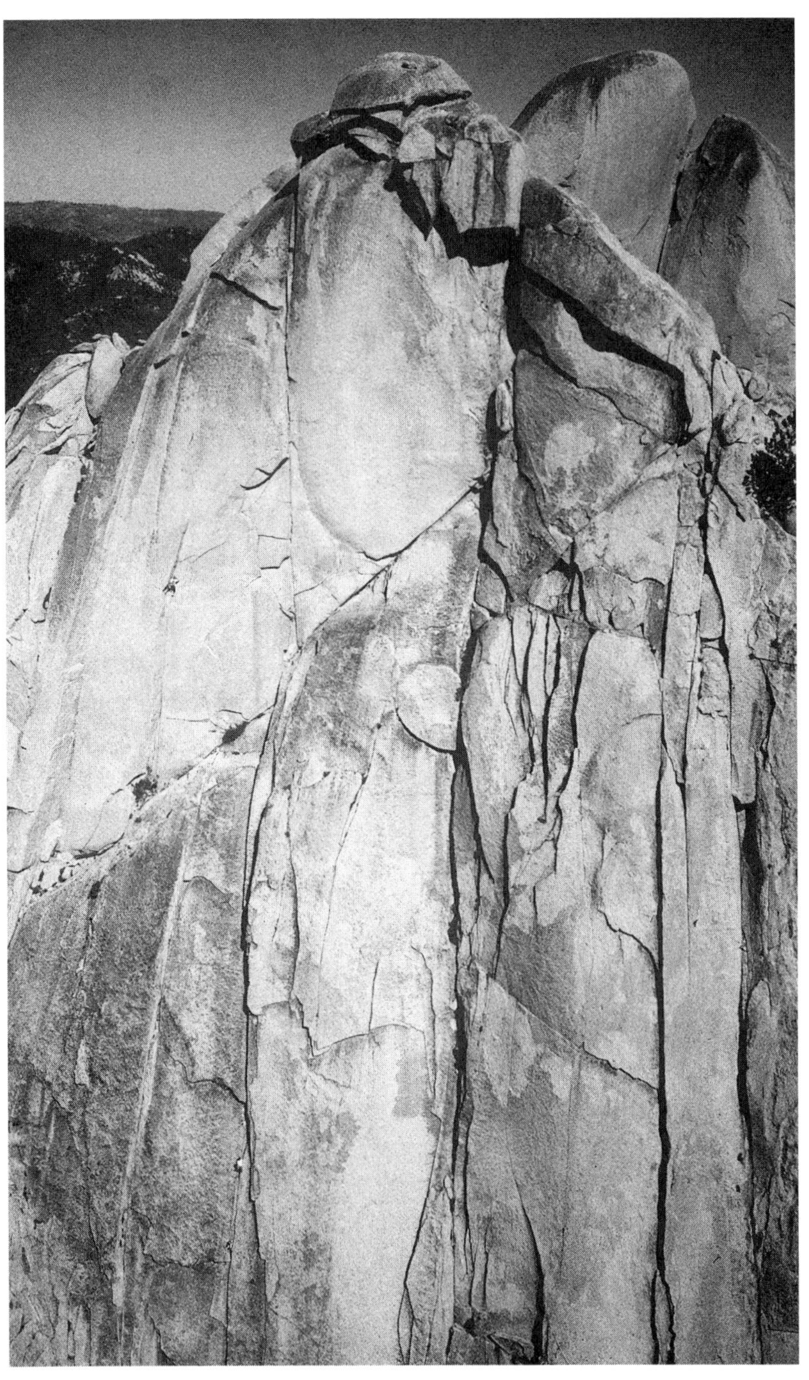

Perfect granite at the Needles of the southern Sierra

swept into the mix and become xenoliths, sort of like chocolate chips mixed up in a cookie batter. On Yosemite's Killer Pillar, the xenoliths are prominent, tempting sport-climbers to link knobs in creation of some very un-Yosemite routes. Often, because they are firmer and finer-grained, such inclusions resist erosion and stand out as blobs, knobs, and *chickenheads* large enough to wrap a sling on. Not all chickenheads are built of xenoliths, however. Others are either a resistant coalescence of minerals in the melt or fragments of a hardened surface left after surrounding rock has weathered off, formations typical of Arizona's Cochise Stronghold or Idaho's City of Rocks.

Once exposed to the earth's surface, the rock is attacked in a multidimensional onslaught. On an up-close scale, the attachment of individual crystals is weakened by chemicals in the water. The surface of such granite decomposes into gravel, and then sand. On the drive up toward the good white granite of Tahquitz Rock in southern California, the road passes through such sections of decomposing granite, road cuts that look more like beachside dunes than bedrock. In Idaho's Sawtooth Mountains, a range known for its outstanding granite, Mount Heyburn's *Stur Chimney* (5.6) finds a way up the best of granite, but all around it the rock seems more like dried oatmeal. The alternating solid rock and weathering gravel gives the range its characteristic sawtooth profile.

In addition to the chemical weathering that breaks down rock on a crystalline level, there are mechanical forces wearing the rock down and creating the surface features important to climbing. Running water can wear deep grooves like otter slides in the rock. In the Sierra, eons of water cascading down Charlotte Dome's south face and Lembert Dome have created smooth troughs so deep they can be chimneyed, with stone fins between so thin that little windows have worn right through. There in the Yosemite high country of Tuolumne Meadows, the main sculptor, however, was water of the frozen variety, glaciers. Ice sheets, thousands of feet thick and with an underside laden with broken rock debris, ground and polished the surface smooth. On a larger scale, the moving ice steepened valley walls and rounded out river valleys.

The last important granitic process for the climber to understand is exfoliation, the sheeting of layers parallel to the surface, like skins of an onion. New Hampshire's popular *Standard Route* (5.5) on

White Horse Ledge and North Carolina's *Great Arch* (5.5) at Stone Mountain both follow arching corners formed by the peeling off of such an exfoliated sheet. Yosemite's Half Dome, seen from the Cables hiking trail, is another outstanding example of large-scale exfoliation. And the sheets are alive. Climbers bivied on the face of Half Dome during an earthquake heard the pinging noise of pitons falling past as the exfoliation slabs expanded. On New York's Poke-O-Moonshine, a large Hex left under an overlap the season before was found on the ground in spring, crushed from the groaning expansion and contraction of the great sheets of rock.

So far the discussion has focused on intrusive igneous rocks, those formed deep within the earth. But when the molten rock spills into cracks or onto the surface itself, the climbing medium takes on wholly new characteristics. All along the west side of the Hudson River, north of New York City, is a line of steep cliffs known as the Palisades. Here, fluid rock poured out and cooled near the surface, forming a resistant layer of a fine-grained rock called basalt. Most of this New York basalt is loose and off-limits to climbing, but elsewhere around the nation, it's a stone quite suitable for climbing. Paradise Forks and the Overlook in Arizona, the Crooked River climbs at Oregon's Smith Rock, and the many newly developed cliffs along the Columbia River in Washington State are characterized by vertical, polygonal columns, requiring good jamming skills in the parallel cracks between and creative, groin-tearing stemming on the fine-grained, flaring walls.

The East has very little volcanic rock worth climbing; out West, where relatively recent tectonic activity has spewed lava into great beds in the Northwest, down through California and into Arizona and New Mexico, volcanic climbing has become a regional specialty. The oddest incarnation of volcanic rock is probably the welded tuff, first publicized at Smith Rock but later discovered in many areas to the south. Here, as part of a massive explosion of lava and hot gas, ash rained down in a fiery layer. Where the cloud was hot and thick enough, it "welded" itself together, forming a rock that looks a bit like hardened mud but, once cleaned of the loose sections, makes for some fine sport climbing. Queen Creek in Arizona and Owens River Gorge in California are two of the best examples of places where welded tuff is attracting climbers from around the world.

Sedimentary Rock

With rock under attack wherever it's exposed to the elements, there's an endless downhill migration of sand grains, usually toward deep basins in the sea. Pile enough grains atop each other, and the process of rock building begins anew. Tremendous pressures and heat from the buildup are the conditions in which the grains are fused back together to form the second major type, sedimentary rock. In places, especially in the arid southwestern deserts, the layers of sand are obvious, the process of sedimentation easy to imagine. In the East, the sedimentation is just as extensive but harder to see because there's less uplifted topography and the region is covered with a thick forest. Up in New York at the Gunks, a north-south fault line has uplifted and exposed the horizontal beds to full view, but down in the sandstone belt of the Southeast, most of the exposures are limited to the canyon walls of gorges like those at the New River, the Red River, and the lesser-known Little River in the northeast corner of Alabama.

The terms sedimentary rock and sandstone conjure up images of soft, dangerous climbing terrain. In places this is so. Some of the layers in Utah's canyon country can be scratched with a fingernail. Even well-placed camming units have sheared from such soft rock, leaving parallel tracks, scars inside the crack. On the famous *Supercrack,* a small widening of the crack continues to look more and more like a foothold as thousands of boots have parked there for a rest. Yes, some of the layers in Utah and other sedimentary areas are little more than a vertical beach, soon to become individual sand grains once again.

Survival for many of these softer layers depends on the presence of a *caprock,* a harder layer above that protects the less durable rock from the elements. Caprock determines almost all of the topography in Utah's canyon country. Almost every slender tower is topped by a harder rock, and from almost every summit, one can look out in all directions and see towers of just about the same height, protected by remnants of the same resistant layer. Looking down onto the White Rim in the Canyonlands, it's easy to see how this hard layer protects not only the canyon walls but also the summits of the myriad spires scattered throughout the maze below. This is differential weathering, a process fundamental to rock climbing. Softer material erodes quickly, leaving in relief the harder materials. Hard crystals stand out on a long-weathered granite surface. *Huecos,* or hollows, form when a hardened surface is removed and the softer interior rock is exposed to the weather. *Dikes,* intrusions of igneous rock into cracks in older rock, wear away into deep gullies if the newer rock is softer, or stand out as defined ribs if the new material is more resistant. As seen in the maze of the Canyonlands, where each layer offers a resistance different from the others, the differential weathering erosion is obviously the artist responsible for the sculpture's grand design.

Give it enough time and pressure, and percolate the right cementing agents between the grains, and sandstone can be as hard as good granite. Eldorado Canyon near Boulder, Colorado, one of the most important areas in American climbing history, is one such example of really hard sedimentary rock. The Nuttal sandstone of New River Gorge in West Virginia is another. The pebbly white stone at the Shawangunks is as hard as anything in the climbing world; in fact, with only hand drills available during its glory years, new-route climbers would search for every possible alternative before subjecting themselves to the agonizing hour it took to drill a good bolt hole.

Most sandstone is laid down in water; the Mediterranean is one such place where, no doubt, future rock is being manufactured. So is the Gulf of Mexico, as the brown Mississippi and the Rio Grande carry earth from the vast stretches between the Rockies and the Appalachians. Many sandstone deposits are evidence of onetime basins where sediments collected and built. Sediments, however, can be deposited in other ways as well. Eldorado Springs Canyon is rock that was once a huge alluvial fan, a tilted, delta-shaped deposit formed in a valley where debris was carried from the higher mountains to the west. Such alluvial fan deposits are everywhere in the West; from seemingly every valley in the arid basin and range region, broad, inclined fans of sediment spread out onto the flats beyond. Sediment carried by moving water can be larger and more varied than that settling in relatively still water. Eldorado's tilted planes are constructed of all sizes of grains, from hard-to-see silts to pebbly gravels that needed the force of moving water to carry them along. Rock made of varied grain sizes is called conglomerate.

A few years back, American Fork Canyon near Salt Lake City became strangely silent as locals moved over to Maple Canyon after the discovery there of one of the most bizarre climbing surfaces imag-

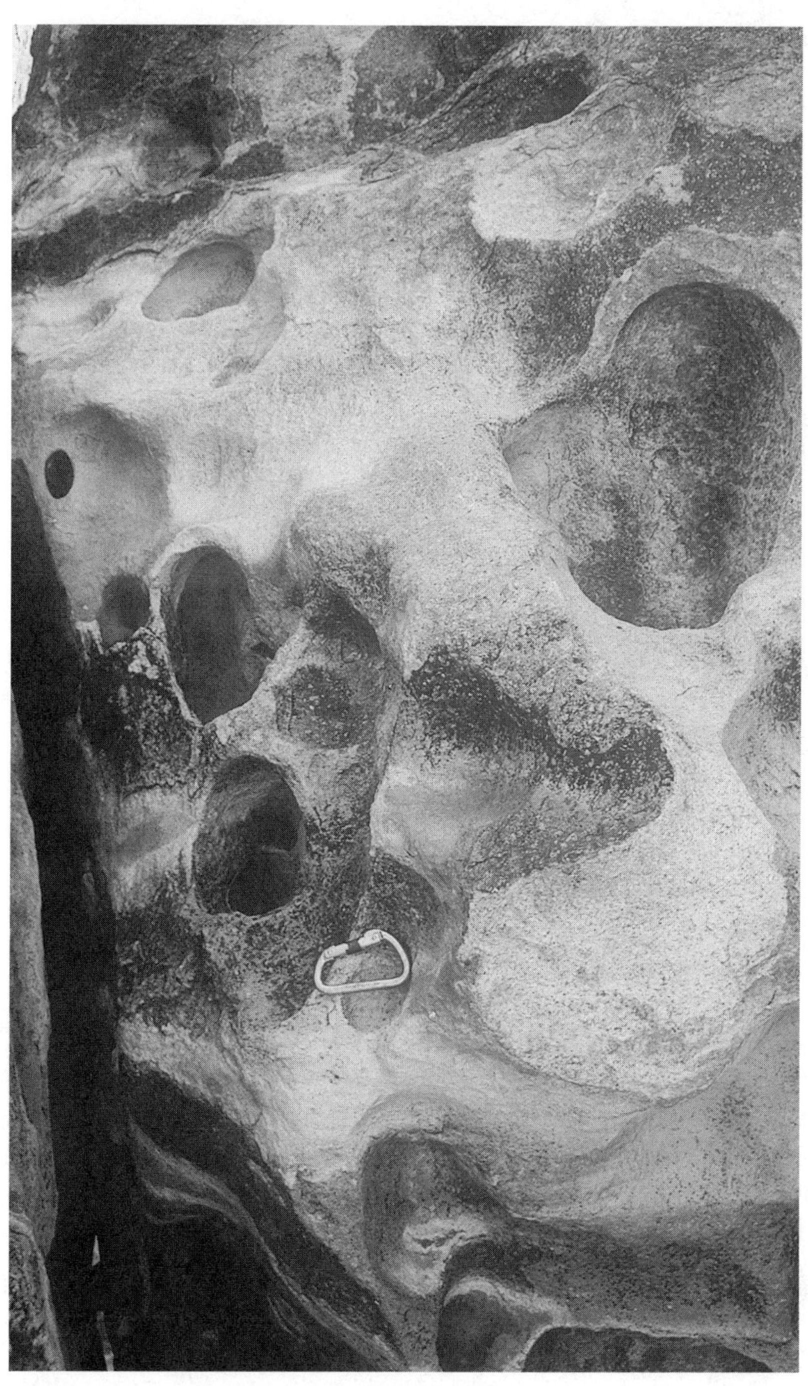

Differential weathering at Hueco Tanks, Texas

inable. The alluvial forces at Maple Canyon must have been terrific, for the grains that make up the sedimentary rock are as large as grapefruits and volleyballs, some even bigger. On a climb, you're too focused on clinging to the stream-rounded balls or lunging for the hollows left when the stones were dislodged for any coherent geologic conjecture. But afterward you stand in awe of the fluvial chaos that must have been responsible for washing grains so big into the pile.

Or if not water, then wind. Today's African Sahara is a sea of wavelike dunes, hundreds of feet thick, moving windward across the vast desert. Two hundred million years ago, the American Southwest looked much the same, the result being the thick deposits of sand like the renowned Wingate layer, the rock of the endless Indian Creek handcracks and countless towers like Castleton near Moab. Unlike the diverse water-borne deposits, the sand blown about in the desert wind is finer and often more rounded, and so there isn't an inherent crystalline structure to define the way the rock cleaves. At the Gunks, there's variety in the bands of rock, and the layering is preserved. As such, Gunks climbs are *bucket ladders,* steep lines of positive and predictable holds, each tilted twenty-two degrees in the climber's favor since that's the angle of the uplift as a whole. No such layering exists in the wind-borne sands of Wingate, and so the rock cleaves according to the demands of gravity, by splintering vertically under subtle upward pressure or the collapse of underlying structures.

The Wingate rock, renowned for its vertical cracks, holds up against the weather with the aid of a thin surface layer called desert varnish, a blackening where minerals have coalesced, coating the rock. Where this layer is broken, the rock is redder and softer. In fact, on the edges of many of the classic cracks, like *The Incredible Handcrack,* the varnish has worn away and the edges are quickly rounding out. Desert varnish is only one of several mechanisms whereby the surface of a rock takes on a hardened, protective coating. On the granites of Arizona's Cochise Stronghold and especially Idaho's City of Rocks, the surface hardening has created an armor-plated surface that, when violated, quickly allows the rock underneath to wear away. At the City, the plates become the best of handholds, solid, incut edges that make climbable the most unlikely expanses. Up in the Stronghold, climbers tie off the plates with slings for protection and even slot nuts between the plates.

One of the most vital rock mediums in the world is limestone, a sedimentary rock composed of the calcareous hard parts of tiny marine animals. Some of the rock is built of tiny shells, most too small to see, that accumulated on an ancient seafloor. Other limestone is formed from the precipitation of minerals from calcium-rich waters. Scuba diving in active marine environments, such as in the tropics, one can see the thin accumulation of such material on wrecks and rocks, the undersea dust that slowly covers a wreck and even more slowly fills in the basin. Now think about Rifle or Mount Charleston: if you can imagine how long it took for such accretion, then you are well along in acknowledging time's role in building and sculpting your local crags.

Metamorphic Rock

Take either igneous or sedimentary rock and bury it deep, heat it up, and twist it around, and the internal crystalline structure metamorphoses into a new kind of rock. Sandstone subjected to such abuse becomes quartzite. Limestone becomes marble. Shale becomes slate. Granite becomes schist. The process of metamorphosis is complex, creating so many incarnations of the stuff that it's almost impossible to make any sweeping generalizations about metamorphic rock, other than that it is often sharp-edged and unpredictable.

The most easily recognized metamorphic rock in American climbing is the striped granitic gneiss at Mount Lemmon above Tucson. Alternating bands of light and dark rock, with sharp crimp edges where the bands meet, is the hallmark of climbing at Mount Lemmon. *Hunchback Arête,* a 5.11 overhanging edge, is one of the most photographed situations in climbing, partly because, if you hold the camera just right, it looks as though the climber is thousands of feet off the desert floor, but also because the banded grays and yellows beautifully depict the metamorphic magic of Mount Lemmon.

Metamorphic rock is everywhere and of every degree. In some places the metamorphosis has left the rock nearly in its original condition, crystals more solidly interlocked but, overall, pretty close to the former igneous or sedimentary form. The quartzite conglomerate of the Gunks was hardened at great depth and pressure, but it retains the unfolded horizontal bedding of waterborne sandstone. The

Colorful metamorphic banding characterizes Mount Lemmon, Arizona

granitic gneiss of the Adirondacks' Poke-O-Moonshine is very nearly granite, its metamorphism discernible only by the slightly lenticular shape of the individual quartz crystals. Yet some high-mountain metamorphic rocks look like taffy bent under the inexorable pressures of plate tectonics. Up close, like at Rumney in New Hampshire, the metamorphic schist offers sharp-edged holds in an unpredictable maze.

Back to the Journey

It's arguable that no nation on earth shares the diversity of American rock. It's equally doubtful that any climber could get to know it all. It takes time on a particular type of rock to know just how much pressure to put on a smeared foothold and to predict what that hidden handhold will feel like once you've latched on to it. Traveling climbers, by exposing themselves to a variety of rock types, surely build a repertoire of tricks and techniques, but the smart ones begin conservatively when they arrive at a new area. They start with routes well below their maximum grade, their minds and muscles adjusting to the new terrain. The not-so-smart ones all seem to have a story about a huge fall taken on a route that "wasn't that hard," but was early in their visit. The foot slipped when it seemed secure. Or the bucket didn't turn out to be a bucket after all.

Edward Whymper succeeded in making the coveted first ascent of the Matterhorn in 1865 by heading up the imposing Hornli Ridge while others were trying the Italian side. Whymper's understanding of layering and tilting told him that the climbing on that face would be steeper but the holds much more secure than on the down-sloping plates of the other side. Today's climbers sampling the vast rock of America would do well to follow Whymper's lead, learning a little about the rock before heading up.

Wallface in New York's Adirondack Mountains

3 LIVE FREE OR DIE

High on the East's tallest cliff, in northern New Hampshire, is the Old Man of the Mountain, a profile naturally sculpted in white granite and a symbol of what it means to be a New Englander. His lines are sharp and angular, his expression a stoic frown. He looks down from Cannon Cliff, not to welcome tourists who travel Route 93, but to remind them of the Granite State's motto: "Live Free or Die."

The culture and values of the Northeast continue to be defined by those of the region's first settlers. In 1620 when the Pilgrims first stepped from the *Mayflower* out onto what would later be known as Plymouth Rock, they were stepping into a harsh world, one whose stony soils would frustrate farmers, where weather was a cruel antagonist, and in whose woods lurked godless natives bent on bringing them down. And so by necessity they dug in and defended; ironically, however, they established a society as intolerant as the one they had escaped. It's been said that the Puritans came to the New World so that they could freely live their Christian faith and, under the banner of religious freedom, would force everyone else to do the same. The siege mentality with which they built Governor John Winthrop's City on a Hill continues to define the New Englander.

It's a mentality that persists even today, an attitude forged of an almost incomprehensible blend of free thinking and intolerance. On the surface, it's just plain Yankee conservatism, but deeper than that, it's a sense of mission, an adherence to values that don't fit neatly into the political spectrum and a refusal to be influenced by the upstarts elsewhere around the country. From afar, the place seems rife with contradiction: Massachusetts was the only state of fifty to reject Nixon and Vietnam in the 1972 elections (down with American imperialism), while New Hampshire continues to reject a state income tax (too socialist). The Granite State only recently folded under national pressure to become one of the last to recognize Martin Luther King Day. Right next door, Vermont, a state with as many cows as people (and as many Saabs and Volvos, it seems), has the country's only Socialist congressman and the nation's first civil-unions laws allowing gay marriage. Simply put, Yankees think for themselves, resist simple definition, and decline to struggle over what others might see as philosophical contradictions.

The Adirondack Mountains of northeastern New York State provide a fitting metaphor for all the Northeast. Geologists refer to the range as "new mountains of old rock." Even today, peaks are rising as quickly as some of the world's youngest and most jagged alpine summits. The anorthosite core that makes up the range continues to rebound from Pleistocene ice and rise in response to the continental drift away from Europe. There's new and independent thinking growing in a world drifting away from its European roots, yet the core and the process is rooted in bedrock traditions.

On the cover of Ed Webster's guidebook *Rock Climbs of the White Mountains* is Chris Gill on the first free ascent of *The Grand Finale.* The granite is cold and sheer. Below is the rich hardwood forest, foliage in full color. And there's Chris, during an era when climbers elsewhere were caught up in the wildly colored Lycra phase, wrapped in an old-fashioned swami belt and wearing a red plaid flannel shirt. New mountains of old rock. Live free or die.

Roots in the Past

There are really three major centers of northeastern rock climbing today: the Adirondacks and the Shawangunks of New York State and the White Mountains of New Hampshire. Elsewhere, Connecticut has a small but energized climbing scene mainly around the excellent dolorite of the *trap rock.* Maine has the sea cliffs of Acadia National Park and the alpine rock of Katahdin up north. Massachusetts has a scattering of crags around Boston and west in the Berkshires. Vermont lacks good rock like its neighboring states to the east and west, and Rhode Island lacks the topography to offer much climbing other than the fine bouldering at Lincoln Woods. Yet blessed with good rock or not, every northeastern state has a hard-core climbing population willing to travel.

Like the region itself, rock climbing in the Northeast is a direct descendant of Europe; nowhere in America are these roots so tangible. In 1916, in two separate places in the Northeast, climbers employed a safety rope to guard themselves as they took to steeper ground. In the Adirondacks, John Case used the skills he'd learned from European guides to explore the relatively modest crags near his summer home near Keene Valley. His principal student there was young Jim Goodwin, who became the area's lead high-angle explorer.

Goodwin would go forth to make first ascents of many of the Adirondack cliffs during the 1930s, including the Big Slab at Chapel Pond. Case made regular excursions to the Alps, but in the States neither he nor Goodwin strayed too far from the Adirondacks. From the beginning, the Adirondacks would be an island unto themselves, a tradition that continues today.

The same year of Case's first American climbs, climbers used a rope and a belay on some outcrops around Boston, christening Beantown's tradition as one of the major climbing cities in the nation, a reputation that grew with the early exploits of Quincy Quarries, included the accomplishments of the Harvard mountaineers, and climaxed with the dominance of Henry Barber in the 1970s. Central to that early Boston scene was Robert Underhill, one of the most influential climbers in American history, the undisputed dean of American climbing during the 1930s and '40s. Underhill had also learned the craft from guides in the Alps but, unlike Case, spread the word throughout America. With his wife, Miriam (formerly O'Brien) Underhill, he left his mark in Wyoming's Tetons and Idaho's Sawtooths, and especially California's Sierra, where he introduced modern belay technique and made the first ascent of the steep *East Face* of Mount Whitney.

In the fall of 1928, Underhill made the first ascent of the largest wall east of the Rockies, the 1,000-foot Cannon Cliff in New Hampshire. It was a spectacular ascent, but it would be eclipsed the next summer when Hassler Whitney and Bradley Gilman, drawing upon their own experience climbing in the European Alps, climbed the blocky knife-edged ridge near the south end of the cliff. At 5.7, the *Whitney-Gilman Ridge* was a remarkable climb. In 1929 it was one of the most technically difficult and committing climbs yet done in the New World. High on the route, the climbers were forced onto the dark north-facing wall that overhangs the Black Dike for the crux moves. A year later, Ken Henderson would jam a pipe into a crack here in the hope that the rope of a falling leader would catch on the pipe, a kind of rudimentary fixed protection. The pipe pitch gained a fierce reputation, and the pipe itself became something of a landmark, most latter-day leaders using it as a foothold.

Henderson was another of the northeastern climbers who, like professors Underhill and Whitney, exuded class and dignity, even while high on a route. Henderson was particularly dapper, wearing a jacket and tie for all his ascents. It's been a relatively recent development that climbers would wear athletic clothes on the rock. Climbers earlier wore what we'd now call a sports jacket well into the 1940s, and knickers would be in vogue right into the early 1970s. For leading climbers like Henry Barber, a neat appearance was part of the statement he made about self-control. A shirt untucked, even on a gymnastic crux, would show weakness.

Closer to New York, a small group was tramping around the Palisades and Hudson Highlands when they were joined first by Fritz Wiessner and later Hans Kraus. Wiessner had come from the rich and bold climbing culture of Dresden and is credited with "discovering" the Shawangunks. Like Underhill, he would travel extensively, putting in cutting-edge crack climbs wherever he went. Routes like *Minnie Belle* at the Gunks and *Vector* at Connecticut's Ragged Mountain were among the hardest in the country. (Guy and Laura Waterman write in their excellent *Yankee Rock and Ice* that while the 1937 *Mechanics Route* at Tahquitz in California is generally acclaimed as the country's first 5.8, two travelers who climbed *Vector* within days of their ascent of the *Mechanics Route* said "emphatically" that Wiessner's 1935 route in Connecticut "was a far more serious lead.")

The Granite State

Though the whole rolling topography of the Northeast is decorated with outcrops suitable for climbing, if you had to pick its cultural and spiritual locus, it would probably be the tourist town of North Conway, New Hampshire. It's a busy place and a magnet for climbers and hikers. Mount Washington, at 6,288' the Northeast's highest summit and, because of its misleadingly benign appearance, one of the world's deadliest mountains, rises above the main strip of outlet malls and climbing shops along Route 16. The congestion is awful. On a summer weekend, it can take a half-hour of agonizing stop-and-go driving just to make it from one end of the small town to the other. And agonizing it is, for beckoning off to the west are two big white sheets of granite: White Horse and Cathedral Ledges. (Elsewhere we might call them cliffs or walls; New Englanders refer to them as ledges.) It's a town steeped in climbing, and in the 1960s and '70s it spawned a rich climbing scene, mainly connected to the professional guide services of Eastern Mountain Sports and International Mountain Equipment. With the climbing schools came the guides, the region's hottest climbers, early heroes of a burgeoning subculture.

The influence of the guide remains strong today. The climbing schools of EMS and IME, along with a number of independent professionals, and led in many ways by everyone's mentor, George Hurley, define the climbing scene. They organize rescues and decide fixed anchor policy, all the while swarming the popular moderate routes. Nowhere are the guide and his clients so ubiquitous. On summer weekends, the classic moderates like Cathedral's *Thin Air* (5.6) and White Horse's *Sliding Board* (5.7) and *Standard Route* (5.5) see lines of helmeted trios, led by a lean guide wearing a light pack and a pair of approach shoes. Their presence is both irritating and educational. They clog up the routes, yet intermediate climbers within earshot can't help but come away enlightened about safety tips or the nuances of a particular route. Still, if you want to get on one of those classic midgrade routes on a weekend, you'd better set an early alarm clock.

Climbers come to North Conway principally for multipitch routes. Cathedral Ledge is about 500 feet high with climbs of three to six pitches. White Horse is a bit taller, around 700 feet, and over in Franconia Notch, Cannon Cliff rises more than 1,000 feet above the huge talus slope at its foot. Though there are indeed some half-rope sport climbs, visitors are usually looking to get high off the deck and to grapple with the enticements and anxieties that accompany exposure and commitment.

The rock is granite and it's excellent: long, arching exfoliation slabs and sharp-edged finger cracks, wide expanses of crackless gray stone and lofty ledges with solitary pines. Somehow the rock seems just right for the place. Like the culture and history, it is deep and timeless, so unlike the fragile and temporary sedimentary beds of the Colorado Plateau. There you feel as though you're climbing on a layer recently laid down and soon to blow away. Granite is different. Put your hand on it and imagine its depth. Climb on granite and you are climbing on the earth itself.

Cathedral Ledge has an auto road to its top, and from a railing drilled into the edge of the cliff, tourists can look out over the sweep of Mount Washington Valley and across to the ski area at Mount Cranmore. The rusted carcass of an automobile lies among the rocks and trees below the cliff; no doubt there's a story here. The road also makes climbing on Cathedral Ledge a spectator sport. From the ground, it defies reason how someone could stick like a fly on what seems an absolutely sheer wall. Along the road, trunks are open, ropes draped over roofs, and climbers are racking up. Tourists pulling their cars over to gape upward are reluctant to disturb the ritual to ask the predictable but necessary "How do you get the rope up there?" But once on top, when they see the chalk-covered hand reach up to grab the railing for the final mantel, even the most reticent onlooker just has to ask, "How long did it take?" "Why don't your shoes have any grips?" "You mean women do this too?" At first the climber's ego relishes every question. Then the interrogation wears thin, even annoying after a while, and local climbers know how to exit the cliff while avoiding the lookout. Yet the savvy veteran who didn't bring approach shoes realizes that to work such an encounter skillfully is to end up with a ride back to the bottom, beer in hand from the visitor's cooler: "Yeah, it was a tough one—had to pound in a couple of croutons in one place. But the rope held, and thank god, we made it."

Next door is White Horse Ledge, comprised really of two faces, one a steep, crackless, south-facing wall and the other a smooth, water-striped friction slab, the best of its genre in the eastern United States. Years back, locals say, the outline of a horse could be discerned in the dark stripes on the slab, thus the name. Today the image is gone, but the cliff continues to draw the eye from vantage points all over town and especially from Echo Pond public beach at its base.

The friction climbing, pitch upon pitch of inclined rock with minimal protection and bolt belays, is super. It's on climbs like *Sliding Board* (5.7) that one truly understands that real friction climbing isn't moving from bump to bump or searching out subtle edges; if you need to choose foot spots, then it isn't really friction climbing. If, however, the surface is so uniformly smooth that it matters not a bit where you place your foot, then the emphasis shifts to body position and momentum. This is friction climbing. Step high, move up to the side and directly over the foot. Keep as much rubber as possible on the rock. When you sense that ever-so-slight downward slide, it's time not to look back at the last bolt but instead to swallow hard and step up again. Climbed in the first-generation smooth-soled shoes of the 1960s and '70s—the old PAs, RDs, or even EBs—*Sliding Board* was well named.

The bottom of the slab is low-angled, really just an ankle-bending walk. Guides tell stories of kids and dogs getting stranded by scrambling just a little too high. Off to the left, however, the wall rears upward to near vertical. Unlike Cathedral with its obvious crack lines, the South Buttress of White Horse is just a blank wall. Lots of face holds, but no alluring lines, and certainly no evident protection. Even with a vital climbing community in North Conway, very little was done here until British expatriate Paul Ross arrived. He was astounded that such a vast expanse of rock had been neglected; nor did the lack of protection cracks seem to matter. His first route, *The Eliminate,* was a mixed free and aid climb right up the biggest part of the wall. Other routes followed, most wandering to connect holds and drilling stances. With most of the routes established on the lead, the South Buttress remains today the realm of experienced climbers, those with the composure for long run-outs and the nose to sniff out a route amid a maze of dead ends and misleading combinations of face holds.

The views from on high are expansive, but reflect the disturbing sprawl of a vacation town. Below the South Buttress is a huge new hotel and golf course, part of the exclusive planned community of Hale's Location. The hotel is palatial, built to look like one of those old New England inns. Out on the golf course, carts scurry to and fro while tanned men and women in bright green pants and white visors cluster around numbered flags. Hundreds of feet above on the orange-white wall, a pair of tiny climbers seem glued impossibly to blank stone. The putters don't notice, too busy concentrating on the important business at hand.

Cannon Cliff, over on the west side of the mountains at Franconia Notch, is a different setting altogether. Here a thousand-foot wall looms over a thousand-foot talus slope in a tight mountain pass where the weather howls and splintered slabs lie ready to slide at a climber's touch. On Cannon, it isn't crag climbing; it's mountain climbing. Although the granite up close is much like that at Cathedral or White Horse, the overall experience of climbing here

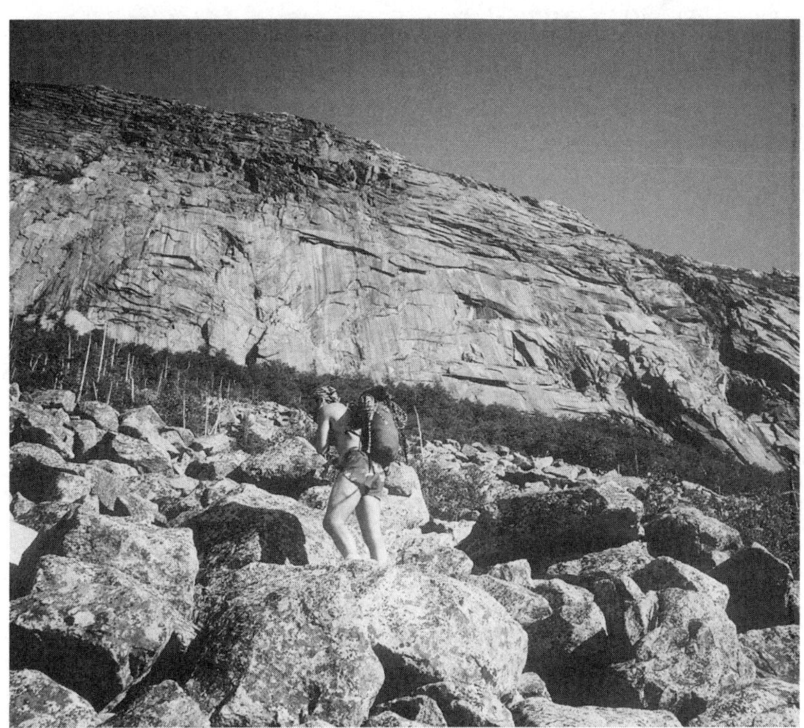

New Hampshire's Cannon Cliff, the East's tallest

makes North Conway seem a planet away. There is no road to the top, no lineup of tourists watching every move through binoculars, no nearby town or swimming hole, no scene. It's a big and dangerous cliff, and many lowland crag climbers choose to stay far away.

Even as the two New Hampshire climbing centers were being developed, there emerged two distinct cultures that kept them generally isolated from each other. Cannon climbers saw the North Conway crew as pretty boys in pretty clothes, squeezing insignificant lines between only marginally significant ones. The Franconia climbers were irreverent, almost surly, more adventurous than gymnastic, burying the rule book deep in the bottom of their rucksacks (even below their bolt kit), and doing whatever it took to get up the wall in one piece.

Notorious disasters have taken place on the big stone of Cannon Cliff, including the 1968 death of former Surgeon General C. Everett Koop's son David, a Dartmouth student killed by a sliding block apparently dislodged by his piton. Five years later, two climbers ripped a belay anchor on the same route, *Sam's Swan Song* (5.7). Up close, the granite is superb, fractured in grand symmetry, with long, sweeping corners and blank, unclimbable slabs. Yet the less-than-vertical angle of the cliff, the classic exfoliation properties of granite, and the freeze-thaw cycles typical of northern New England make for a surface that seems alive and angry. Climbers approaching from below have been swept back down the talus by avalanches of loose stone. Others have watched huge sections just fall away when the weather was fine and nothing could be held accountable except the sad realities of gravity and potential energy. The good sections are great—granite identical to the best of Yosemite. But every route has its loose sections, and when one refers to someone as a "Cannon climber," one has succinctly defined a personality type.

ROUTES FORGED OF PRAGMATISM AND TRADITION

The 1970s in New Hampshire was a period of ethical wrestling during which two climbers emerged side by side whose influence resonates today. Henry Barber was a brash Boston teenager with a reverence for the British traditions of clean climbing and the nerve to practice it; Paul Ross was a Brit with an ironically pragmatic approach to big-wall trickery. The decade was marked by Barber's methodical free climbing of the old aid cracks and by Ross's forays out onto the blank areas, drilling and hooking unabashedly and making damn sure that no ethics police patrolled an unwilling climbing community.

Barber was perhaps the most important climber of the decade, and not just in the Northeast. Trained by the conservative Appalachian Mountain Club and steeped in the British rock ethic of Joe Brown and Don Whillans, Barber climbed to make a statement. His routes weren't so much exhibitions of what *could* be done as they were demonstrations of how things *should* be done. Tall, strong, and confident almost to a fault, Barber strode the base of New England cliffs in uniform: clean white trousers, a webbing swami for a harness, a tidy rugby shirt or even a collared dress shirt à la Henderson) and always, always his trademark short-visored cap, a classic look so much a part of the classic values he espoused.

Paul Ross, on the other hand, was the authentic Brit, a real, not vicarious, partner of Brown and Whillans. He was older when he arrived, and he came with a solid résumé of climbs in Great Britain and the Alps. To New Englanders nursed on such conservative treatises as Geoffrey Winthrop Young's 1920 *Mountaincraft,* British climbers were the world's cleanest. Just to hear his thick accent was to imagine Ross made of the same steely fiber as the Brits of lore. New Hampshire climbers emulated the British, creating a scene that was the offspring of British rock climbing tradition. The pub scenes in North Conway, the irreverent puns and innuendo coloring the guidebooks, the homey feeling, the honest friendships, the historical chronicling of climbing activity—all of these were pulled, either directly by travelers or vicariously from the legends, right from the British model.

Yet there was something impish and irreverent about Paul Ross, and when he moved from Outward Bound's Hurricane Island School in Maine to Tom Lyman's Climbing School in New Hampshire, the place would never be the same. Ross was more a man of tools than technique, an aid climber who could pick out disconnected natural features with full confidence that he could hammer his way from one to the next. Ross immediately picked up on the big-wall work of Steve Arsenault and Joe Cote, even in an era when it was going out of fashion. Nor was he concerned about the grumbling coming from the new kids. He pointed out in his 1978 guidebook about freeing his old aid route *The Prow* (now 5.11+) that the first free ascent was a multimonth siege while the original aid route took just a day and a half. "Which is the better style?" he asked.

Today the two schools of thinking happily coexist. Good, clean, classically protected cracks remain most popular, and the legacy of Henry Barber still looms over the Mount Washington Valley. The upper left wall of Cathedral, where he did many of his free ascents, is still known as the Barber Shop. Yet North Conway is a climbing center, and it attracts top eastern climbers looking to push boundaries. Bolted face routes are going up between traditional crack lines, and though there was a bit of a fracas a few years ago when every climber wanted a policy but no one could agree on just what that policy ought to be, there's peace today among the practitioners. Some routes require a little trickery, a little Paul Ross pragmatism. And others seem to ask for an adherence to the old-style, swami-belted, ground-up traditionalism.

THE ADIRONDACKS: FOREVER WILD

While New Hampshire and New York's Shawangunks have bustling and competitive scenes, the Adirondack region is distinguished by its very lack of one. The Adirondacks are a vast collection of walls and slabs, many of which are far from the small towns scattered throughout Adirondack Park. Lake Placid, the winter Olympic site in 1932 and 1980, is probably the first destination for the visitor, or historic Keene Valley, but one is hard-pressed to find a bar or coffee shop where climbers collect, where everyone seems to be wearing sticky-rubber approach shoes or talking the talk so familiar to the club.

With John Case's 1916 ascents on the cliffs on Indian Head or around Chapel Pond, the Adirondacks of northeastern New York have one of the longest climbing histories in North America. Yet even with its traditions, good rock, and diverse climbing, the region remains a bit of a backwater in relation to its neighbors to the south or east. Big-name rock climbers seldom visit. It rains a lot. There aren't any résumé-enhancing routes. Nor is it likely that any of their accomplishments will make it into national print. Most Adirondackers consider it an unwritten rule not to publicize the region. The nasty weather associated with the region might, however, ironically help open the floodgates, as the region's reputation for ice climbing grows. Visits by Alex Lowe and Jeff Lowe, among others, have shown the place to be among America's best, and the climbing media is beginning to cast light on the winter climbing here. Will such attention expand to the summer rock climbs? Probably not as long as there remains such a dearth of bolted sport climbs.

Essentially and fundamentally, the Adirondacks is a park, a sanctuary from the craziness elsewhere and a model of what a place can be if left alone to heal. All facets of the region—from its architecture to its arts to its rock climbing—reflect the special heritage that is at the core of the Park.

In the early 1800s, America's concept of wilderness was much different from the one we hold today. Explorers of the region saw the mountains and the trees only as impediments to their utilitarian visions. In fact, Thomas Jefferson, looking upon Lake George in the southern Adirondacks, said the place was one of the most beautiful in the New World, one that would be even more so when the lands were cleared and farms dotted the rolling hills. The Iroquois hunters who passed through simply called the place Couchsacrage, or "dismal wilderness." (Without going too far afield here, one might speculate on this same ambivalence toward things wild that gnaws at climbers today. "Yes, it's a beautiful piece of rock, and won't it be even more so when a line of bolts leads to a chained anchor?")

There's a blessed irony behind the creation of the Park. It wasn't the manifestation of a mature wilderness ethic by New Yorkers. Instead, it was for much more pragmatic reasons that the idea of an Adirondack Park took root and became law. In the late 1800s, New York led the nation in forest products, but the logging industry's tactics were shortsighted. The slash left to dry after the logs were removed made excellent kindling, and in the early 1900s fires swept the region bare. Once the lands were cleared, either by design or by fire, the landowners simply stopped paying state taxes, and the land quickly reverted back to the state. Rather than letting private owners once again do such damage, the state adapted a law declaring that all wild forestlands remain "forever wild," not because of the aesthetic value of wilderness, but because without a thick forest cover up north, the rivers would run dry in the summer and flood in the spring. And so long before Americans learned to grasp the intrinsic value of wilderness, New York State had created one of the largest parks in the country.

At 6 million acres, Adirondack Park is about the size of the state of New Hampshire. Not only is it vast, but its composition is also unique in that it's a patchwork quilt of private and public lands. The public lands comprise just under half of the park and are protected forever from development, while the private lands are under strict development guidelines that cluster human activities into hamlets and keep the hillsides wild.

Predictably, when big government imposes itself onto a rural population, there grows the classic ideological rift pitting environmentalists against proponents of home rule. When the Park Agency, for example, refused to grandfather an old road leading into the Pharaoh Wilderness, blocking its entrance with huge boulders, the rocks soon appeared on the lawn of one of the agency officials, "stones of shame" painted across the largest one. Though the restrictions are controversial, there's no debating the results. Today's lowland forests are covered with a rich blend of deciduous trees, the big three hardwoods of the mature Adirondack forest being maple, beech, and yellow birch, while the opportunistic pioneer species of paper birch and balsam fir cover the higher elevations. To the uninitiated, the endless miles of deep, rich forest look undisturbed and original. It's this forest, almost as much as the routes themselves, that defines the Adirondack climbing experience.

The rock is mainly anorthosite, a billion-year-old formation similar to that which makes up the white parts of the moon. Most climbers simply call it granite because it has been so thoroughly metamorphosed that it looks more like a massive igneous rock. The best examples of this anorthosite are on the many cliffs and slabs around Chapel Pond and on the legendary wilderness cliff of Wallface Mountain. Chapel Pond's cliffs are essentially roadside crags. There, right in view from Route 73, are all kinds of climbing, from the steep and imposing 350-foot Washbowl Cliff, so named for the tiny pond hidden above, to Chapel Pond Slab, with its 700 feet of easy friction, to the relentless cracks of the Spider's Web, an overhanging wall laced by sustained cracks, from fingertip to off-width. Most climbers here, however, congregate at the lowly Beer Walls, probably because the routes are moderate and top-roping so convenient.

The quintessential Adirondack cliff, Wallface is the East's largest wilderness cliff, almost 700 feet high and six miles from the parking lot at Adirondack Loj (for *Lodge;* another regional peculiarity is the vestige of phonetic spellings introduced by Melville Dewey, founder of the Lake Placid Club and father of the Dewey Decimal library system). It's a place that appeals only to the oddball few. Some say it's the best of wilderness experiences. Others, having been lost both on the rock and in the tangle of trailless blowdown on top, vow never to return. No other cliff, however, so fully captures the Adirondack experience. The approach is arduous; the five-mile rolling trail is followed by a half-hour of scrambling over and burrowing under house-sized blocks choked with nasty vegetation. Above, the rock is weathered rough and sharp, loose slabs tilt crazily from slightly overhanging headwalls, and birches are everywhere. It's a whole lot of work, yet the feeling of being "out there" is unmatched in the eastern United States, and for these qualities, Fritz Wiessner called it his favorite Adirondack destination.

Well to the east of the mountains and off near Lake Champlain is Poke-O-Moonshine, an Iroquois name meaning "rough and smooth." The 400-foot cliff is mainly "smooth" and sheer granitic gneiss interrupted at rope-length intervals by horizontal intrusions, dikes of easily shattered "rough" rock. Poke-O has the hardest routes and the most contemporary feel of any Adirondack cliff. That it sits well away from the High Peaks climbs around Lake Placid and Keene Valley means that it's less constrained by the hard traditional ethic that prevails elsewhere in the park. Poke-O has the only real sport climbs in the Adirondacks, but beware: If there are any gear placements available, even on what is essentially a clip-up, there just won't be a bolt. Although Wallface climbers ought to know how to use a compass, Poke-O climbers need to be adroit in placing tiny wired chocks.

In such a vast, unregulated area as the Adirondacks, no dominant idea as to how the game should be played emerged until well into the 1980s. The earliest pioneers, Fritz Wiessner, Jim Goodwin, and John Case, seemed to enjoy being out in the wild more than anything else, and their routes were more just wilderness experience than high-level technical rock climbs. Case never pounded a piton in his life, considering such an act akin to an admission of incompetence. Nor did he ever fall. Goodwin was a prolific hiker and explorer; technical rock climbing was just one small element of a much broader game of mountaineering. Wiessner liked Wallface best of all, not because of the quality or difficulty of the climbing, but because it was so far from the crowds.

The strongest influence in the 1950s and '60s came from the Canadians, who saw cliffs like Poke-O-Moonshine as their local crags. Montreal, after all, is only about ninety minutes to the north. The group was influenced by French mountaineers in general and led by Englishman John Turner in particular. Like the Europeans, they were free with their pitons and didn't mind grabbing a sling or two to get through a difficult passage. Turner, on the other hand, was clean and daring. While his contributions at New Hampshire's Cathedral Ledge (*Recompense* and *Repentance,* both 5.9, for example) were well acclaimed, his Poke-O routes like *Bloody Mary* and *Positive Thinking* (also 5.9s) were equally long and hard, but too far from the American mainstream to attract much attention.

As the clean-climbing revolution was being waged so vigorously elsewhere, in the Adirondacks climbers still poked along in relative obscurity, never adhering to one school of thought or another. Local Poke-O climbers, led by Gary Allen and Geoff Smith under the club banner "Ski to Die," did their share of rappel bolting and aggressive cleaning of cracks. At the same time, a few visits from New England by Henry Barber, Rick Fleming, and Steve Larson modeled for the growing Lake Placid and Keene Valley climbers an admirable purity of style.

All the while, as a more coherent nucleus of local climbers established itself and matured, climbers generally came to acknowledge that their activities were part of a much broader context, that Adirondack Park, considered by some to be a Central Park for the world, was no place for drilling and chipping with abandon. If there was to be a sanctuary from the frenzy of the citified world, so ought there be a sanctuary from the frenzied climbing scenes emerging elsewhere. Supplementing this thinking was the physical nature of the place. There's exposed rock everywhere, some of it difficult miles from the road. Climbers haven't invested much time or effort to "work" routes so far from the car—they'd rather climb. And those who do wish to explore new terrain know that there won't be much notice, not much glory for the effort.

The Adirondack region is too vast, too spread out, and its climbers come from too many different places for there to be much concentrated discussion about ethics. Yet as the years go by, the place is increasingly known for its wilderness and traditional approach. The cliffs are hard to access, the routes sometimes hard to follow. There aren't any "status routes." In fact, there are fewer 5.12s here than at any major climbing area in the country. The cracks are dirtier than you'd like, and lichen covers all. But talk to a visitor, and you'll hear the same refrain: "It's sure good to get away from it all."

THE LEGENDARY GUNKS

When envisioning northeastern rock climbing, one's imagination usually travels north—to the Adirondacks or White Mountains—to rough weather and smooth slabs and multipitch walls soaring above a rich boreal forest. Just seventy miles from New York City, however, is one of the most beautiful and important climbing areas in the nation. With the urban area so near and with so many people on the carriage road and trails around the cliffs, the place feels more like a city park than a true wilderness. It's close to the highway and heavily traveled, a single compact escarpment clearly delineated as sedimentary rock with its predictable horizontal strata and intimidating overhangs, so different from the smooth granitic rock elsewhere in the Northeast.

The Shawangunk escarpment is about seven miles outside of New Paltz, a college town, home of the state university. It's a town unlike any other. The cliffs bring the climbers, the college draws the kids. Sprinkled among these two groups are some friendly but seedy-looking types attracted to or leftover from the college scene. Bikers in leather and aging hippies, both anachronistically refusing to accept the passing of the '60s, mingle on street corners. There are head shops and organic food marts, along with countless offerings to stay healthy or drink hard. Bacchus is the bar of choice today. The better spot used to be P and G's up the street; it was the grubbiest place imaginable, where customers were encouraged to carve their names in the tables and where a patron might roll in on skates, wearing nothing but satin hot pants and buffalo horns, and no one would take notice as he bellied up to the bar. After the pickup truck smashed through the front window, they fixed the place up. These days it's a mite too respectable for climbers.

The climbing history at the Gunks reflects the same irreverent nonconformity. In the tradition of the British example, early climbers in the Northeast tended to group and form clubs. The Harvard and Yale Mountain Clubs were two of the most prolific. The most influential, however, was the Appalachian Mountain Club, based in Boston, but reigning all over the Northeast. At the Shawangunks, the Appies developed a safety code that went so far as to require special certification for leading. In their conservative dominion over the area, they kept even competent climbers on the easy routes for long periods of apprenticeship. Every repressive regime, however, has within it the seeds of its own demise, and in the case of the Appalachian Mountain Club at the Gunks, the rebels called themselves the Vulgarians. It was a title to which they pledged strict allegiance.

In the 1960s, while the Appies were teaching safe techniques on

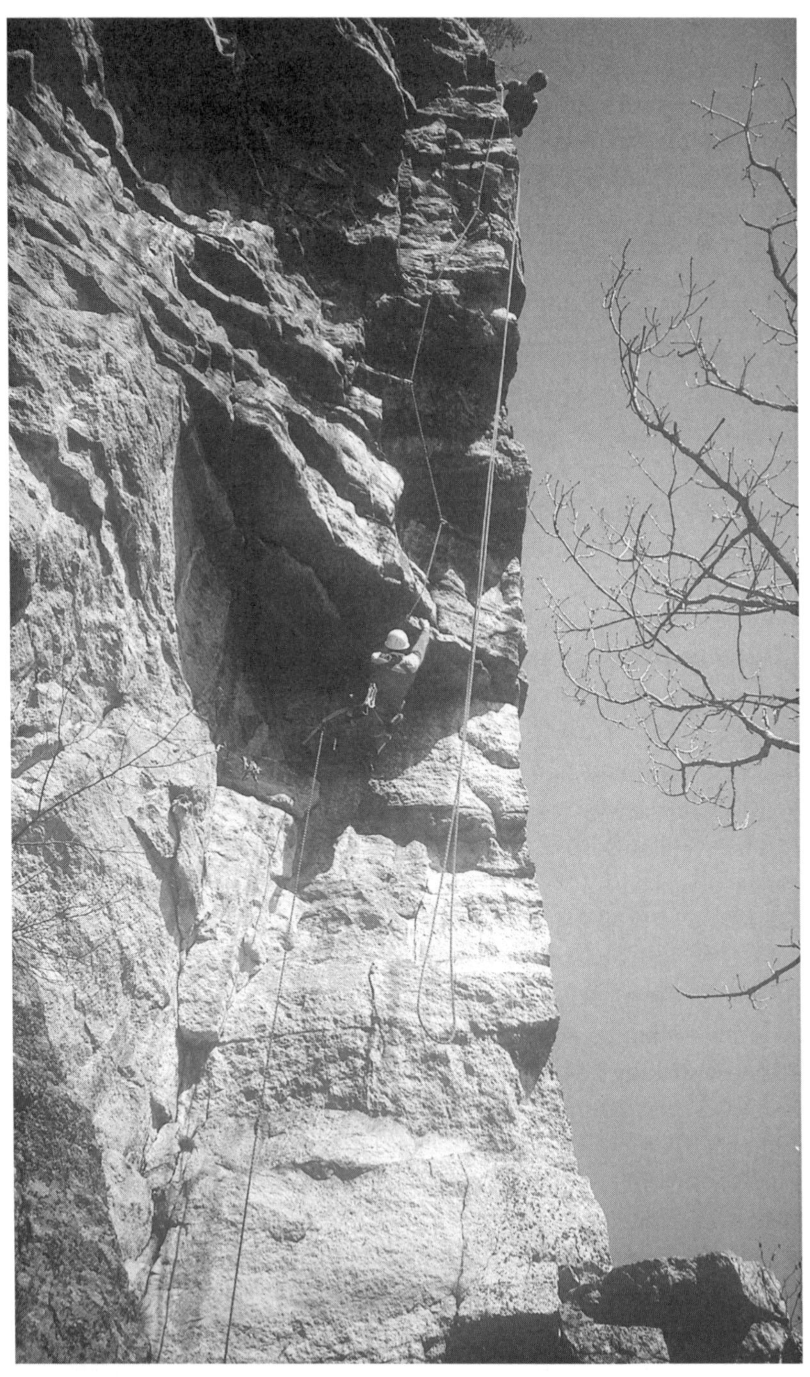

Steep rock and strenuous climbing at the Shawangunks

the historic routes of Wiessner and Kraus, the Vulgarians were probing the limits toward and into the 5.10 range. While the conservatives were following such innocuously named routes as *Beginner's Delight* and *Layback* and *Easy Overhang,* the Vulgarians were establishing *Dick's Prick, Swinging Cunt,* and *Vulga-Tits* (a proudly all-female ascent). The cultural war waged by the Vulgarians included pissing from the roof of a New Paltz bar on emerging Appies and turning over one of their cars in defiance (OK, it was the wrong car, but it's the thought that counts). The symbol of the Vulgarians was the black-and-white photo of Dick Williams leading the big roof of *Shockley's Ceiling.* Nude.

Many witnesses to their antics dismissed the Vulgarians as immature jerks, basking in their own self-importance. But as the years pass, their stature as rebels against authority grows. Yankees still value the individual over the collective and encourage free expression over the tyranny of organization. Pissing off the roof of a bar onto the head of a fellow climber was little more than an impulsive and obnoxious gesture by drunks, but the passing of years and the simplification that accompanies the telling and retelling of a tale have elevated the deed to a dimension akin to tossing a box of tea from a ship into Boston Harbor.

Most of the Vulgarians still climb, but few have made it their life as Dick Williams has. His climbing shop, Rock and Snow, is one of the best stocked in the East, and it's a first stop for visiting climbers. If you are looking to hook up with a partner, you can head right to the Uberfall, the climbers' hangout at the base of the cliff, where notes are posted, daily fees collected, and vicious boulder problems cruised by locals so familiar they seem almost a part of the landscape itself.

Most striking about the Gunks is its capacity to absorb so many people, especially important with New York City an easy day trip for millions. Neither the Adirondacks nor the Whites could handle the pressure of being so close to the city. Even though each is so vast and varied, the trails would become muddied and trampled, the relatively few easy and moderate routes would be hopelessly jammed, and any feeling of wilderness would be lost.

Yet somehow the Gunks survives. Some might prefer solitude over loud and distinctly New York accents shouting "Ya got me?" just a few feet to either side, or the befuddled novice leader decorated with shiny new gear and holding open Williams's thick guidebook calling up, "Yo. What route you on?" But there's a certain pleasure to be among other climbers, to be part of such a distinctive scene. In a way, it's like a rock gym without a roof: ropes everywhere, advice ringing out all around, and chalk marks leading out to even the most unlikely roofs. The sign below the cliff calls it a multiuse area, but on a weekend when the sun shines, one has a hard time imagining successful bird-watching or peaceful hiking.

It's a place defined by the rock itself, a quartzite conglomerate bedded in straight horizontal layers—an almost snow-white aggregate of pebbles and sand grains held together as tightly as the hardest granite. The routes have little loose rock, yet the horizontal ledges that run across the cliffs collect debris; many Gunks climbers wisely wear helmets, for there is always someone above, usually a beginning leader dragging a rope across just such a ledge as he follows an easy zigzag line above yours.

The climbing at the Shawangunks is very different from that at other northeastern areas; in fact, it's almost unique. Rather than requiring the endurance or patience necessary to take on a long granite dihedral, for example, it demands strong arms and a long reach. It's often brutish climbing—hard, strenuous cruxes between good hands-off rests. The holds are often big and predictable, and though the protection isn't always what you hope for (flexible cams or tied-off Friends make a huge difference), the deadly run-outs on sharp, secure holds are accepted as routine parts of almost every climb. Sure, many routes involve subtle footwork or excruciating crimping on microflakes, but most routes just take strong-armed jug hauling. Some describe the rating of Gunks routes simply as a function of the distance between buckets. If it's a short pull, the route is easy. If you've got to crank higher, holding on from, say, your midchest level, then the climb is in the 5.10 realm. Strength is vital for most routes, and when one refers to someone as a Gunks climber, it isn't to locate the person geographically. It's almost akin to saying the person is a gym climber: a strong-armed roof specialist.

Climbing exclusively at the Gunks does not make a well-rounded technician, and climbers from the Adirondacks or New Hampshire like nothing better than watching such a Gunks climber struggling up a long finger crack or smooth granite corner. Yet those same North

Country climbers get a well-deserved reciprocal spanking when they sneak down to the Gunks and hunker under a roof that blocks out daylight and whose grade seems a cruel mistake.

The Shawangunks isn't all terror and overhangs. In fact, some of the friendliest climbing anywhere can be had there. No place in the country has such a proliferation of easy and moderate routes (there are more than four hundred routes under 5.8), and aspiring leaders can simply open the guidebook and find a three-pitch route of exactly the grade they are looking for. How many places nationwide can boast steep and overhanging routes at 5.4? Climbers from the big areas out West use the grade to suggest an unroped approach or a scrambling finish. Those climbers should get on Fritz Wiessner's 5.4 *Gelsa.* The route's third pitch is an overhanging line of long reaches, so steep that beginners have trouble just keeping their feet on the rock. Only at the Gunks do climbers proudly proclaim that they lead 5.6.

Years back, when climbers carried a hammer and a rack of pins, the Gunks seemed ideally protectable. The horizontal cracks tilt back perfectly for the best piton placements, so much better than in Yosemite granite. During the 1970s when the clean-climbing revolution was sweeping like a storm wind across the American climbing scene and when purists began working the aid from artificial routes, the Gunks bristled with good resident pitons. You could leave your hammer at home, but the routes weren't truly clean. Over the years, the pins gradually rusted out or broke off.

The horizontal cracks that made nailing so easy were a quandary to the climber with a rack of shiny new Hexes and Stoppers: Not only is it inherently tough to arrange solid protection in a horizontal crack, but it's even more so when you have to hang on long enough to place it. On low-angled rock, you can stand and work out the gear; it's quite another thing to be dangling under a big Gunks roof, fiddling with a nut that won't hold anyway or stuffing a blind camming unit into a crack just out of sight over the lip. Arm strength and confidence just drain away, and even if the gear is finally good, there's not much left in you to give the move a full go.

In the 1980s when the Euro influence made Smith Rock the model for a burgeoning game called sport climbing, it seemed as though the Gunks might go the way of so many areas nationwide and that bolts would quickly fill the blank areas between natural lines. The cliff lies on private land, however, a tract held in preserve by the Mohonk Trust. Wisely, a hard line was drawn before too many brandished their Bosch drill: no physical changes, no bolts or unapproved pitons, would be allowed. The very few bolts (on *Arrow,* 5.8, for instance) were grandfathered in. But overall the Gunks retained its old-world character. You earn your routes here.

The bolting ban has had an obvious impact on several facets of the game at the Gunks. Climbers still talk about 5.9 and 5.10 routes as hard. It's not a place to tick high numbers for their own sake. There's pride in a bold run-out or a clever arrangement of opposed chocks in a horizontal crack. And though the crowds are amazing, there isn't much half-rope hangdogging. People still go there to "do" routes rather than work them. They climb at the Gunks to feel the satisfaction of long, back-stretching reaches and the happiness that accompanies fingers latched securely onto a flat, pebbly surface. They go to scare themselves for a moment, to dig deep for short bursts to good ledges, and to enjoy sitting high on a ledge, relishing the breeze and the expansive views over the Hudson River Valley to the east.

Small Crags and a Hunger for Sport Routes

When it comes to climbing practices, the Northeast remains decidedly traditional. There are fewer sport routes in this section of the country than anywhere else. Part of this has to do with the nature of the rock. The granitic rock that dominates the Northeast has obvious natural lines, and as one North Conway native explained, "A really appealing natural line is much better than another stupid clip-up." A bigger part of this, however, is the depth of the northeastern tradition that hovers over the place. Up in New Hampshire, one climbs in the footsteps of great traditional climbers like Underhill and Wiessner and Barber. In the Adirondacks, the guidebook takes a heavy-handed approach in placing the climbing ethos firmly within the broader context of the preservation of Adirondack Park.

Down in Connecticut one man, Ken Nichols, has waged a dedicated campaign to keep the trap-rock cliffs bolt-free. Nichols has so zealously guarded his view of proper methodology that northeastern climbers see him and the Connecticut trap rock as inextricably woven together, so much so that many avoid the place because its anxiety level is simply too high. Nichols' guidebook of the region is Bible-thick, a figure of speech deliberately chosen here. Most of the first ascents are his, and his efforts to avoid bolting include filing chocks to the half size for specific placements and even protecting routes with homemade skyhooks held in place by light ropes cinched to the ground (as many as seven on one route). Nichols is an excellent and passionate climber, but a route that requires seven tied-off skyhooks isn't the kind of route that will see a waiting line. Had Nichols not built Fort Connecticut, the place might be overbolted now, or even closed. But the pressure under the cork could well blow sky-high when the oligarchy topples.

Dominant personalities and wistful romancing about traditions have made the Northeast a hostile place for sport climbing. Yet climbers, both the pragmatists and the newcomers, hunger for gymnastic clip-ups. The craving shows up in Kingston Quarry, near the Gunks, where the rock is limited but the rules aren't. It shows up in quarries and hidden crags on the periphery of Adirondack Park, where hard routes have been established, but hush is the word for fear that someone will object. And it shows up on smaller cliffs in New Hampshire, like Sundown Ledge and especially Rumney.

The newcomer and the old-timer sit together to talk about New Hampshire. The gray-hair closes his eyes and sees a Chouinard Stopper dropped deftly into the fine fingertip layback of Cathedral's *Recompense* (5.9); the kid sees the overhanging, sharp-edged pump-fests at Rumney's Wiamia. He's not alone. Once-humble Rumney has emerged as the state's most popular climbing area. As at so many other places, the early sport routes at Rumney took a beating. In fact, more than fifty bolts were chopped by visiting Ken Nichols in response to some rappel-placed bolts in Connecticut. Judged in the context of the big granite cliffs of New Hampshire, the bolting at Rumney seemed blasphemous to some climbers. But everywhere, the nature of the rock often dictates the way it will be climbed. Rumney wasn't quite the limestone choss pile awaiting excavation, like some of the more noteworthy sport-climbing venues out West, but the complex waves of ripples, the grippy feel of the rock, the big, crackless, overhanging planes of schist call for an approach much different from that required of less-than-vertical granite.

Rumney is now the best and busiest sport-climbing area in the Northeast, with 5.13s and 14s and a cadre of young climbers you haven't yet heard of but will. The best is David Graham, from Maine. Maine? When news of his high-end routes was printed in *Climbing* and *Rock & Ice,* a lot of climbers scoffed at the thought of some young kid from a climbing backwater attaching big numbers to routes they hadn't heard of. That is until Mr. Graham went west and quickly dispatched many of their biggest and baddest sport climbs. For many around the nation, it was validation for Rumney, proof that these 5.13s and 14s are, in fact, real 13s and 14s.

Maine, a place they call Down East, is probably a good place to close. There, on the rocky, windblown coast, is America's best sea-cliff climbing, a pursuit made noble by the British. Go down to the Maine seacoast. Smell the salt air and feel the crashing waves beneath your feet on Otter Cliffs at Acadia National Park. Or better yet, venture onto the hulking Great Head, sticking out into the cold North Atlantic, where the swirling rock offers little protection and the pounding surf will make you pay for a mistake. From its top, you might sit and look out to sea and reflect upon the connections: techniques and values from across the sea laying the bedrock foundation for one of the country's bastions of traditionalism.

West Virginia's New River Gorge

4 THE STEEP SOUTH

On an afternoon in October 1987, a pinnacle of stone teetered from its perch on the spine of West Virginia's Seneca Rocks and exploded in the talus hundreds of feet below. The Gendarme, an icon of southern climbing, was gone.

Countless climbers had stood atop the spire since its first ascent in 1939, and even though the route to its summit was only 5.4, the maneuver was notorious, both because a slip would be fatal and because the spire itself seemed so fragile. None of those who performed the ritual stunt actually fell, but their skepticism about its fragility proved justified on that October afternoon.

More than just a 30-foot spire of rock, the Gendarme was the symbol of southern climbing and the legendary climbing store of the same name. In parking areas around the country, you'll see the store's logo decal, copied somewhat from a classic photograph in the Alps, with a lone climber balanced on the listing pinnacle. Like all good bumper advertisement, the decal characterizes the car's owner—in this case announcing that he has been to Seneca Rocks and, more, that he is an old-school trad climber; for no place in America represents old-style, ground-up, undergraded climbing like Seneca. Photographer Harrison Shull claims that if you can climb 5.10 at Seneca, you can climb 5.10 anywhere. True.

Yet as the Gendarme was falling, so was a new kind of climbing burgeoning and budging aside the legendary traditionalism of the South. In the sandstone gorges of Kentucky, West Virginia, Alabama, and Tennessee, steep cliffs of horizontally bedded sandstone were showing themselves to be a sport-climbing resource rivaling any in the world. Years ago in the minds of outsiders, the South was only Seneca Rocks and the granite domes of western North Carolina. How quickly these old-school climbing areas have been eclipsed by discoveries in the great southern sandstone belt, where modern sport-climbing attitudes and staggeringly steep rock have come together to redefine southern climbing. And though the islands of traditionalism will surely endure, it will be the sandstone, solid, overhanging, and endless, that will etch the South onto the map of vital American climbing regions.

Dixie

No region in America has been so parochial, so defended, so consciously regional as the South. It's a place that still flies the flag of the

Confederacy, where "y'all" isn't just a manner of speech but a password, where bumper stickers read "I'd rather be shooting Yankees." On one house in Alabama are two hand-painted signs, one proclaiming that "Jesus loves you" and the other warning "This house is protected by automatic shotgun." To the proud owner there's no irony.

The South is distinctly aware of its roots, its secession from the Union, and its capitulation in the Great War of Northern Aggression. Southern culture is distinctly homegrown but, as with its newfound climbing celebrity, it's a culture that continues to emerge into the national consciousness. Thus, the tension isn't only between North and South; it's also between old and new. Much of today's South is gleaming and modern, closing the final chapter, in a way, of Reconstruction. All the while, there's a collective wistfulness for the antebellum regality of the region's past. The dichotomy shows up in southern climbing as well, with cutting-edge sport routes exploding across the Cumberland Plateau, while militant islands of traditionalism hold strong in the older climbing regions in North Carolina and West Virginia. Visit the South for the best of every kind of rock climbing and for a cultural experience distinct from all others.

The first thing you'll have to do is slow down. There's a different clock in the South, one that allows time for conversation, for savoring a moment. You'll feel it in the shops and diners. You'll feel it at the cliffs. "How y'all doin' today?" is not just a polite manner of speech. The greeter actually wants to know. When an out-of-towner is seen at the crux of a puzzling move, a smiling group will congregate below. "OK now, git your foot up on that there shelf to the left. Good." The beta flows excessive and generous from folks who truly hope you'll succeed. In busy places like the Gunks or Yosemite, where climbers have been swarming for years, you sense less eye contact. Walk the crags of the South and people notice you, smile, wonder where you're from, especially pleased if it's a long way off. They're happy to have visitors from afar, company at the crags, affirmation that their routes are worth the miles.

The language of the South is more soothing than efficient. Yankee bluntness is replaced by the gentility of southern understatement. The Yankee is task oriented and will tell you what's on his mind. The southerner is more patient. He'll dance around a topic, and you'll just have to read between the lines. Author Tom Wolfe, visiting Atlanta to promote a recent novel, told his audience that he liked southern indirection, that he didn't even mind vicious personal attacks one bit, provided they were couched in softened, roundabout terms.

Southern climbers, too, will understate a point. "Kinda isolates your fingers, doesn't it," says Kentucky climber Porter Jarrard about the pockets of Red River Gorge. There's a knowing smirk on his face as you reach for more ice and ibuprofen after having been graciously "home cooked" on one of his routes. Southern hospitality is at its ironic best when climbers there use the term "home cooked" to describe what elsewhere climbers call "spanked" or "sandbagged." Southerners are self-consciously southern, so much so that you even suspect at times that, in the presence of outsiders, they mimic themselves by exaggerating their accents, talking "up the holler," aware that they are part of the overall show and unwilling to let their audience down. Southern climbers talk a lot about "rednecks," either in self-deprecation or as apology for what they perceive to be their image in the outside world.

In 1993 New River guide Steve Cater and friends produced a film called *The South's Steepest,* an action-packed show of six of the most dramatically overhanging routes in the South, from Moore's Wall in North Carolina to the New River Gorge in West Virginia to Red River Gorge in Kentucky and Little River Canyon in Alabama. The film was a statement to the outside world that southern climbing had arrived. In some ways it was like so many other climbing videos of the age: hard rock music accompanying dizzying footage of muscled climbers hanging stubbornly on viciously steep stone. But its secondary agenda was to perpetuate the stereotypes of the South, to harden in the national mind-set the idea that these were a bunch of good ol' boys out having some fun.

There was Doug Reed, the best of his generation, calmly explaining how, on an earlier training day after having climbed about a dozen 5.12 routes, his body just quit and he "tore a big piece of muscle right off the bone." There were longhaired, shirtless boys with bellies uncharacteristically ample for climbers describing the horrors of trying to approach an unclimbed wall through the jungle of "rhodos" (the rhododendron jungles that obscure the cliff bases and tangle the approach routes throughout much of the South). One of them fired up a thick joint, talking about "Kentucky's best tobacco." And there, way out of place, was J. B. Tribout, French superstar, just settin' on the porch with the rest of them, his thick accent in marked contrast to the drawl around him, raving about the routes and talking incredulously about Doug Reed's diet of beer and potatoes. The duality in the message was clear: these southerners are bad boys, but their routes have Tribout's international stamp of approval.

Rock climbing is little known to most southerners. Kids in school who have discovered the local gym or crag aren't heroes, but weirdos. There's not much support in a land where the holy sports trinity is car racing, bass fishing, and football. Climbing is a game practiced by few and hidden in the jungled seclusion of sandstone canyons, out of public sight and mind. Sport rappelling is a different story. Nowhere in America does rappelling have so strong a following as it does in the South, a popularity related to the huge influence of the military in the region. Walking the base of Whitesides, near Cashiers, North Carolina, one is befuddled by the fragments of rugs strewn about in the woods, hanging tattered from the branches of trees, until a local explains that these were used to pad the rough edges of the 600-foot free rappel, a far more sensible use of the cliff than actually trying to climb it.

Yet southeastern climbing has old roots, dating well before the 1940s, when the military used Seneca Rocks for training its Tenth Mountain Division for combat in World War II. But only recently has the South emerged into the national climbing consciousness as one of the nation's bona fide climbing centers. Much of this emergence has been the result of a change in climbing attitudes, the shift that accompanied sport climbing and acknowledged that routes of a half-rope length or less were real climbs. The objectives of old (big walls or alpine summits, routes that went somewhere) were steadily replaced by the short, hard sport climbs, routes that end at a bolted anchor 50 or 75 feet off the ground. Once small-cliff sport climbing became acknowledged as worthy in its own right, the South instantly became one of America's major climbing regions. Some even say that the overhanging sandstone routes of the South are the best of their genre in the country.

Island of Tradition

America has been moving away from Europe for a lot longer than most realize. It wasn't with the Declaration of Independence in 1776 that we separated. No, it really began around 170 million years earlier as North America was shoved westward, a pressure emanating from the mid-Atlantic rift valley, one of the world's most active seismic regions. Here the American and European crustal plates continue to pull apart from each other, leaving a great crack running from Iceland almost to Antarctica, a chasm lined by undersea volcanoes and regularly shaken by earthquakes.

The folding that resulted from this continental drift shows up plainly in the Appalachian Mountains. The parallel lines of hills that bend and wrap around New York and Philadelphia look, on a map of Pennsylvania, like the folds in a blanket. The giant ripples on the map make for some of the windingest roads in America, stranding settlements in the hollows and isolating the residents of Appalachia from mainstream culture. Subsequent erosion of those ripples also defines the climbing terrain up in West Virginia's Seneca Rocks.

The flat beds of conglomerate sandstone that make up the Shawangunks in New York stand on edge in northern West Virginia. It's the same rock, the same collection of quartz pebbles, white walls streaked in rust, the same obvious bedding planes, the same slippery and insecure step-ups, the same nasty, pebble-lined cracks. Yet the formation is on end. It's been crumpled up from its original horizontal orientation and stood upright. The horizontal crack at the Gunks is a vertical crack at Seneca. The Gunks ledges and roofs are steep dihedrals at Seneca. Up close, you can't tell the difference between chunks of the two rocks, but once you're up on a route, the places are a world apart. Seneca Rocks is an extraordinary fin of stone jutting above the North Fork of the South Branch of the Potomac River. It's the only major eastern summit that requires a rope and a belay. It's also the only eastern mountain that seems likely to blow over in a stout wind. It's the kind of feature that draws attention, breathtakingly for the first-time visitor, and it's the kind of place that begs to be climbed. And so of all southern climbing areas, Seneca Rocks has the oldest and richest history.

The first ascent of the technical South Peak was probably made by surveyor Donald Bittinger in 1908, most likely following what is now called *Old Ladies,* 5.2. In the years to follow, locals made countless daredevil scrambles, and occasional visitors employed up-to-date rope work to add a few new routes to the mountain, but war in

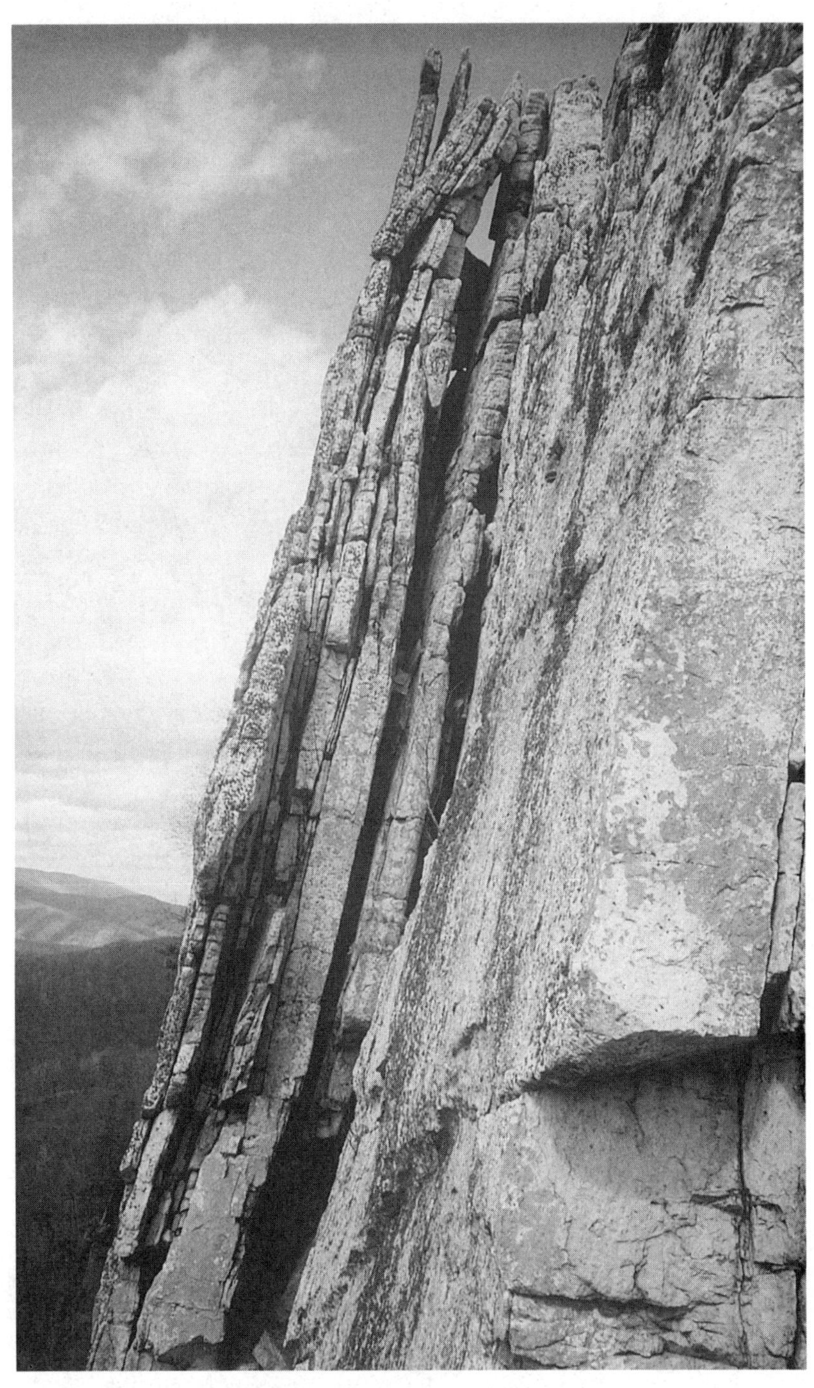

Sedimentary beds pushed up vertically at Seneca Rocks

Europe would be behind the most furious burst of activity at Seneca. The famed Tenth Mountain Division used the walls as training grounds so aggressively that one section would forever be known as the Face of a Thousand Pitons.

Today, despite its hammer-wielding heritage, Seneca Rocks retains a reputation for clean and adventurous climbing. It holds tight to old-fashioned ideas about commitment and grading, ideas shared at traditional fortresses like Granite Mountain in Arizona and the New York cultures of the Shawangunks and the Adirondacks (though with a recent bumping up a notch of many of the climbs in the new Seneca Rocks guidebook, locals sadly acknowledge that the Gunks now can lay sole claim to the world's hardest 5.9s). Climbs at Seneca are as rewarding as they are arduous, since many traumatic and sustained routes end right on the summit ridge, a spine no wider than a sidewalk in some places. Atop a classic like the 1958 *Soler* route (5.7), you can set your helmet down and contemplate the hundreds of feet of air, both in front of *and* behind you, as you belay your second. And as you grapple with the fragility of the blade you're perched upon, you can also begin planning your rappels, part of a descent that will seem more like getting off in the big mountains than from the tidy lower-offs at the other crags.

The inconvenience of climbing at Seneca Rocks filters the crowds, especially now that places like New River Gorge have exploded with routes. Interesting that those two crags should exist in the same small state. Seneca is tall and dangerous. The New is compact and controlled. Seneca routes wander. Those at the New fire straight up to the anchors. High grades are frustratingly elusive at Seneca. At the New you can tick off dozens of career highs in a two-week stay. Though the two places nestle in the valleys of the same Appalachian state of West Virginia, they occupy the extreme ends of the American climbing spectrum. Some climbers will appreciate the variety. Most will hunker down at one place or the other.

FIRST IN FLIGHT

People don't talk about North Carolina as a climbing region—they talk about *western* North Carolina. Visitors to the South hear about those western North Carolina guys as traditional, fiercely ethical, militant, crazy. They hear about the "running belay" of Stone Mountain, where the belayer charges downhill to shorten a leader fall to keep the unfortunate slider off the ground. They hear about the *Dollywood* pitch on the mythic Whitesides (big jugs, wild rides), of leaders using a pad of sticky rubber under their skyhooks in order to place a bolt from a sloping edge. They hear of a climbing population that sneers at the sissies who drill on rappel. Over and over again, visitors are reminded that the adage "when in doubt, run it out" is not just a hollow saying in North Carolina. It's religion.

Physical elements contribute to the adventure and the attitude in western North Carolina. The rocks are big, and at times protection is hard to find. Additionally, many of the climbing areas are relatively far from civilization. Wildest is Linville Gorge, a 2,000-foot gash, the deepest canyon in the eastern United States and home to the North Carolina Outward Bound School. Second only to the Adirondacks' Wallface for remoteness and multipitch adventure, Linville attracts climbers willing to thrash in the underbrush, race the clock, and adroitly read the complicated sequences required by the metamorphic quartzite.

Linville Gorge is a collection of separate big exposures of rock. Closest to the road is the popular Table Rock, standing proud above the canyon rim, visible for miles. It has routes in every grade, routes up to four pitches long, and even a small selection of bolted 5.5s and 5.6s. It's a good place to begin the exploration of the area before venturing down toward the biggest feature, the North Carolina Wall, where the climbing is more remote and more committing. Visitors usually wander around lost down there for a while before the landmarks begin to take shape. It's the kind of climbing that reminds you to bring a headlamp.

Down in Linville Gorge, the scale and the adventure attract climbers more than the quartzite rock itself. The real rock of renown in North Carolina is granite, clean and smooth, with all the features of the best of Yosemite, part of a huge batholith that pokes through the surface typically in the form of big exfoliation domes. The quintessential granite dome climbing, and the ideal introduction to the genre, is Stone Mountain, up north in the Piedmont west of Winston-Salem. It's a remarkable place, demanding still feet and an emotional detachment from the reality that you're 50 feet out from

Stone Mountain's smooth granite requires confidence and concentration

that lonely bolt halfway up the pitch. Such a predicament places demands on a climber that just won't come in the gym.

Friction climbing, a term too liberally applied to a range of subtle face-climbing situations, means sticking to the rock solely from the sticky contact of shoe rubber to a smooth surface. It's not crimping subtle edges, or footsing back and forth between inobvious bumps. Friction climbing means that it doesn't matter where you stand. It's all in *how* you stand. A beginner may well be able to follow the hard routes at Stone by simply keeping an upright body position and padding uphill. After all, a slip can be held by the slightest tug from above. A leader, however, inevitably finds the incline steeper, the surface smoother. Fifty feet out from the last bolt, a fall is unthinkable. But no matter how much you meditate, how pure your thoughts, how deliberately still your breathing, your hands invariably sweat as shoe rubber oozes slowly downhill. Step up, wriggle the foot ever so slightly to set the crystalline surface into the soft rubber. Now move over, directly onto the foot, keeping the weight just so. Breathe. Believe. Keep your heels down even as your eyes glue to the bolt hanger so many miles away. Don't reach too high; it will only make your feet slip. You don't like it but there's no place to hide, no ledge up there that will give you a break. Only the outline of a bolt hanger high on the horizon. You reach the belay with a glad-to-be-alive glaze in your eyes.

Those old quarter-inch Rawl split-shaft bolts have recently been replaced by beefy half-inch Petzl Long Lifes in an effort by the Carolina Climbers' Coalition, led by Sean Cobourne and supported by the Access Fund. Good thing, because those old quarter-inchers really got slammed when they had to take the force of two leader falls, one the leader himself and the other hurtling down-slope through the trees.

When Stone Mountain climbers talk about the running belay, they are referring tongue-in-cheek to a method so different from the running belay of British tradition. The Brits used the term to describe putting a piece of protection between themselves and their belayer. The gear was called a runner, a term more broadly used today to refer to a sewn or tied shoulder-length sling. Stone Mountain climbers use the term, well, a bit more literally. Based upon the premise that a belayer can run almost as fast as a leader can fall, the method demands that the belayer charge downhill through the woods when the leader takes off. Done correctly (with a track star for a belayer and a leader who fights the fall by paddling uphill at the cost of a little shoe rubber), a leader can be held at the bolt. Such tactics explain why some of the routes might have the first bolt 30 feet up and the second well over 60.

Typical of granite domes everywhere, the principal process of erosion is exfoliation or sheeting, and nowhere is this process so evident as on Stone Mountain's easiest long route, *The Great Arch* (5.5), a three-pitch, flawless, right-facing corner that runs right up the middle of the wide south face. It's one of the few stress-free leads, and with protection all the way, it gives the newcomer an opportunity to leave the layback at times and experiment with the uncertainties of pure friction climbing without the consequences of the run-out. Out to the right, on the other hand, are some sustained 5.9s with only a bolt or two per pitch.

Stone Mountain is the purest friction experience, its only eastern rival being White Horse Ledge in New Hampshire, the other state whose license-plate motto says as much about the climbers as it does the general population. In New Hampshire the tags say "Live Free or Die," a climbing tradition that thrives in the Granite State. In North Carolina, it's "First in Flight," a spirit engendered at Kitty Hawk and alive both on and off the big granite walls.

INTO THE LOOKING GLASS

Perhaps the staunchest of all western North Carolina conservatives are those clinging to the odd-shaped "eyebrows" of Looking Glass Rock, a 700-foot granite dome off the Blue Ridge Parkway in Pisgah National Forest. Most other granite domes are blank, save for the cracks in exfoliation corners. No fiddling with gear on such blank expanses. Instead it's either a bolt or a run-out. Looking Glass, on the other hand, is pocked by a million horizontal depressions, some with pretty deep cracks, others sadly shallow. Trouble is, you can't tell the difference from below. Sadder still is that these eyebrows are usually dipped slightly downward, and the only way to move past is to turn a sloping hold into a better undercling by deftly, and sometimes dynamically, high-stepping up and onto the shelf. Sadder, because if the next eyebrow is rounded and crackless, you can't reverse your moves. There's no choice but to repeat the maneuver and hope for the best, all while your clever nest of camming devices grows increasingly distant below. The prospect of a fall weighs heavily because the angle is all wrong: not as steep as the sandstone crags where you can simply take to the air and flap your wings, but neither so low-angled as at Stone Mountain, where you can effect a four-point, hand-slapping slide while your belayer sprints off into the trees.

For their first foray into the Looking Glass, most people choose the *Nose* (5.8), the classic route established in 1966 by Steve Longnecker, Bob Watson, and Bob Gillespie. Longnecker is still a feature at the rock, seen frequently instructing groups, telling groaner jokes. When he first launched upward on the mountain's first technical route, he recounts, he was wearing old-style lug-soled shoes—something to consider when your modern sticky slippers begin to ooze downhill. In the '70s, a coterie of local climbers continued that brave tradition, keeping bolts to a minimum, patient enough to know that every route has its time, willing to let an unprotected line sit idle until someone gathers the nerve.

Looking Glass is a big piece of rock, with three distinct sections for climbing, each with its own approach. Not all of it is eyebrow horror shows. There are also some excellent crack climbs, steep corners, and dicey aid routes, many of these requiring odd *circle heads,* a copperhead-type bashie designed for shallow horizontal cracks.

WHITESIDES

Next to Kitty Hawk, North Carolina's other undisputed launch site, is the hulking Whitesides Mountain, biggest cliff in the South, a huge, smooth wall of swirling metamorphosed granite. It's long and blank and mottled, low-angled down low, then rearing up in the middle. The unusual surface of the rock makes for some creative face-climbing opportunities, but unlike the jointed and exfoliated granite in the Sierra or up north in New Hampshire, the rock here lacks continuous cracks. Routes are hard to find and follow. The challenge comes more from the run-out unpredictability than the actual difficulty of the moves.

The easiest free route on the big rock is the *Original Route.* Most of the climb is moderate fifth class, with some route-finding confusion and a few potentially fatal run-outs on easy terrain. The crux is a short 5.11 bolt ladder of rusted quarter-inchers, graded 5.10 when Bobby Rotert first free-climbed the pitch in 1977, a year after he had added his own first route to the face, *New Perversions* (reported to have protection on only three of its eight pitches). Given the reputation of some routes such as this and others that snake up into the overhanging blankness, newcomers have little choice but to try the *Original Route* as a Whitesides entrance exam. Better to be run out on 5.7 than to be dangling high on a headwall route, mouth dry and arms melting, knowing that 50-footer is just moments away.

In 1985, an incursion from Tennessee resulted in the first route on the headwall section: a hard mixed free and aid route called the *Volunteer Wall.* Initially some North Carolina boys felt threatened by the success of Arno Ilgner, Eddie Whittemore, and Mark Cartwright, from the Volunteer State. Sentiment soon turned to admiration as other climbers sampled this and other Ilgner routes. Yet before long, the admiration would turn to incredulity as Ilgner shifted styles and established *Warrior's Way,* a steep 5.12 with enough bolts that others might actually come to repeat it. By the time Ilgner put up *Warrior's Way*, he had already demonstrated his mettle: on *Volunteer Wall* (which he later free-climbed at 12a in 1990) and on *Little Miss Dangerous* (5.12a), he had logged so much air time that most other climbers simply stayed away from his routes.

Even with a few exceptions to the Rotert-style horror shows, Whitesides continues to define the western North Carolina experience. It's a hard-to-read cliff, a cliff where fool optimism is requisite. Climb up into the unknown. Have faith that, somehow, a solution will reveal itself. Head this way or that (it's going to be a coin toss), believing that you've chosen right. It's steep enough that you'll survive a fall. But don't think about this. Disregard the distance that is stretching out between you and your last decent piece of gear. After all, you didn't come here to have fun. You came so that, at a later date, you could sit with friends and strangers around a fire at any climbers' camp in America and hold the group spellbound as you described your brush with the infamous Whitesides.

A Tennessee Excursion

It wasn't for lack of rock that the invaders from Tennessee strayed over state lines to put up the *Volunteer Wall,* for the Volunteer State has as much rock as any place in the South. In fact, pioneer and promoter Rob Robinson says confidently that there's more climbable sandstone within reach of Chattanooga than any city in the United States. Protests from Boulder notwithstanding, he might be right.

Chattanooga, known by romantics for the famous Choo-Choo, by history buffs for its Civil War battles, and by the Cherokee as their name for Lookout Mountain, is a climber's city, a town ringed by thin lines of light-colored cliffs poking out above rich hardwood forests. The city lies in a basin between flat ridgelines, and everywhere you look, there's rock. There's good climbing right up there on Lookout Mountain, but if you only have a few days, better to follow your eyes out across the curving Tennessee River, to leave the posh cliff-top neighborhoods near Sunset Park and head into the hills to places like Suck Creek, or, best of all, to the Tennessee Wall.

The Tennessee Wall burst hard into the awareness of American climbers in the mid-'80s mainly as a result of the routes and writing of one climber, Rob Robinson. His first route, *In Sight of Power,* was a literal reference to the hydroelectric station below, but more significant, it referred to the vision he had for the future of the Tennessee River Gorge. Within only a few years it would have hundreds, then thousands, of good, solid rock climbs, crack and face and roof climbs. The variety of climbing experiences distinguishes the T Wall from many other of the growing list of sandstone destinations along the Cumberland Plateau. It's not all just multitiered roofs. The Tennessee Wall has a supreme collection of crack routes, some in the very moderate 5.8 range.

It was 1985 when Robinson and Arno Ilgner first started poking around the Tennessee Wall, a time just before the lid blew off American climbing styles, the year before the French invasion of Smith Rock and the country's first 5.14. The timing was important. Had the cliffs of the T Wall been more like the majority of southern crags—all roofs and few cracks—the visitors might have been awed by the possibilities, cursed that lack of protection, and then walked on. But like the New River Gorge, the Tennessee Wall is infinitely protectable, and the routes that jump out on first inspection are vertical cracks, lots of them. The Tennessee Wall and the others surrounding Chattanooga will continue to offer bolted sport routes as explorers continue to search, but they'll forever have that traditional flair, for it was in old-school, ground-up, clean-gear style that the first generation of routes was forged.

Complementing the crack potential around Chattanooga are countless other sandstone exposures. Two of the best in Tennessee are Obed, up north of Chattanooga, and Foster Falls, an hour west of the city. Foster Falls is an outstanding little area, compact, easily accessible. Nashville's Eddie Whittemore, of Whitesides' *Volunteer Wall,* was almost solely responsible for the development of this southern gem of a climbing area. The routes are solid and steep, with flat, secure holds. There's good parking at the start of the Fiery Gizzard Trail (the more you explore the South, the more you'll appreciate the place names), a short path around the rim of the falls to the steep walk down. It's a small and tight-walled place, not expansive like the T Wall. But inch for inch, it's as good as southern sandstone can get.

More extensive than Foster Falls, and more recently developed than the cliffs around Chattanooga, is the incredible line of crags along the confluence of the Obed River and its tributary Clear Creek. The Obed Wild and Scenic River lies just west of Oak Ridge, Tennessee, known for the Oak Ridge Boys and the Oak Ridge research laboratory that played a key role in the Manhattan Project to build the atomic bomb. Numerous exposures above the Obed River and Clear Creek typify the best and steepest of the Cumberland Plateau. And if you really want to see steep, visit the high-ceilinged chamber they call the Stephen King Library.

The big roof, 40 or so feet above, is flat and blank. It stretches out over the ground for about 30 feet. Hard to imagine it being climbable. Yet there's a skinny high school kid with a baseball cap launching out. What's he holding on to? How can he be so relaxed dangling possumlike upside-down while he traverses what looks like an overturned parking lot? Three more moves and he's got the lip, where a locking carabiner dangles as a lower-off point. "Damn, it's rusted tight." He switches hands. Feet dangle. "Can't git the somebitch open, and I forgot to bring a draw." An eternity passes before he finally lobs.

There was a time when *Foops,* the big 5.11 roof at the Gunks, was dramatic. *Kansas City,* close by at the Near Trapps, nudged it aside, and mortal visitors who stood underneath could only imagine climbing out a full twelve feet to the lip. Then in Yosemite, Ron Kauk discovered *A Separate Reality,* a 5.12 hand crack splitting an even bigger roof. Surely the limit had been reached. But that was all before places like Obed and Foster Falls, Little River Canyon, and countless other exposures of good overhanging sandstone were discovered all over the central Southeast. Yet still it's off the national map. People tend to doubt such stories of giant ceilings, dismissing them as what Huck Finn would call "stretchers." Or even if they thought the tales true, people shy away from so long a drive, especially with the South's reputation for bad weather, multiday pelting rains so unlike the sunny West. So even with America's largest climbable roofs, the sandstone canyons of the Cumberland Plateau stay just outside the national limelight.

A Bridge

The local chamber of commerce claims that the river is the oldest in North America, second oldest in the world. Odd that they'd call it the

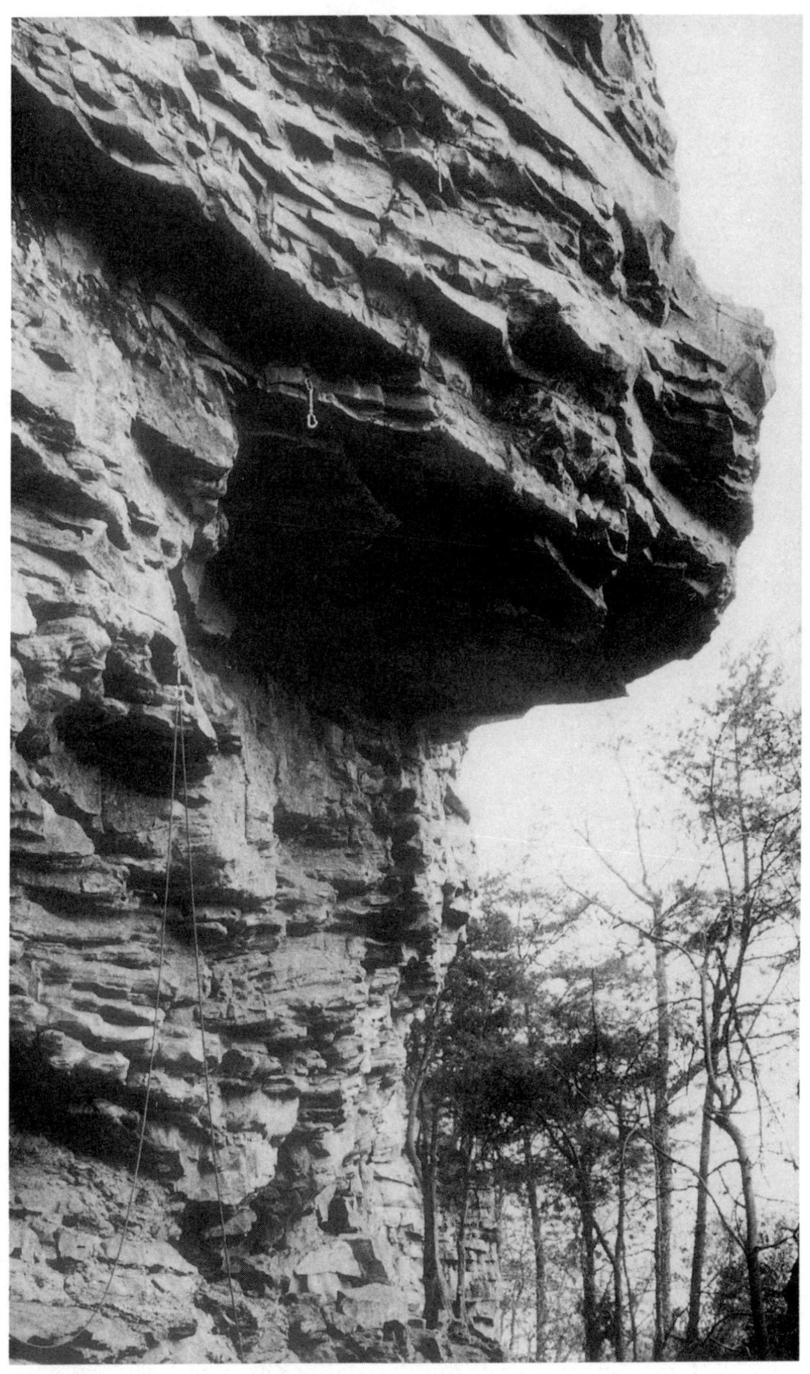

Obed, Tennessee

New. Seen through a climber's eyes, however, the blend of old and new makes the New River Gorge one of the best rock resources in the country. In 1977 the great bridge was christened, a 3,000-foot span across the gorge. At about the same time, local climbers began poking around, noticing with every new route that, although the height wasn't much to brag about, the quality of the crack climbing had few rivals. They raved about their discovery, but it still took a while for their invitations to be accepted by other climbers. By the mid-1980s, however, the New had established a reputation as one of the best crack-climbing areas in the East.

A walk along the Endless Wall tells why: It's an uninterrupted four-mile cliff band with no break easier than 5.0 for its entire length. And every fifty feet or so is a vertical crack, most running the full hundred-plus feet up the face. For single-pitch crack climbing, the New River Gorge is as good as it gets, from *Leave It to Jesus* (11d fingers) to *Celibate Mallard* (10c tight hands) to *Springboard* (soft 10a and perfect hands) to *Crescent Moon* (eight inches wide and only 5.7?) to *Timberline* (a wide 10b where Andy Zimmerman installed two sawed-off logs, prototypical Big Bros, as fixed protection). For its first few years, the New River Gorge was decidedly trad, a crack-climber's paradise, routes so obvious and so well protected that bolts just weren't an issue. A fixed log or a jammed chockstone perhaps, but no need to drill.

Yet it wouldn't be long before climbers looked right and left from the crack lines and saw the square cuts and *letterboxes,* lines of solid crimper holds. Without the constraints typically self-imposed at older climbing areas and perhaps in response to the stern limitations of places like Seneca Rocks, the New River crew didn't agonize over the fairness of bolting hard-to-protect routes, nor did they go hoarse arguing about whether or not the gear was placed on lead or rappel. There was just too much to do.

For easterners, the New River is a great bridge between old and new, traditional crack climbing and new-wave sport climbing. Neither gets in the way of the other. The West Virginia motto is *montani semper liberi,* "mountaineers will always be free." You feel it at the New, the freedom just to climb. Residents of West Virginia call themselves mountaineers, but not in the sense to which we climbers have become accustomed. No, a mountaineer is a hill person, independ-

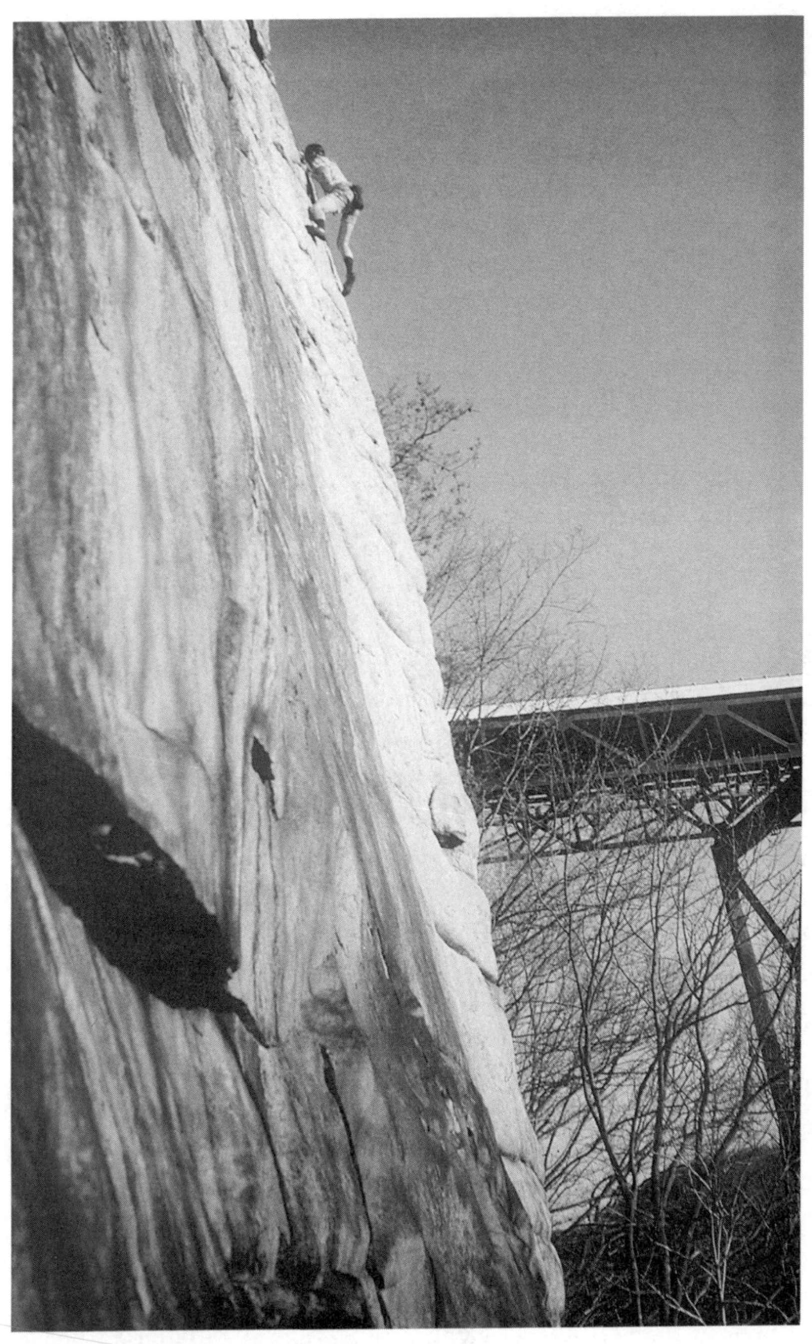

The big bridge at New River Gorge helped open up the region to tourism and recreation.

ent, proud, isolated. The mountain people of West Virginia were for many years a people cut off from the rest of the world, physically by the tortuous landscape and economically from the vibrance of the eastern cities. Yet the eastern prosperity was fueled by coal, and West Virginia was a leading producer. The 100-foot layer of Nuttal sandstone is the caprock over the softer, coal-rich rock below. In the late 1800s and early 1900s towns sprang up all along the river gorge, and miners worked for as little as a dollar a day, hacking coal from tight shafts, dying early from black lung. When coal went bust, the region had very little to support it, and the Appalachian poverty only deepened. With the bleak outlook for such a region in the throes of a dying coal industry, any economic injection is welcome indeed. Recreation, thus, plays a huge role in the lives and futures of the people of Fayette County; it's a place that appreciates its visitors.

Climbers weren't the first recreationists to discover the New River. In the 1960s word was out among white-water rafters and kayakers that here was some of the best high water anywhere. The New River offers miles of excellent rapids before it joins the Gauley, just past the cliffs of Bubba City. Upstream from this confluence, the Gauley has earned a fearsome reputation, and today it draws hundreds of spectators to notorious sections such as the Room of Doom or Sweat's Falls to watch bug-eyed boaters eat it, a bit like the hordes who flock to Indy just to see cars crash.

The people of Fayette County must wonder what's gone wrong with the rest of the world, since everyone coming their way, it seems, is hell-bent on self destruction. To them, the boaters and climbers seem almost timid next to the BASE and bungee jumpers who put up fifty dollars a shot to leap from the 876-foot-high span on the annual Bridge Day. Scores line up to take the plunge while thousands pack the bridge and cliff tops to watch this aerial circus, held on the third Saturday of every October. Seen next to the jumpers, then, the climbers who invaded the area didn't seem too threatening. Odd dressers, to be sure, what with their earrings and brightly colored tights. But they buy a lot of beer, so they can't be all bad.

The explosion of New River Gorge into the imagination of American climbers was set off first by an August 1984 cover shot in *Climbing* magazine of Tom Howard pulling the roof on *Supercrack,* with the river, the railroad tracks, and the endless line of cliffs drifting back into the fog, and later by Pennsylvania climber Rick Thompson, whose guidebook advertisements proclaimed the place to be the crack-climbing Mecca of the East. His book *New River Rock* was enthusiastic and well illustrated. Any climber fingering its pages would be drawn toward the place. With a new-route explosion under way and spanning both the traditional and sport era, new climbs went in at an almost daily pace.

Big Red

Kentucky was neutral in the Civil War. It was a society founded mainly on personal gain, and its first settlers saw no reason to fight one another. Well into the late 1800s most roads were private toll roads, and a trip across the state could require fifty stops to cough up some change. It's a land known for bluegrass and fine horses, for Bourbon whiskey and some of the best climbing in the South.

When all the southern canyons are explored, all the escarpments of the Cumberland Plateau discovered and documented, the state of Kentucky will probably show the most rock, will probably turn out to be the mother lode of southeastern sandstone. Already well known to climbers everywhere is the Red River Gorge, with its complex tributary drainages. The Red has more than a thousand high-quality routes, and climbers there say they've developed only the most obvious, easily accessible cliffs. The countless little subcanyons that splinter off in dendritic patterns in all directions will likely triple the amount of climbing we see there today. But Kentucky climbing doesn't end with the famed Red River Gorge. To its south, running into Tennessee, are the vast canyons of the Big South Fork, potential for at least as much climbing as in the Red.

The Red River Gorge is one of the more recent southern entries into the national climbing scene. New River Gorge had been explored and hyped in the national climbing press. So had the greater Chattanooga area, with the Tennessee Wall having been included in a *Climbing* article on the ten best crags in America. And long predating these sandstone regions were the bastions of traditionalism at Seneca Rocks and North Carolina.

When historians piece together the process of discovering Kentucky climbing, they'll probably divide it into two eras: before

Porter and after Porter. Porter Jarrard, viciously strong and endlessly searching out new hard sport routes, is responsible for more of the current batch of hard routes than all other climbers combined. Originally from North Carolina, Jarrard had climbed quite a bit out West and elsewhere in the South, and he was particularly active in West Virginia's New River Gorge, where he served an informal tutelage with New River's strongest climber, Doug Reed. Reed and Jarrard were part of a group that brought bolt-protected climbing to the New River, putting up climbs that would eclipse the well-known crack routes. Although Reed had been around long enough to have been influenced by the chock revolution and the emphasis on clean climbing, Jarrard bore no such ethical burden.

Jarrard claims that when he first became aware of Red River Gorge, he "was sitting in the can, reading an old issue of *Climbing*" and an article by Martin Hackworth. A few trips later he was so hooked that he moved to Kentucky and got to work. Beginning in 1990, he began putting up as many as a half dozen routes a week. On rainy days he'd just explore, hanging a rope down over the best-looking route and installing bolts where he thought they made sense. Sometimes he wouldn't check first on top-rope: the holds were everywhere, and even if the sequence wasn't obvious at the time, surely such a sequence would emerge later. Once the bolts were in on a particular route, Jarrard would typically look left and right for more. Tensioning off directional gear, or even hooking from side pulls, Jarrard would in very short time have a wall with several unclimbed, bolt-protected lines. It was like setting the table for a feast, and Jarrard had little trouble attracting partners for a climbing day that would surely bring the participants first ascents.

Jarrard is a geographer, working with the state to map out the recreational potential of the Red River Gorge. His home office is walled with maps and aerial photographs that show a landscape looking like little more than a crumpled sheet of paper. Indeed, it takes a geographer to decipher central and eastern Kentucky's chaotic topography. It's classic Appalachia with ridges and "hollers," steep and junglelike, ideal in years past for hiding stills and running moonshine, and ideal today for growing marijuana, said to have recently replaced tobacco as the state's number-one cash crop.

But as climbers know, seeing a field from the air doesn't mean it can readily be accessed on foot. In fact, agents looking for dope often have to rappel to get to the crops, under the hidden gaze, no doubt, of the angry farmers. Climbers say that these frequent helicopter inspectors are probably the only visitors who won't be challenged by the militant growers. Though no violence has been reported, explorers looking for new cliffs fear inadvertently stumbling onto a million-dollar crop patrolled by armed guards.

"Experience is not rewarded at the Red." So says Gina Bochiccio, geology instructor and climber from nearby Lexington. At first the warning sounds like the typical steep-rock climber's admonition to the newcomer not to hang around and get fancy with the feet. There's just not enough time as the clock ticks away and the fingers melt. But there's more to the warning than that. It speaks of the rock itself, an incarnation of sandstone unlike any other in most climbers' backgrounds.

Fabulously colorful and swirling with motion, the rock in Red River Gorge is a delight just to watch. Iron-lined glassy pockets, protruding little mouths like pouting lips, and rounded tubes that at first look like solid hand railings but, in fact, are more like slick PVC pipes. And pockets all around. Some, like those on *Mississippi Moons*, are big enough to stand in. Others, like the basketball-sized hollows on *Jac Mac,* require all kinds of knee locks just to hang on. But most of the pockets are for the fingers.

Sedimentary rock, more than most types, is readable, has a predictability to it. In the Southwest, it is splintered into towers and cracks that run uninterrupted for hundreds of feet. Hard to climb, maybe, but at least easy to read. Look up at *Supercrack* or any of the other features at Utah's Indian Creek and there's no wondering what it will take. Same for the more predictably layered sedimentary beds of places like Foster Falls or Obed in Tennessee, or the Shawangunks in New York State. You know there's a hold up there and, not only that, based on the way the rock breaks along horizontal planes, you have a pretty good idea of what the hold is going to feel like.

Not so at the Red, where it's impossible to know what any particular hold is going to feel like or which of the hundreds of alternatives happens to be the sequence until you're hanging dejectedly on the rope, fingers throbbing from having tried every imaginable way of grasping the pockets until flame-out. The Red River Gorge is a decidedly uncooperative place for the aspiring on-sight climber. It's too complex, hard to read. It doesn't give you the time to figure out the moves. It demands to be inspected and tick-marked. It's a multifingered affair. Instead of slapping a hand onto an edge where the fingers function together as one, imagine lunging toward a bowling ball, drilled with a multitude of holes, and having to get every finger just right. Routes such as these are the bane of the on-sight climber, even one with fingers of steel.

Lexington attorney John Bronaugh is a trad climber from way back. His guidebook *Red River Gorge Climbs* is not only clear and excellent, but only slightly below the surface it has an agenda: to portray the Red as a traditional area where the crack climbing is as good as the clip-ups. It's a purposeful juxtaposition. On the book's cover is Jeff Moll, crimping out the outrageously steep *BOHICA* (5.13) at the Motherlode, but on the back is a handcrack dihedral as smoothly alluring as any in Indian Creek or New River. Nor is the duality limited to the graphics. There are charts with grades and route type, as if to say, "OK, there are lots of bolt routes here, but trad climbing still prevails." As of his 1998 printing, the scorecard had traditional climbing holding a strong but dwindling lead over sport climbs, 631 to 355.

Eastern Kentucky, land of anomalies, has nudged its way into the elite areas of American rock climbing. It's a place where sandstone isolates the fingers like the nastiest French limestone, where the burgeoning climbing scene is not a redneck saloon but a gourmet Portuguese pizza house. It's a place where some of the best climbers are just kids with no respect for overhanging impossibilities, kids who get rides to the cliffs from their parents.

THERE ARE LOTS OF PLACES to get home cooked in the southeastern United States. Like everywhere else, the well-bolted sport climbs, those you can train for in the gym, will continue to get the most traffic. At the same time, the hard traditional routes in the fortresses of conservatism like Seneca Rocks and western North Carolina will repulse much of a new generation of climbers, the Gendarme standing sentinel or not. The granite expanses, thus, will retain their nobility among the diehards. More climbers will go where the clipping is easy, and in the new South, the potential is endless. The cliffs discovered so far are only those happened upon by a small group of explorers. Most come back from their excursions in the unnamed canyons of the Cumberland Plateau with eyes wide and claims that there's more good rock here than anywhere else in America, provided climbers are willing to thrash a bit in the rhododendrons, to sweat buckets in the heavy southern heat, to wipe spiderwebs from their faces and scare snakes from their path, and, most of all, to launch out on some of the most overhanging sandstone terrain on the planet.

5 TALES FROM THREE CITIES

Red Rocks. So big, so wild, so close to Las Vegas.

Picture a map of America, posted on a wall. Now start sticking those colored pins into all the climbing areas and watch the clustering. Yes, Tim Toula's highway bible for the itinerant climber, *Rock 'N' Road,* describes rock climbing in forty-nine of the fifty states (with folks still crawling through the jungles of Louisiana, confident that they'll find a hunk of sand solid enough to call stone and high enough for a fifth-class move). But still, the pins will group up, mainly in the mountain states, and as you plan for your next climbing trip, a few hub cities will be obvious to you. Three of these cities—Boulder, Salt Lake City, and Las Vegas—will probably attract more pins than the rest, and you know that if you've got limited time and unlimited ambition, these are the places you'll want to visit.

Physically, one can make a lot of comparisons among the three cities in terms of their climbing topography. Each sits on a western flatland at the foot of something big. From each, high-walled canyons of varied rock cut into the mountains. Accessible from each city is a lifetime of climbing, where if you don't like one kind of rock, simply go to a different canyon; where if you want something bigger, you need only head up into the nearby high mountains; where if the weather isn't just right, simply move to a place higher or lower, in the sun or in the shade. And if you want to mingle, each has vibrant gyms and rock shops where talk of climbing is in the air.

Yet every bit as intriguing as the physical comparisons are the social contrasts between the places: eco-chic Boulder, land of Teva sandals and herbal teas, beautiful tanned college kids and computer nerds, rusted Volvos held together by duct tape and Phish stickers; straight-laced Salt Lake City, streets radiating from the great Temple, numbered sequentially to the thousands, an almost all-white population steeped in the same quiet confidence as their prophet Brigham Young when he arrived with his band of pioneers in 1847 and declared, "This is the place"; and crazy Las Vegas, land of mirrors, where vice is virtue, a strip of unabashedly dishonest facades of glass and glitz, where a dammed river generates the electricity for a billion lights to shine on a happy population of damned souls.

The Edge

At the western edge of a thousand flat miles of American heartland, layers of red rock tilt upward against the base of the Rocky Mountains.

The image is distinct all along the front of the range, from Colorado Springs north to Fort Collins, as line upon line of inclined sandstone slabs rest against the foothills of high, snowy mountains to the west. It's the edge of the Plains, the base of the great mountains. And even to the nongeologist, it's evident what's happening here. Mountains are being pushed from out of the Plains and the layers of flat red rock below are bending upward and lapping the edge of the uplift like breakers on a beach. This is Colorado's Front Range, literal edge of the Rockies and metaphorical cutting edge of American climbing.

The Front Range, running north and south from Boulder, offers the full spectrum of rock climbing, from bouldering to mountaineering. There's soft sandstone at the Garden of the Gods and hard sandstone in Eldorado Canyon. There's short granite cragging in Boulder Canyon and multipitch granite climbing at Lumpy Ridge. There's urban climbing close to the road, and there's the wild domeland of the South Platte River. Crowning all else is the abrupt eastern edge of the mountain range at Rocky Mountain National Park. For the breadth of climbing possibilities and depth of the climbing culture, Boulder has long been seen as the original hub city of American rock climbing.

This status was confirmed in 1977 with the publication of *CLIMB!*, by Bob Godfrey and Dudley Chelton, describing the history and capturing the flavor of climbing in Colorado. It was a regional book, but it grabbed the attention of climbers nationwide. As the book was passed around among groups of climbers, and as copies on climbing-store shelves grew dog-eared from the greasy fingering of climbers too cheap to buy, Colorado's rock walls grew higher and the characters loomed more vital and eccentric in the collective mind. Within a few years, climbers everywhere knew the Diamond and the Black Canyon, the Flatirons and the narrow red walls of Eldorado. They knew Pat Ament and Jim Erickson, Dave Breashears and Layton Kor. So enticing were the photos and so riveting were the stories that by the time the reader would finally visit Eldorado Canyon to see it in person, the reality couldn't match the regality that the book had bestowed upon the place.

Sit at an outdoor table at a brew pub in the Pearl Street Mall in Boulder, Colorado, and you know you are in the midst of an outdoor recreation center. It's still a place where climbing is richly embedded in the culture at large, not the strange outlet of a fringe that it has been elsewhere in the country. Grab an edition of Boulder's paper, *The*

Daily Camera, and you'll see editorials blasting the Parks Commission's fixed-anchor policy or notices announcing plans for a chalk cleanup at Flagstaff Boulders. Climbing is so integrated into community life that talk among climbers moves beyond beta and bolts and on to movies or mountain bike trails. There's no need to obsess. It's an active and healthy town, home of La Sportiva and Trango, of Celestial Seasonings herbal teas and Boulder Beer's Redpoint Ale, and of *Rock & Ice* magazine. It's upscale, intellectual. Boulder's statistics show more residents per capita hooked up to the Internet, more with master's degrees. Perhaps less empirical are visitors' observations that the women are blonder, the men slimmer and more muscled. Everybody runs. There are more Volvos and Subarus and golden retrievers and bikes with fat tires. The sky is usually blue, and things feel unreal to the working-class climber on a two-week holiday.

Above town, thousand-foot sandstone slabs called the Flatirons are the symbol of the city, backdrop to almost every postcard available in local shops. The Flatirons stand for Boulder's place at the foot of the mountains, the edge of the Great Plains. Still faintly visible are the initials CU, painted on by college kids. In his guidebook to the region, Richard Rossiter writes that he knows of no other outdoor pitch in America climbed almost exclusively on a painted surface. At the south end of the Flatirons, Eldorado Canyon forms a big-walled gateway to the mountains, through which generations of American climbers have passed on their way from the small crags to the big climbs of the West.

With the Flatirons right at the edge of town, it was inevitable that the dramatic rocks would tempt an ascent even before the advent of rock climbing as we know it today. The Third Flatiron, best of the series, was first climbed by Floyd and Earl Millard in 1906. It wouldn't be until the 1930s that modern rope technique came into popular practice, and so this ascent and the many others to follow for the next two decades were done a bit recklessly without a safety rope. That's nothing. In the 1950s Dale Johnson climbed the route in roller skates, and in the '70s Gary Neptune climbed it nude. Malcolm Daly soloed the climb without using his hands. The Flatirons are so deeply woven into the mystique of Boulder that even the best and most jaded climbers are still drawn to what some consider the best beginner climbing in the country.

The Flatirons formation of uptilted sandstone runs north-south along the edge of the range, breached by two gorges, Boulder Canyon to the north and Eldorado Canyon to the south. "Eldo" is the mandatory stop for visitors to Boulder. The Dyno-Mart, best-named grocery store near any climbing area, marks the turn toward the odd little town of Eldorado Springs, a chaotic collection of cottages below the entrance of the spa and pool, its parking lot jammed on a hot summer day.

Eldorado Canyon is steep-walled and narrow, with high red cliffs of hard, tilted sandstone. Streaks of lichen, golden, red, and lime, paint the walls, changing hue with the season. The left rampart of the entryway is the Bastille, so named for its supposed resemblance to the prison of French Revolution notoriety. The revolutionary aura looms even higher than the rocks themselves. People don't go to Eldorado just to climb. They go to immerse themselves in something bigger, to climb routes of a day when the first ascent meant something; for every climb in the canyon is a story well known to a generation of climbers. It would be sacrilege to enter without first learning the great tales.

Yet as the sport moved on beyond the confines of places like Eldorado, even on a summer day the canyon no longer seems the hotbed it once was. It isn't as packed and frenzied as one might expect. Of course, there's the perpetual waiting line for the *Bastille Crack* (5.7) and *Werk Sup* (5.8) to its left, and across the river there's usually an instructional group on *Calypso* (5.5). But most of the other high routes are empty. Old-timers will show up after work; their footwork tells of thirty years' practice. These gray heads still find satisfaction in old-school traditional climbing, knowing that the grade numbers won't impress anyone. They've grown up. One of them called Boulder a retirement community for climbers: "If not rock, then shuffleboard." Young sport-climbers will be off to other places, claiming that they want harder routes, but in fact unwilling to jump on the poorly protected, so-called easier climbs of old. The aura of boldness lingers even if the canyon has lost its place at the cutting edge.

Another reason Eldorado is slipping from the minds of today's new climbers is that it's so damn tricky to climb there, requiring skills that the gyms and the sport routes just don't teach. You have to be really good at placing gear, knowing when to add a runner, when to oppose that RP so it won't lift out when you pass. You have to know how to read sequences and how to down-climb when you have guessed wrong. Two parallel routes on the Bastille drive home the point: the *West Buttress* (5.9) and the *West Face* (5.10). The crux sequences of both routes seem obvious from below: just follow the cracks. But both routes require stepping off to the side at just the right place for a face-climbing sequence invisible from below. If you get beta from a local, no problem. But leaving the crack and heading out into the unknown without any assurance you can get back is really unnerving. Climbing in Eldorado isn't the predictable bucket pulling like at the Gunks. Eldorado routes are complex mazes of sidepulls, underclings, and hidden holds. No wonder Boulder climbers got so good.

The *Bastille Crack* is the most obvious line on the left wall of the canyon, starting right from the road, an approach so short that passing cars are in danger from falling carabiners. The climbing is steep and dramatic, continuous at 5.7, and polished smooth from thousands of ascents. The edges of the crack feel like the stone railings in a medieval church, worn to an oily sheen from the many hands sliding over the surface. What used to be secure laybacks and jams twenty years ago are a little scary now, though good protection eases the mind a bit.

You kind of expect to find bolts and chains at the top of a route these days, but the rigging atop the Bastille seems a bit much, unless you know of Ivy Baldwin. Eldorado Springs was quite the resort spa years ago. The Eisenhowers even honeymooned here. Between 1906 and 1948, stuntman Ivy Baldwin would walk a tight wire strung across the canyon, much to the delight of visitors below. He made his last trip at the age of eighty-two. Fifty years later, the remains of his wire lie rusting away on top of the Bastille. There, from the top of the Bastille, one has a clear view across at the legendary *Naked Edge.*

Few routes in American climbing history have the aura of the *Naked Edge* (5.11). When the sun is just right, the knife-edged arête stands out in obvious relief, the best line in all Eldorado. The route starts well up the Redgarden Wall, after a diagonal fifth-class scramble up from the *Redguard Route,* and, in five exposed pitches, tests the competence of climbers in all the skill areas. The first pitch is a 5.11 finger crack. The second is 5.10 face climbing up the edge itself, and

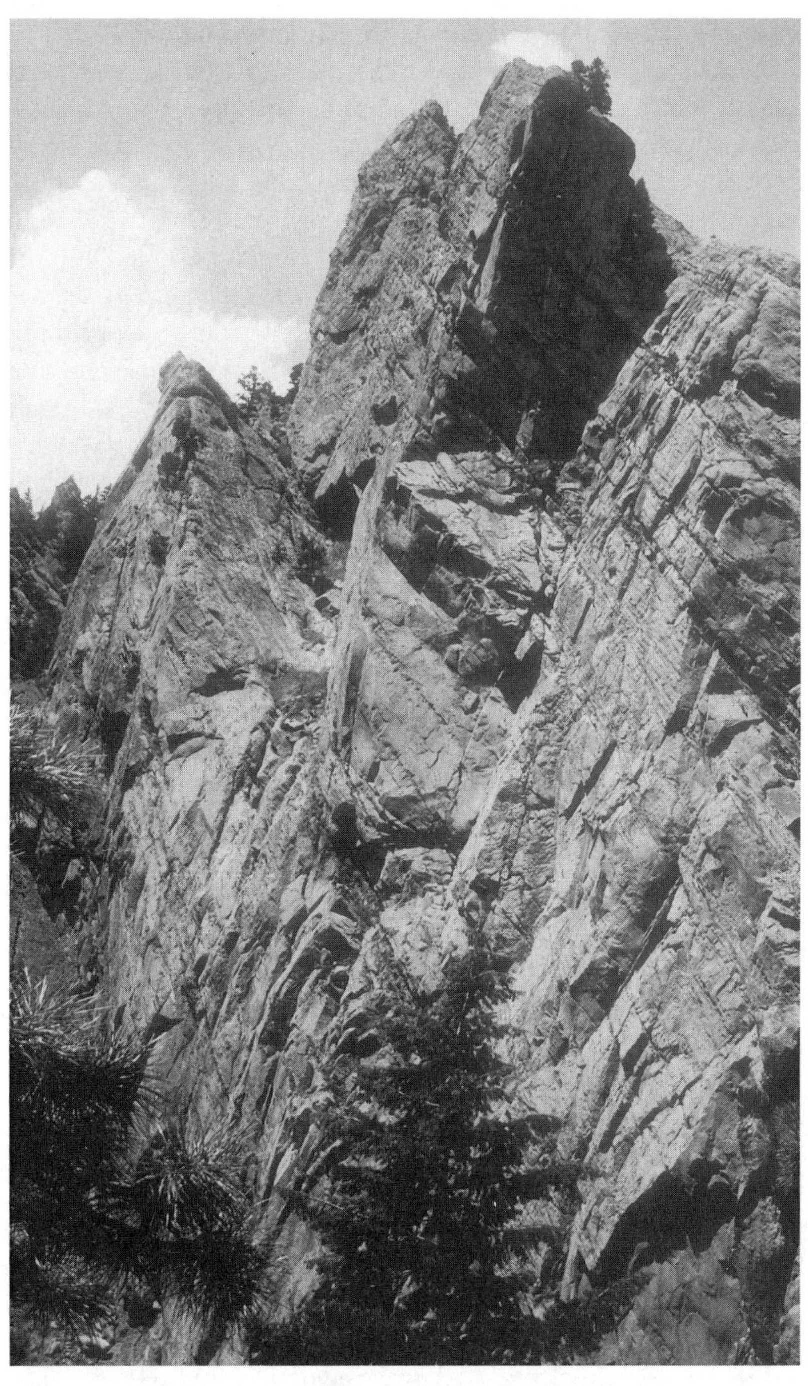

Eldorado's historic Naked Edge *route climbs the central ridge.*

when the leader disappears around the left, the second is left to contemplate the legend that a rope will cut here should the leader fall. Higher, the technical crux is an insecure struggle out of a shallow chimney box, but the real thriller is the last pitch, a handcrack in an overhanging dihedral, 700 feet of air below and as climactic as a finish can be. A numerical grade doesn't apply here. 5.9? 5.11? Hard to say. The moves aren't that bad, but lots of climbers who did just fine on the harder sections below have failed here. The exposure overwhelms. And it's hard to be smooth when you are hyperventilating.

The *Naked Edge* was a physical edge, but it was a metaphorical one as well, a leading edge that the best of a generation would push. Lots tried the route, but when the legendary Layton Kor failed, its reputation loomed bigger than ever. Kor came back in 1964 with Rick Horn and completed the line, rating its hardest aid pitch at A4. The climb was finally freed by Jim Erickson and Duncan Ferguson. Erickson had come to the University of Colorado in 1967 after having learned to climb at Devil's Lake, Wisconsin. Over the next decade, his name would come to stand for purity of climbing style. In Erickson's code of ethics, to use the rope in any way was to taint a climb. When he'd fall on a route, he would simply pull his rope, sometimes not even returning for another try. Erickson became one of the most influential climbers of the 1970s. The high standard held by such a climber influenced a generation of Americans and was one of the chief barriers to the introduction of sport climbing. Erickson's success on the *Naked Edge* changed a country's perspective on what was possible.

Maybe the high point of all Boulder climbing came when young Dave Breashears (later of Everest and IMAX fame) climbed a one-pitch route on Mickey Maus Wall called *Perilous Journey.* This 1975 ascent is considered by purists to be the highest expression of the sport, basically an unprotected free solo, dragging a rope in case there happened to be good protection—there wasn't. Had this route waited a few years, or had it been somewhere else, it would now be just one of a thousand bolted 5.11s. Climbing needs routes that few climbers will ever do. Like an endangered species that few will ever see, such routes' existence is vital.

One of the remarkable aspects of Boulder is the variety of climbing. On the north end of town, Highway 119 heads up toward

Nederland through Boulder Canyon, a scattering of walls on featured granite. It's the perfect complement to the tricky sandstone of the Flatirons and Eldorado Canyon, giving Boulder climbers a venue to escape the red sandstone for the world of granite cracks and the subtleties of crystalline slabs.

First cliff on the right is the Dome, with its wandering and lower-angled climbs above the paved running/bike track. It's a popular place, though it lacks the dramatic verticality of the steep walls of Eldorado. As the road twists higher out of town, passing numerous crags along its way, the last rock encountered before the winding road emerges onto the high valley of Nederland is the odd pinnacle of Castle Rock, a 300-foot miniature mountain, its summit inaccessible to hikers. The approach couldn't be easier because the road wraps around the base. On the back side are two historic and excellent routes, *Athlete's Feat* (5.10) and *Country Club Crack* (5.11). *Athlete's Feat* is an especially significant route, bringing together Boulder climber Pat Ament and California star Royal Robbins in 1964. Four short pitches of hard face and crack climbing made it the hardest multipitch route in the country at the time. The pair also came close to success on *Country Club Crack* to the right. This is handcrack climbing at its best, though the boulder problem start is hard and the upper crack is a bit greasy.

Just above Castle Rock, the road levels out at more than 8,000 feet into the town of Nederland, where the cars are older and rustier, the overalls baggier. Dreadlocks are not a statement in Nederland—they are the norm. At the Wolf's Tongue Brewery, you'll share the bar with Trustafarians, eastern suburban refugees, halfway through college and still driving a Saab. There have been some impressive drug busts in Nederland. Higher still, the road snakes its way through high pine forests and expanding alpine views toward Rocky Mountain National Park.

Rocky Mountain National Park

About an hour's drive northwest from Boulder is Rocky Mountain National Park. It is a climber's park, a perfect place to make the move from multipitch cragging to alpine climbing. The approaches are generally short for the mountains, the territory well mapped out by guidebooks. One guide boasts, tongue in cheek, that there's even good cell phone reception from most of the climbs. The park is a perfect link between the crags and the mountains.

The bustling commercial center of the region is Estes Park, which is not a park but a town at the edge of a park and the starting point for most climbing. It's packed with everything you'd expect in a tourist town, from gift shops and movie theaters, condos and pizzerias, to lots of people jammed on the sidewalks enjoying their commune with nature, their attention fixed on store windows instead of the big peaks lined up outside of town.

Unless climbers are bent on finding T-shirts, souvenir coffee mugs, or postcards, they'll be more interested in two other elements of Estes Park: Komito's Boot Repair and Lumpy Ridge. Steve Komito has been fixing climbing shoes since the '60s. He was once a regular partner of Layton Kor, sharing the rope on such first ascents as *Outer Space* in Eldorado. Komito humbly referred to himself in those days as "Layton Kor's piton retriever." The shop has long been a locus of activity, a meeting place for climbers and a source of route information. But you didn't come here to schmooze or fondle shoes; you came to climb. And if you just arrived from sea level, best to start with a rock climb or two at Lumpy Ridge, a fine collection of domes and towers at the edge of town.

If Lumpy Ridge were anywhere else but across from the majestic crest of the Rockies, it would be a destination climbing area. Given its awfully mundane name and its submissive place in the shadow of the Diamond and Hallett's north face, it remains humbly out of boastful talk and tick lists. Which is just as well. Lumpy Ridge is one of the most beautiful places to climb granite in America, especially when it's not swarming with climbers. The ridge is comprised of several separate towers and domes, all good granite, and most with routes in the three- to six-pitch range. The rock is excellent, featured granite, smooth slabs separated by splitter cracks. Multipitch routes in moderate grades are the mainstay here, though as is true everywhere, vicious hard routes abound as well.

From a belay ledge high on one of the granite towers, you look over the pastures of the McGregor Ranch and out to the crest of the high Rockies. Left end of the panorama is the square-topped Longs Peak, highest in the park. The sheer east face, known as the

Hallett Peak: alpine climbing on Colorado's Front Range

Diamond, can be seen from many vantage points below. Off to the right are the steep walls above Bear Lake, the north wall of Hallett Peak being as imposing as any in the range.

The north wall of Hallett gets bigger and more ominous the closer one gets. By the time you've arrived at the Bear Lake parking lot, the daunting wall dominates the view. It's the quintessential north face, the way an alpine wall ought to look: steep, dark, and brooding. A little imagination and it can be the Eiger, right here in Colorado. Hallett immediately drew attention from climbers, and when Ray Northcutt and Harvey Carter climbed its third buttress in 1956, their route was considered the boldest climbing in Colorado. Northcutt described the route in the 1959 *American Alpine Journal,* building up the intrigue surrounding this north face. Californians Yvon Chouinard and Ken Weeks later went up one afternoon to check it out for a future ascent. They started up around four in the afternoon, intending just to have a look. It was still light when they topped out, having spent just four hours to knock off what was supposed to be a major alpine challenge. The big north face was slightly diminished after that, and even more so when Layton Kor soloed it in an hour and a half, claiming that wherever you reach, there's a handhold.

For many years *Northcutt-Carter* on Hallett Peak was a stepping-stone route for climbers entering the world of alpine rock climbing. It had the look, the route-finding difficulties, the long run-outs on big sharp holds. In the summer of 1999, it would be more than myth that peeled away from the big north face. A large chunk of *Northcutt-Carter* crashed to the ground, leaving the lower portion of the route unclimbable and its future as an American classic uncertain. Other climbs on Hallett that fill the void with high-quality introductory alpine climbing are the *Jackson-Johnson Route* and the *Culp-Bossier Route,* both left of Northcutt and Carter's 1956 line.

The glacial action that scoured out the steep faces of Hallett Peak is also evident in the deep basins to the south. Sky Pond sits in one such basin, under the most serrated crest in all the West, the Cathedral Spires. This is summit climbing at its purest, with the most dramatic being the top of the Petit Grepon, a blade of rock thirty feet long and a dozen feet thick at its top, six pitches above its only slightly wider base. It looks to be little more than a stone wafer ready to blow over in the next hard wind.

It's impossible to stand on a spire like the Petit Grepon and fail to reflect on the fragility of the mountains, the steady wearing away of solid rock and toppling over of teetering spires. Time takes on a renewed significance when we think about how long ago this great buried mass of rock was crumpled upward from continental collision, how much later the great masses of ice deepened the valleys and steepened the headwalls, leaving fragments like the Petit Grepon to be toppled soon after by rain and ice and the relentless pull of gravity.

Farther south in the lineup of summits and basins is Black Lake cirque, where Spearhead rears upward in front of the two faces of Chiefshead. Here the climbing is smoother, less broken than Hallett Peak or the Cathedral Spires. Spearhead is more like the classic granite of Yosemite, cleaved into more continuous cracks, the slabs not so featured. Right of the pyramid-shaped face is the *Northwest Ridge* route, a good candidate for one's first alpine rock climb. It's long and moderate, with lots of variations possible, and, best of all, it finishes on the sharpened tip of the Spearhead. To its left are two fine but harder routes. *The Barb,* at a gentleman's 5.10, follows thin cracks on a not-so-steep face, and left of this, *Sikes Sickle* draws one up into a bizarre bomb-bay chimney (what a place to be) 700 feet above the base.

The centerpiece of climbing in Rocky Mountain National Park is the Diamond on the east face of Longs Peak, one of the premier alpine walls in America. Unlike the rugged, broken profiles of many of the other high-country routes in the park, the Diamond is cleaved sheer, vertical in places, slightly overhanging in others. The entire face stands above 13,000 feet, the base of the wall higher than most summits in the park. The Diamond is the most coveted climbing objective in all Colorado. At first, applications to climb on the Diamond were denied. Ray Northcutt and Layton Kor thus opted for the lower east face via a route they called *The Diagonal.* It was the biggest climb done to date in Colorado, yet with the real prize looming overhead, it was a consolation award. After their success, coupled with the recent forty-five-day siege by Warren Harding and partners on the 3,000-foot wall of El Capitan in Yosemite, park officials finally changed their stance and sent applications for an attempt on the Diamond to all who had sought permission earlier. The bureaucratic process allowed two Californians to step in front of the Colorado climbers who consider Longs Peak to be their home turf.

Bob Kamps and Dave Rearick were outsiders to the Colorado scene, but they were capable climbers with rich experience on Yosemite granite. They also had access to a collection of hard steel pitons manufactured by Chouinard. Over a three-day period in 1960, and with a support team at the ready should assistance be needed, the two pushed a line right up the longest, steepest, most central section of the wall, a line they called *Ace of Diamonds* but now is better known as *D1.* Their feat was celebrated in *Time* magazine and the two were stars of the Estes Park summer rodeo parade.

The Diamond is only a third the size of El Capitan, but the altitude, remoteness, and weather make it a serious undertaking. The sun leaves the east face before noon, and ice forms in cracks even in the summer. In the years following its first ascent, climbers approaching the Diamond would come prepared for at least a three-day ordeal, the first humping loads to Broadway ledge, a third of the way up and the start of the difficult climbing. Days two and three would be spent getting up the wall and back to civilization. A Diamond climb was a major undertaking, mainly artificial and often with a bivouac on the face.

As with so many of the icons of Colorado climbing, the next three decades would see a steady erosion in the mythic stature of the

Diamond. The first and most significant assault was the free ascent by Wayne Goss and Jim Logan, experienced climbers but by 1976 no longer part of the younger crew pushing the standards around Boulder. Their success was shocking, at least as significant as Erickson and Ferguson's free climb of the *Naked Edge.* In 1978 Charley Fowler soloed a linkup near the center of the face in an hour and a half, saying it felt "casual." Sad, in a way, that the name stuck. The *Casual Route* (5.10) was one of the final blows to the Diamond's mystique, cleverly linking the easy sections of several routes for a startlingly easy route that seldom exceeds 5.8. In the old days, a Diamond veteran would be accorded unqualified respect. Today, when someone tells of doing the Diamond, it's just as likely to be an intermediate climber in tow of a professional guide.

What happened on the Diamond is what has occurred at many of the big, popular walls around the country. Some call it cragification, the steady process whereby a big, threatening face gets more user-friendly. With familiarity, the cliff seems smaller. Someone will feel like caretaker of the place and install rappel bolts as a service to the community. Each belay ledge now will seem closer to the ground, and the big routes become a collection of individual pitches. You don't have to do the route; you can instead just head up until things get hard, you change your mind, or the clouds move in. It's a safer, more popular, sanitized version of what once was a big deal. Even with the fixed rappel route and the detailed route topo, however, the sun still fades out of sight before noon, lightning still crackles across the high peaks most summer afternoons, the temperature still drops into the 20s even on July and August nights. The likelihood of failure is still high, and if the Diamond's aura rubs so dull that regular folks stop taking it too seriously, then we can expect some spectacular disasters up there.

AND THERE'S MORE

While Boulder itself is a climbing hub, the activity is spread wide, in part because of the restrictions imposed on new bolts in Eldorado Canyon and the Flatirons. In the years when sport climbing was gaining a foothold, Boulder was one of the first places to struggle with, and then generally embrace, the new methods. The main force here was the colorful and controversial Christian Griffith, who vocally broke with the traditional locals and began putting up face routes in the 5.12 and 5.13 range, linking lines of weakness between the established routes in the canyon. Like everywhere else in the throes of change, there were angry letters to the magazines, angry conversations at the crags. It was hot for a while. In contrast, when the wave of change hit Smith Rock, few were around to complain. Once seeded, sport climbing grew rapidly on the Front Range, creeping from Eldo and up onto the back side of the Flatirons, where the inclined sedimentary bedding made for some wildly gymnastic routes. When the park stepped in and placed severe restrictions on bolting, things quieted down almost as quickly as they fired up.

With sport climbing firmly established elsewhere and with the dearth of opportunities right in Boulder, Colorado climbers spread out and new areas were discovered. First was Shelf Road, south near Cañon City, developed initially by climbers from nearby Colorado Springs. Generally vertical, and with moderate routes available to regular folks, the limestone cliffs at Shelf Road edged their way onto the list of most popular climbing areas in Colorado. Cañon City calls itself the "climate capital of Colorado," and as such, there's year-round activity at Shelf Road.

A short time later it was Rifle Mountain Park, far west of the Front Range. Rifle is a big, steep-walled canyon, known for hard, strenuous, sequential routes on angular, blocky limestone. Shelf Road was a fitting start to the limestone era, but it was soon eclipsed by the higher overhanging walls of Rifle. Now that other, bigger limestone cliffs, mainly around Las Vegas, have been opened up, Shelf Road has slipped back from the front page, though Rifle holds its own today as one of the country's premier sport-climbing venues.

But there's still a lot more available a short drive from Boulder. At the other end of the spectrum from the pumpy clip-ups at Rifle is the rolling dome land around the South Platte River, just south of Denver. Here in the cool pine forests is a vast array of climbing possibilities on golden and pink granite. It's a place with a deeply held tradition of adventure climbing. Top-down sport routes are as disdained as boastful reporting of first ascents in the national magazines. Even with metropolitan Denver so near, the Platte is a climbing area that still hides in relative obscurity.

Some of its areas, like Turkey Rock, site of the most intensive crack-climbing development on the entire Front Range, see a lot of traffic. It's close to the road and splintered into so many vertical cracks that it seems made for rock climbing. Not too far from Turkey Rock, however, is Big Rock Candy Mountain, known for long routes (up to fifteen pitches), long run-outs, and questionable bolts. Then there's Cynical Pinnacle, the most prominent feature in all the South Platte. *Wunsch's Dihedral* (5.11a) and the *Center Route* (5.9+) are two of the best crack routes. The rock is coarse and excellent, the lines unmistakable, and from the pinnacle's top, endless miles of green trees and golden granite stretch out in stark contrast to the dark caves of Rifle.

This Is the Place

In 1964, the same year he teamed up with Pat Ament for *Athlete's Feat,* Royal Robbins also joined future Salt Lake City mayor Ted Wilson in Little Cottonwood Canyon and established another challenging 5.10 line, the *Robbins Route.* It was the same year George Lowe and Mark McQuarrie free-climbed *The Coffin* at 5.9. A year later the pair did the *Dorsal Fin* at a stout 5.10d. Shortly thereafter the Lowe-McQuarrie team was attempting a new route on the Church Buttress in Little Cottonwood when McQuarrie fell, cutting his rope on a sharp flake and crashing to his death into the church archives parking lot. The triumph and the drama of Salt Lake City climbing, one could argue, were every bit as rich as those of Boulder, and stories from Cottonwood should have become just as richly a part of American climbing lore as those so thoroughly told from Boulder. But Salt Lake City is not a land of self-congratulation. Different things mattered, and no one collected the tales in a book. Mark McQuarrie died near the door of the Mormon Archives, the most complete repository of genealogical records in the world, so precious that they are kept in a bombproof vault blasted into the white granite of Little Cottonwood Canyon. That McQuarrie's name in American climbing remained obscure, but that the residents of Salt Lake City sought to keep the world's most meticulous records so that the dead could remain in the hearts of the living says a lot about the stark difference between Salt Lake City and Boulder. Boulder relished the moment, yet some of its climbers ascribed eternal significance to their deeds. Earthly self-absorption is not the way of the people in Salt Lake City.

Take the postcard image of Boulder, nestled on the east side of the great Rocky Mountains, climbers oozing from the town up into fantastic canyons of varied stone, or trekking, heavily laden with mountain gear, up to the high alpine climbs or snow chutes. Take this image and turn it around, and you have Salt Lake City, at the western edge of Utah's Wasatch Range. The city sprawls broadly across the drying shores of the Great Salt Lake, with east-west avenues heading up into the mountains and the canyons: American Fork, Big and Little Cottonwood, where climbers have every choice from granite to quartzite to limestone to the fantastic cobbled conglomerate of Maple Canyon.

A tourist's guidebook to Utah explains that it's impossible to know Utah without knowing what it means to be Mormon. Overlooking this would be like exploring Italy without acknowledging Catholicism, the book explains. True. But at the same time, if too much emphasis is placed on the city's Mormonism, the reality will be reduced to oversimplified images and stereotypical vignettes. Outsiders might see Utah simply as a place where it's hard to find a drink, where maverick Ross Perot beat Clinton in the 1996 presidential election, where, according to a Utah delegate to the Libertarian Party, "the separation of church and state is exactly two city blocks." They are apt to paint in broad strokes a picture of polygamy and intolerance, a city of straight streets and straight people, where the crime rate is low and healthy living is rewarded.

Mark Twain noticed this radiant healthiness in Salt Lake City, saying that "there was only one physician in the place and he was arrested every week regularly and held to answer under the vagrant act for having no visible means of support." He also mused that "heedless people often come to Utah and make remarks about Brigham, or polygamy, or some other sacred matter, and the very next morning at daylight such parties are sure to be found lying up some back alley, contently waiting for the hearse." With a steady migration of outsiders to the city, and with the international status earned by hosting the 2002 Winter Olympic Games, Salt Lake City is changing and growing beyond the stereotypes.

Nineteen-ninety-nine was a tough year for Salt Lake City. There was the Olympic scandal, in which local officials were accused of bribing members of the International Olympic Committee to get the winter games. Such palm greasing has long been an accepted part of the bid process everywhere to be sure, but it was with deep bitterness that residents had to listen to accusations about their own moral lapses. Even though the scandal further polarized the factions for and against the games, the Olympics for long after would be seen as having welcomed the world and cemented the city's image as a place to play. It was along the same lines that the second trauma shocked the city in the summer of 1999. Just as the Outdoor Retailers Convention was about to open, a tornado dropped from the sky and ripped apart the displays, scattering kayaks about the city streets, knocking down big tents, and killing one worker. Had the storm not come during lunch hour, many more would have been caught in the wreckage. Salt Lake City is indeed becoming known as the place for premier outdoor recreation, and even in the wake of the tornado, the convention went on. It was here, by the way, that the U.S. Department of the Interior announced a moratorium on the fixed-anchor ban in wilderness areas. That the announcement came in Salt Lake City confirmed the city's vital place in the outdoor retail industry.

Two occurrences symbolize the city's burgeoning place in the climbing world. In 1988, the first international climbing competition was held on the big wall of the Snowbird Cliff Lodge, up Little Cottonwood Canyon. It was an event that made TV stars of Lynn Hill, Ron Kauk, and Scott Franklin. The Americans did get whipped, however, partly because the old-school traditional approach had left us way behind the French. But it was this same year that Bill Boyle, Jeff Pederson, and Boone Speed began turning nearby American Fork Canyon into the country's first unabashedly modern sport-climbing crags. AF and the countless sport-climbing cliffs developed in the years following would play a big role in bringing American climbing back to the fore.

The second event etching Salt Lake City into the minds of American climbers was Black Diamond's move from California to Salt Lake City. Black Diamond replaced venerable Chouinard Equipment in 1989, when it was restructured as a fully employee-owned

The white granite of Little Cottonwood Canyon, Utah

and -operated company. Its original factory, known as Great Pacific Iron Works, was located near the beach in Ventura, California, because founder Yvon Chouinard liked to surf. Two years after the employees took over, however, the new company peeled itself away from the California scene and moved to Salt Lake City. It was a visible move and a statement about the vitality of climbing places outside the better-publicized areas of California and Colorado. Along with the company came a lot of really powerful climbers.

Salt Lake City is a very positive climbing scene, a scene friendlier than most, where climbers are less apt to take cheap shots at each other than at older climbing areas. Perhaps this is because Salt Lake City is a big place where climbing isn't the only thing that matters. Perhaps it's because the old-timers didn't care to make much of a stink when the new-wave sport climbing hit the nearby canyons. Perhaps it is because there's just so much climbing that there's room for all kinds. It's a climbing city where visitors are likely to run into big shots but where the encounter will be comfortable. It's an open and welcoming scene, one the rest of the city hopes to nourish as it invites the world to its Olympic Games.

What distinguishes the climbing around Salt Lake City is its diversity. There's granite, quartzite, limestone, and conglomerate all within an hour of the city. Longest recognized is the dazzling white granite of Little Cottonwood Canyon. On a drive up the canyon road from town toward Snowbird, the cliffs seem modest, low-angled, part of a fish-eye-lens' view where the glacial, U-shaped valley spreads upward to meet the sky and the rounded rocks are only part of the rubbled hillside. Once you're on the routes, however, they grow in size and steepness. Face climbing is the essence here in Little Cottonwood, but cracks abound as well. Routes can be moderate and friendly or they can be treacherously run out. Modern climbers in sticky-rubber shoes still fall off old George Lowe routes like *S-Matrix,* with its hard 5.10 slab originally done in hiking boots. With all the hard overhanging sport routes around the city, it's the classic white granite of Little Cottonwood that grounds the place traditionally, where footwork is subtle, where nerves and nut-placing ability matter more than muscle. The road emerges at the top of the canyon at Snowbird and Hellgate Cliff, a hulking 400-foot mass of limestone developed by the late Mugs Stump. From the plastic holds of the Cliff Lodge or the limestone pockets of Hellgate, one can see down the round, granite-strewn valley onto the flats of the big city.

Then there's Big Cottonwood Canyon, another collection of good, though shorter, cliffs. Big Cottonwood is a chaotic scattering of crags and buttresses, layered a bit like the Flatirons, with slabby corners and steep, pumpy back sides. It's the kind of rock that won't appeal at first—too jumbled and confused, lacking the sweeping lines of good granite. Up close, the quartzite is covered with sharp positive edges, making it very climbable. Most of the routes went in during a surge in the late '80s, but keep in mind that one of the oldest hard routes in America is in Big Cottonwood: *Goodro's Wall,* an excellent 5.10c done by Harold Goodro around 1949, a typically unheralded achievement.

Sport Climbing

It's been said that Salt Lake City has more 5.14 climbers than any other place in the country. For that, nearby limestone can take much of the credit. The Church of Jesus Christ of Latter-day Saints mined the good white granite up in Little Cottonwood Canyon to build a temple in the city, but climbers like Boone Speed, Bill Boyle, and Jeff Pederson discovered the potential in a softer, humbler rock at American Fork Canyon just south of the city, and at Logan Canyon up to the north. These cliffs, admittedly, aren't much to look at. In fact, having heard exaggerated reports about American Fork, visitors might be disappointed with their first impressions of the place. Unlike the legendary white sweeps of beautiful limestone like Ceuese or Buoux in France, American Fork cliffs are loose, blocky, and ugly.

Russ Clune describes the gamut of American limestone as based on two main factors: the *chossiness* of the rock (*choss* meaning loose, ugly rock), and the amount of glue used to hold it together. Places like American Fork Canyon were hardly climbable until someone hung on rappel, picked out a line, and decided which blocks to pry off and which to reinforce with cement. In addition to the construction of the route as a whole, individual holds that were jagged and sharp, too painful to climb, were "comfortized" with a file or hammer. In the old trad days, routes were discoveries; here they are creations. Though the methods were unconventional, few objected. The limestone rock in most cases held little appeal to the hard-rock climber, and no one could claim that future traditional routes were being stolen by unfair means.

The state of a cliff and its routes has a lot to do with when it was "discovered" and developed. At Shelf Road in Colorado, the first major limestone area to hit the press, the holds are looser and "comfortizing" is rare. Rap-bolting alone was considered blasphemous in many areas, and the early climbers at Shelf were reluctant to take things too far. A much newer kid on the block is Jack's Canyon in northern Arizona, a minor cliff with a growing reputation for fun climbing. And much of the fun, say visitors, is wrapping your hands around perfectly manicured holds and sticking your fingers into smooth and deep pockets that are, well, about the size of a good half-inch Bosch drill bit. Such practices would have led to a lynching just a few years ago. Most climbers today agree that a code of ethics is grounded in the place itself.

Climbing on limestone is a very different experience for anyone schooled on more traditional stone like granite. First, limestone lacks the joint patterns of other sedimentary and igneous rock, breaking down instead by solution, and so there are very few cracks. Hand- and footholds in limestone are often pockets where the rock has dissolved from slightly acidic water percolating through the rock. Some of these solution holes are as big as a house, forming caves and outrageous roof routes. Other cavities are finger-sized—*mono-doigt* they call them, part of the lingering French jargon. Limestone climbing is almost always vertical or overhanging, the bottoms of many cliffs having been scoured out by river action or rockfall. Low-angled limestone is rare. Such rock would have been quickly eroded by the direct contact with the weather, and even if limestone slabs did exist, friction climbing would be a nightmare on the slick surface.

Limestone lacks the geometric predictability found on many other kinds of rock. Granite's exfoliation sheeting and friction qualities allow one to make a pretty good guess from below as to how a particular route might be approached. You can look up at a corner and know in advance what techniques will come into play. The horizontally layered sandstone of the Southeast or the vertically jointed sandstone of Utah's canyon country is also quite easy to read. On the banded stuff, you just reach up until you find a flat hold, and on the vertical cracks, you're looking at repetitive jamming. Limestone has no crystalline orientation to dictate the way it fractures. The edges and pockets seem random, sequences hard to decipher. Faces that look blank might well contain hidden pockets. Broken-up routes that seem well featured might be nearly impossible because everything faces the wrong way.

Limestone climbing is dynamic and creative. Instead of the repetitive movements required by cracks or sandstone bucket ladders, it forces the climber to think and react—fast. The small pockets isolate the fingers. Body positions also need creative accommodation to the multiple direction of the holds. Straight-on climbing might work at the Gunks or on the geometrically monotonous layers of southern sandstone. On limestone, however, you need side-pulls, drop knees, and lots of dynamic movement. Colorado's Rifle Canyon is especially frustrating for anyone aspiring to an on-sight climb: It's almost impossible from below to anticipate how each hold will be best used. The old-school climber who thinks that style points will be awarded for smooth and static control will soon be hanging dejectedly from the rope.

One of the biggest challenges to climbing on limestone is the polished surface of the holds after just a few ascents. Calcite is a very different medium from crystalline rock like granite. Initially the surface might feel gritty, even sharp-toothed. It isn't long, however, until even the good positive holds begin to take on a greasy sheen from repeated use. Old routes in France are frighteningly glassy, especially at cruxes where hundreds of chalked and rosined hands have worked the pockets over and over, and hundreds of dusty soles have ground footholds slick. At limestone areas in America, even where few routes are older than ten years, one can tell easily whether or not the route has had much traffic. It's a problem almost unique in climbing. A route with gritty, secure holds in the beginning can devolve into a shimmering glaze.

All down the Wasatch Range and east into the lesser-known Uintas, the variety continues. Ferguson Canyon offers good, short, north-facing summer climbing when the granite up in Little Cottonwood is scorching. South down the range is Maple Canyon, where an unearthly landscape of cobbled cliffs looks like an inclined gravel pit. Holds are either big, rounded stones embedded in the matrix, or hollows where a cobble became dislodged. It's one of the oddest climbing experiences in the country. The big, rounded stones look as if they would pop right out upon first tug, and so one tends to climb gently at first. But then the pump begins, and as anyone who has trained on big holds knows, nothing burns the forearms like ample, rounded holds. Making the situation even more desperate is the slipperiness of the cobbles underfoot. Feet skate from big slopers, hands strenuously readjust to keep from slipping. Soon the apparent looseness ceases to matter. Just reach up and pull, confident that the chalk up there means someone else has already tested the hold. And out east in the Uinta Mountains, there are hundreds, soon to be thousands, of fine quartzite routes ranging over the entire spectrum of styles from closely bolted sport climbs to bold, ground-up trad affairs.

The number of Utah license plates in the parking areas of the West shows Salt Lake City to be one of the region's most important hub cities. You see, these cars aren't all owned by Utah natives; many are rentals driven by visitors from elsewhere. From the airport, they can head north to the City of Rocks, even up to the Wind Rivers or the Tetons. They can hit canyon country just a few hours to the south. Or looking up at Lone Peak Cirque, visible from all over the city, with its alpine rock climbing on steep, vertically jointed granite high above the city sprawl, they might just choose to stick around town. Utah is the Beehive State, a bustling, industrious state welded with common purpose. To the climber, it's certainly a hive of vigorous activity.

SIN CITY

In 1829 Spanish explorers called the marshy grassland the Meadows, *Las Vegas.* A hundred years later, the already whiskey-soaked town legalized gambling and boomed with workers building Hoover Dam. Today, gambling and entertainment continue to make Las Vegas the fastest-growing city in America, a population exploding by as many as 4,000 newcomers per week, playing host to 30 million annual visitors determined to eat cheap, maybe play a little golf, and stay up all night trying to get rich.

Las Vegas is unique in America. Its strip is a giant amusement park of lavish buildings in playful imitation of international landmarks. One of the first big hotel casinos was the Desert Inn, exaggerated but at least fitting the region with its desert motif. Then, as the stream of neon rolled up the strip, came Caesar's Palace, with its lavish Roman decor, and later the MGM Grand Hotel and Theme Park. Soon it looked as if developers were in competition to produce the most outlandish imported facades. Today, a Las Vegas visitor can be anywhere in the world: the Great Pyramids, Treasure Island, the Arc de Triomphe, Venice, or even high in the blue sky via the Stratosphere Tower, replete with its high-altitude roller coaster. The climber flying in at night to McCarran International Airport is treated to an unearthly light show as the runway parallels the Strip, greens and blues and reds lighting the dry night sky.

It's hard to decide which is more striking, the anomalous proximity of such pristine climbing to the decadence capital of America or just the variety and quality of the climbing itself. Backdrop to the explosion of color and cars, metal and glass, are the high sandstone walls of Red Rocks, one of the richest concentrations of varied climbing in the nation. Just as Las Vegas is every kind of earthly experience, so is it every kind of climbing experience as well. Las Vegas is high-quality bolted sport climbing right next to the road. It is twenty-pitch adventure routes high on a mountain face. It's being part of a tanned and vocal scene at the base of a busy little crag, ropes draped all around. It's standing alone, shivering, on an airy ledge high in a remote canyon many pitches from the ground and even more to the top. With the huge adventure routes at Red Rocks, the overhanging limestone of Mount Charleston just a short drive up the mountain, and lots more unexplored limestone all over southern Nevada, a lot of folks call Las Vegas the best, most complete climbing area in the country.

Drive out West Charleston Boulevard, past Desert Rock Sports and the Powerhouse gym, where an aggressive commercial sprawl surges toward the cliffs, ending at a front edge of plywood and bulldozers. Just ahead is the line where the wave of development will soon crash against the public open-space land of the Bureau of Land Management. In the distance are mountain walls, horizontally striped in red and white, so big that they throw everything else out of proportion. Beneath such giants, cliffs like the Gallery seem tiny and insignificant. But it's the combination of huge, multipitch free climbs in remote canyons, along with short, overhanging, desperate sport routes, that makes Red Rocks so appealing. You can stretch your fingers and test your wings on hard clip-ups one day, and next work your quads in an hour-long uphill march toward a twelve-pitch moderate.

The city of Las Vegas has been cranking right along since the boom days of Boulder Dam construction, through the entertainment era of Frank Sinatra and his Rat Pack, right to today's vigorous attempt by casino owners to make the city family-friendly (in other words, keep the kids busy while their baby-boomer parents gamble away the college funds). Yet there weren't too many climbers among the hordes visiting Las Vegas during its glory years. Even in the early 1970s not too many people had Red Rocks on their must-do travel lists. It was all Boulder and Joshua Tree and the Tetons and Yosemite.

It wouldn't be until the late 1970s that stories about such climbing potential so close to Vegas crept west and east. And still, many doubted that climbs of fifteen or twenty pitches could possibly exist in a land the they pictured as bleak and flat.

Certainly, when Jorge Urioste accepted a post at the University of Nevada Las Vegas to teach cultural anthropology, he didn't do so because the climbing was so rich. Urioste had been a well-known climber in the East, spending summers in the Gunks and winters exploring alpine routes in New England. In 1974 he and his new wife, Joanne, arrived in Vegas and began poking around Red Rocks. For the next few years, they'd have the place to themselves. In 1978 they teamed up with Joe Herbst to climb an incredible eighteen-pitch chimney system on the brooding Black Velvet Wall. Jorge followed the climb with a trip to the hospital for an allergic reaction, and so the route took on the name *Epinephrine* (5.9). Chimney climbing is usually awful: full-body grunting, bad protection, no view. But this isn't granite. It's Aztec sandstone, with flakes and edges, odd hollows and positive holds. It's stuff that wants to be climbed. *Epinephrine* continues to be a favorite route, even in the minds of a lot of jaded locals. It requires fast, efficient climbing. Pitch after pitch roll by and you stop counting. Some of it is indeed a struggle. Tony Calderone described it as "kind of like having rough sex in a closet, but a lot harder on your clothing." And there are some spooky moves on loose flakes up high, but all seems well with the world when you have beaten the clock, topping out with time to savor the view, instead of losing the race and spending a chilly night on the wall, the experience of so many climbers who have gone before.

The Aztec sandstone is a relative of Utah's Navajo Formation. Much of it has a hard, desert-varnished surface that, when worn away, exposes the softer, lighter rock underneath. The result is an amazingly climbable surface. Routes that look like crack climbs from afar are actually face routes that happen to follow protectable cracks. *Crimson Chrysalis* (5.9) is one such route. The crack keeps you going straight for its nine marvelous pitches, but it's really a face route on big positive holds. The main challenge on this Urioste route is its popularity; get there early or take a number and bring along some good reading material.

"The desert is a harsh master. It rewards the strong and the adaptable. The fate of others is extinction. One must learn wisdom of the ways of the desert to be safe within it." So reads the sign at the Red Rocks Visitors Center on the scenic loop drive. The Uriostes did indeed have to adjust to the environment so different from the Gunks or Yosemite. When they arrived in Las Vegas, there was little company and no climbing scene. Like Herb and Jan Conn a generation earlier at South Dakota's Needles, they had the place to themselves and saw climbing in its purest terms, as adventure, not a statement to others about how things ought to be done. Seen through the competitive eyes of climbers elsewhere in the '70s and '80s, the Uriostes relied too heavily on the drill. One seasoned climber called their *Prince of Darkness* (5.10) "the most flagrantly overbolted multipitch route in the country." In what amounted to a direct response to their *Dream of Wild Turkeys* (5.10), adventure climbers Richard Harrison, Jay Smith, and Nick Nordblom added *Rock Warrior,* also 5.10, exposed, continuous, but with very few bolts. But it is still the Urioste routes that get most of the business.

Culturally, climbers have connected Red Rocks more to southern California than to the canyon country of the Colorado River drainage, even though the sandstone climbing is much more similar to Utah's than to the rounded granite of Joshua Tree National Park. The connection comes mainly from the people, principally Californians John Long and Lynn Hill. In 1980 they teamed up with Joanne Urioste to free-climb *Levitation 29,* establishing one of the country's hardest long routes (eleven pitches, sustained 5.11). For a few years, it would be California plates that lined the parking areas, until a local community emerged and the word spread nationally about this remarkable climbing area.

In the years to follow, the energy spread in two directions at Red Rocks: to the short cliffs like the Gallery where top-end sport routes would draw big crowds, and up-canyon to the giant Rainbow Wall, originally a big-time aid route, later free-climbed by the persistent Dan McQuade at 5.12b. The sport venues show up first on the one-way scenic loop. Quick access and a lot of bolts make these crags the social centers of Red Rocks. In contrast, approaches to the long routes can take hours. Given their position in the tight canyons, there's usually shade in the heat of the summer and sun in the cold months. When temperatures are extreme, it's vital to get the orientation right, choosing a climb according to the position of the sun. Long routes mean long descents. Some of these are tricky and require keeping the rope ready for short rappels. The American Mountain Guides Association likes to use these routes for guide testing because they have all the demands of a high mountain environment, minus the ice and snow. Any guide who can quickly read the best descent, knows when to rope and when to scramble, and is able to move a client back safely in a short amount of time at Red Rocks is a strong candidate for certification.

LIMESTONE CAPITAL OF AMERICA?

Mount Charleston is in the Spring Mountains outside of Vegas, a well-named range of cool breezes and ancient bristlecone pines. The air is dry, but the mountain is a water-soaked sponge. Streams and waterfalls are everywhere. The rock itself flows with water, dissolving and percolating the calcite through the layers and gradually coating the underside of the cave roofs. The glassy skin of the rock belies the aquifer inside. Sometimes when a bolt is drilled and the skin is broken, beads of water will drip from the hanger. Or when the clay soil of a deep pocket is removed, the hole becomes a steady seep of moisture. It's a mountain of rounded motion, so different from the angular, blocky rock of Rifle or American Fork.

The way Dan McQuade tells it, Las Vegas is the limestone capital of America, if only for the amount of stone waiting for development. McQuade is a prolific climber and guide synonymous with Las Vegas. On the hard sandstone at Red Rocks, he has established countless routes from the vicious but short sport climbs to the Rainbow Wall. But even with all that good sandstone so near, McQuade has shifted focus to the limestone at Mount Charleston and the endless possibilities in the outback. You can hear it in his voice when he describes his wonder at the features growing and oozing from the orange roofs of Charleston's caves.

Technically, limestone is dead, the boneyard of prehistoric creatures with names like radiolaria and foraminifera. But in other ways, the rock is alive and growing. It's an impression you'll get especially at Mount Charleston. The most dramatic climbing here is on the underside of huge roofs that exit giant solution caves. The surface is wavy and smooth, like liquid swirling and dripping down walls, solidifying into fantastic shapes, fluted fins and weird hollows, rods hanging from ceilings like icicles or candlesticks of melting wax, matted dreadlocks made of stone. The high green forests seem a million miles from the harsh lights and torrid climate of Las Vegas. Of the numerous crags scattered around the 8,000-foot level of the mountain, the Hood is the biggest and best, a single crag with more 5.14s than all of Rifle. Charleston may be alluring, but the entry-level routes generally start at 5.12. It's a reserve mainly for very good and very strong climbers. Closer to town, Waterworld cliff in the Las Madres area has moderate routes (if 5.10 is moderate) with all the swirling surface architecture of the harder cliffs.

The well-known rock up at Mount Charleston and Mount Potasi is only a small fraction of the limestone that forms so much of the Great Basin of Nevada, a vast region inundated again and again by the sea. The Las Vegas area, loosely defined, covers a wide area of the Great Basin, including Clark Mountain in nearby California, the cliffs around Saint George, Utah, and Virgin River Gorge in the northwest corner of Arizona. Clark Mountain was an extraordinary find by Californian Randy Leavitt, who almost single-handedly developed the area. Two routes became well known in the magazines, *The Tusk* (5.14a/b) and *Jumbo Pumping Hate* (5.13), a dramatic, overhanging orange wall as familiar to magazine readers as a Maxim Ropes advertisement. The cliff is high, wild, and hard to get to. Some who have trekked out there call it the best limestone cliff in America. Newcomers to the region will probably want to begin their tour at crags easier to get to and closer to Vegas.

There are beautiful settings like Mount Charleston and the lesser-known Welcome Springs near Saint George, places you'd like to wander even if you didn't climb, environments that expand the dimensions of a climbing day. And then there's Virgin River Gorge, east of Las Vegas in the northeast corner of Arizona. Climbers almost universally describe the climbing as extraordinary and the environment hideous. They savor the routes but agree that the place, as a place, is awful. The Virgin River drains Utah's Zion National Park, and as it passes between Zion's majestic red and white walls it is sadly naive about what lies ahead. If it knew, it would surely find a different route through the rude, buckled canyon it shares with Interstate

15 on its way. Miles of chain-link fencing, hideous scars from massive road-cut blasting, and the incessant grinding noise of cars and trucks whizzing by at seventy-five miles per hour make the climbing here a less than idyllic experience. Cynics even murmur about being irradiated from the nearby nuclear test site. Guidebook editor Todd Goss from Saint George says that climbing in Virgin River Gorge "forces you to live in the here and now. You block out everything" while you focus on the particular moves in front of you, and when you clip the chains, the world comes alive with smells and noise. Areas like Wild Iris and Welcome Springs are wonderful places to be, not just places to climb. The Virgin River Gorge is simply a climbing area.

It's not as though Virgin River Gorge was some hidden gem discovered by a lonely trekker. Anyone driving from Vegas to Salt Lake City would pass within a few hundred feet of the rock, and so thousands of climbers had seen the place before three Utah climbers decided to pull over and check it out. In 1989, on their trip home to Salt Lake City from Red Rocks, Boone Speed, Jeff Pederson, and Vince Adams did just that. Seen through the new lens of modern sport climbing, the Gorge was obviously a major "discovery," with the Blasphemy Wall being one of the single best chunks of limestone anywhere. The numerous hard routes that emerged weren't short and powerful, but long and sustained, usually on tiny holds. Speed's link-up of several routes to create *F-Dude* is described as a full-on thirty-minute burn. In 1997 Chris Sharma added the direct start to Speed's hardest climb, *The Route of All Evil,* and created *Necessary Evil,* hardest routes in America. With the direct start (worked earlier by Speed but never linked), *Necessary Evil* was like doing two 5.14s back to back. Again, it's a long route of tiny holds.

Virgin River Gorge is no place for the untrained or uninitiated. Its entry-level routes are at 5.12. Yet there's still a lot of rock in the canyon around the developed cliffs, including blocky towers that remind one of a miniature Dolomites of Italy. When a place is found and developed so quickly and by such strong climbers, routes 5.12 and up get the most attention. Older areas have a more typical evolution, with the most obvious lines of weakness the first to be explored and exploited. Perhaps there'll be a backfilling of easier routes in the towers and walls by mortals who lack the finger strength of Sharma and Speed.

Boulder, Salt Lake City, and Las Vegas certainly aren't the only hub cities in American climbing. There are lots of places to live and lots of places to visit for the climber who wants a lifetime of climbing on a variety of rock types. There's Tucson, with close-to-the-road sport climbing on Mount Lemmon Highway and wild outback multipitch adventures on remote granite towers, and Flagstaff, nestled strategically between Granite Mountain, the volcanic Paradise Forks, and the spooky sandstone of Sedona. There's Tahoe and Bishop in California, both with the full spectrum of climbing opportunities near. In the East there's North Conway, New Hampshire, with a rich mountaineering heritage, and Chattanooga, Tennessee, buckle of the southeastern sandstone belt, closer to more sandstone climbing than any other city in America. American rock climbers travel. The anticipation of a trip is a powerful incentive to do one more lap at the local gym or top-rope area. With just a week or two to pack in so many climbing dreams, the hub cities are good places to start.

Zion National Park

6 | CANYON COUNTRY

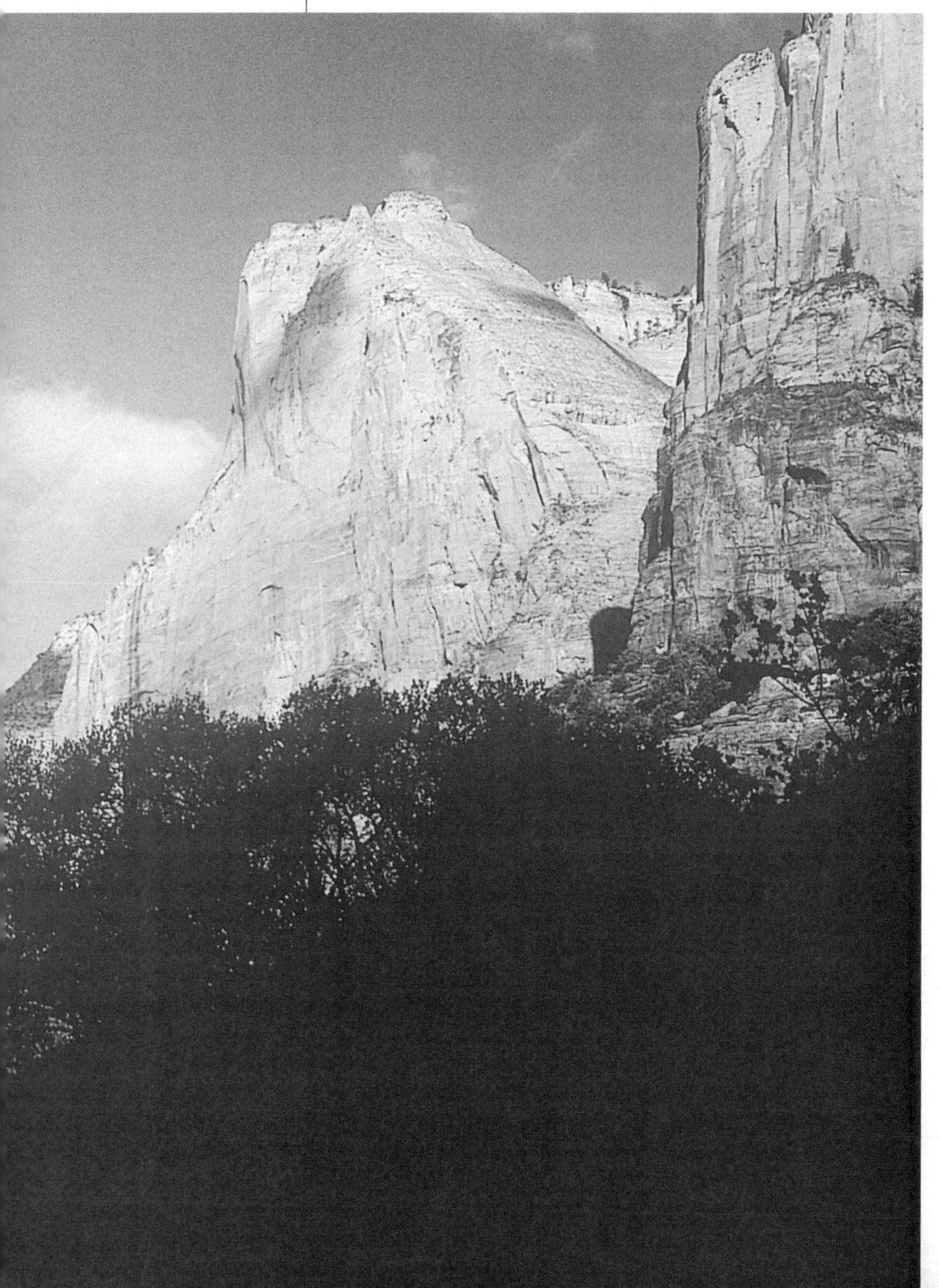

Desert country . . . a hideous Sahara with few oases, a grim bleak harsh overheated sun-blasted God-damned and God-forgotten inferno . . . I am describing the place I love. Nobody in his right mind would live there." Edward Abbey was referring to the desert canyon country of the American West. It's a place deep in the soul of all Americans whether or not they have visited. We grew up with celluloid images of cowboys and Indians stalking each other through the maze of red cliffs. We know its eerie silences, its fragile fingers of rock. We share pictures in our mind: from Georgia O'Keeffe's painting of the sun-bleached cattle skull in the sand to the Chevy truck set by helicopter atop Castleton Tower. The image of canyon country is central to the American consciousness.

Over the last few years (especially since the advent of spring-loaded camming protection) the canyons have become equally central to American rock climbing. It seems that every other issue of the national magazines has an article about jamming the cracks of Indian Creek or balancing perilously atop a crumbling Monument Valley spire. Even outside the romantic context of the Wild West, the climbing would be appealing. But add the surreal and historically vital setting, and the climbing experience is all the more extraordinary.

This is desert country, home to one of the world's greatest concentrations of vertical rock, layers upon layers running uninterrupted for hundreds of miles, cracks by the millions. It's an enchanted land of color, massive red walls streaked in black, all under a perpetually blue sky. It's a land of delicate purity, where a footprint in the desert soil will last 250 years. It's a place where we tread gently.

It is a soft place, where fingernails can scratch marks into stone, where handholds soaked by an afternoon thundershower lose half their strength, where rappel rings blowing in the steady winds wear curved grooves in the rock. It's a temporary place, where a bolt placed thirty years earlier sticks halfway out as the surface wears away around it, where rivers excavate the land and carry it away, right before our eyes. It's a place that asks us to contemplate Time and our own place in it.

The watershed of the American West is built upon two geomorphological oddities. The first is the Great Basin, basically the whole state of Nevada and much of Utah, a giant sump with no outlet to the sea. To the north, the Snake River leaves the Tetons and cuts across the volcanic tablelands of Idaho before joining the mighty Columbia River on its way to the Pacific Ocean. To the south and east, the Colorado River wanders through fantastic stone canyons as it carves its way to Mexico. And to the west is the granite barrier of the Sierra Nevada. Inside is a giant depression. A few muddy streams enter, but none leave. The lowest regions of the basin are the flat, alkaline bottoms of lakes dried up long ago.

The other odd thing about the western drainage is the course of the Colorado River and its feeders, right across an uplifted plane called the Colorado Plateau. It's as though the river foolishly chose to flow right through the bulge of the plateau instead of sensibly skirting around it. At first it looks as though the river had begun atop the high plateau and for eons has been hard at work digging a trench back toward base level. In fact, it is the land itself that is rising, and the river just stays where it is. Rather than spilling off to the side when this broad area was pushed slowly upward over the ages, the river held its own, cutting deep canyons into the red layers of sandstone. The river's capacity to remain generally in place no matter what's happening beneath tempts us to personify it, to ascribe human moods and aspirations to it. It seems to know its place and stubbornly refuses to be redirected. It's an overly romantic view, of course, but it's one that takes on even more meaning downstream where the river is blocked to form Lake Powell and Lake Mead. The concrete dams are among the most massive structures ever built, yet they too are temporary. The river deposits an incredible three cubic miles of rock annually into Lake Powell alone, intent on filling the lake in a relatively short time. And around the edges of the dam, where concrete meets stone, there is an ominous and increasing gush of water. Nature isn't likely to submit to our intrusion.

The Colorado River begins in the melting snow of the Rocky Mountains. Clean, icy water trickles from under a summer snowpack. One such trickle joins another and another, and the trickles become streams, the streams converge, and a river grows. At Grand Junction, Colorado, the Gunnison River adds to the flow. Farther south, the big Green River comes in from Wyoming's Wind River Range and doubles the size of the Colorado where they converge below Island in the Sky in Canyonlands National Park. By now the rivers have clouded up with sediment. Sometimes the Colorado is the muddier of the two; sometimes it's the Green. For a while downstream from the confluence, the cloudier and the cleaner halves of the river run side by side until the two big rivers mix. More rivers join and more rock is carved as the Colorado makes it way to Mexico and the sea.

In places, more than 2 billion years of earth history lies open for review. At the bottom of the Grand Canyon is the hard, dark Precambrian gneiss. On top of this are numerous layers of sandstone and limestone, each with a tale of climate change, of advancing and retreating seas, of deserts and dunes moving like great waves across a Sahara. Seen from above, the Colorado Plateau is a complex maze: Not only are there endless, twisting side canyons, but the whole drama has multiple levels, one superimposed upon the next. At first look, there's no apparent pattern to it: Towers and canyon walls seem chaotically strewn across a flat plane. Yet the Colorado River, the main river with its tributaries fanning out in all directions, forms a pattern elemental to all nature, like a great tree or our own capillary system. Tiny feeders, nourished by the melting snows of the Rockies, join in larger, wider arteries carving their way through the plateau to the sea.

In the canyons is the story of life on earth, from the fossilized hard parts of the earliest tiny organisms to the footprints and bones of dinosaurs in the real Jurassic parks of the West. The layered rock tells of a human history too, of ancient peoples dwelling in cliffs, farming and trading peoples whose descendants would be subjugated by the Spanish for gold and Jesus. The canyons became homes to Mormons, looking for and finding Zion, and hideouts for rustlers fleeing the law. As settlements increased, there were feverish battles over water, the winners building great recreational lakes and drawing electricity from the moving water to build cities and make a desert bloom. The network of rivers that drain the Colorado Plateau converge finally near Las Vegas. From the desolate to the desecrated, from the sacred to the stained, the river is witness to it all.

THE BLACK CANYON OF THE GUNNISON

Most of what we see in the desert Southwest is young sandstone, with the harder, older rock hidden deep underneath. The bottommost layers in the sequence of rock are Precambrian gneisses, schists, and granites, exposed only in a few spots in the West, such as the Black Canyon of the Gunnison River in southwestern Colorado. (The term "Precambrian" refers to the first 85 percent of total earth history; to the nongeologist, the term just means *old.)* The Black Canyon of the Gunnison is a great water-carved gash in the rolling chaparral of southwestern Colorado. It is the narrowest, deepest, most intimidating place in all the great drainage. It's a place most climbers have heard of, but few have visited. Its reputation is just too daunting.

The canyon isn't really black. In fact, seen from below, looking up toward the light of the sky, the walls are light and colorful, striped in places with squiggly pink bands. But looking in from the rim, one feels utter darkness, more an impression than a literal picture. From its edge, it seems an awful crack in the earth, jagged-edged and narrow, no place you'd like to be. At 2,200 feet from rim to river, the walls are higher than Half Dome, yet it's only 1,800 feet across. With a good pair of binoculars, you can see tourists and their cars on the other side. You can even read license plates. No other canyon in North America is as deep and as narrow as the Black Canyon. More than anything else, it's this combined impression of depth and narrowness that makes the canyon the most intimidating spot in American rock climbing.

Though the rock is some of the oldest exposed in the West, the canyon itself is relatively new. Like the Grand Canyon, the Black Canyon demonstrates the awesome capacity of an angry, debris-laden river to hold its course and its level even as the land around it rises and becomes a broad hill. The Gunnison River originally flowed between two volcanic highlands, where it had carved a shallow course in the soft volcanic and sedimentary rock. Once the land began to rise, the river was trapped, or entrenched, in a pre-uplift valley. And because the uplift is generally dome-shaped, there are no major tributaries, and thus nothing to wear down the canyon rim from the side. Most canyons, the Grand Canyon, for instance, were widened not by the main river itself, but by the tributaries that flowed in from side canyons, spreading the walls of the canyon while the main river carried away their debris. Entrenched on an elevated plateau, the Gunnison lacks the tributaries, and so the down-cutting of the river far exceeds the wearing away of the sidewalls.

Yes, there are good geology lessons here at the Black, but to a climber in a campsite on the rim, the science just doesn't seem important. Instead, for newcomers especially, there's just the pit in the stomach. On the night before a climb, you can't simply sit there in your tent and wait. You are drawn instead to the edge to have a look, straight down 2,000 feet to the churning river. In the moonlight, the walls seem eerily white and the noise of the river is clear. Stories you've heard about the canyon rise from its depths and hover, stories of loose rock and the sulfur smell that follows crashing blocks, tales of unprotected and loose bands of pink crystalline pegmatite, stories of unplanned bivouacs, of deaths and near deaths, stories told by climbers who say they won't be back. You look up at the sky and hope it will rain.

It all seems so backward, leaving the car at the top of the climb and heading down an interminable gully to the base of the wall, only to top out right back in camp. Black Canyon descents are notorious for loose rock and head-high poison ivy. One route down is known as the S.O.B. Gully, a name that fits. The other main descent is the Cruise Gully, named not for its ease but for the climbing route, *The Cruise.* This one, too, is a son of a bitch. Either way, it can take more than an hour to reach the bottom of the canyon. To the ambitious trout fishers who share the path, the rope-draped climbers heading downhill must seem nuts. But remember, at the end of the day, when the sweating anglers are trudging back up, the climbers are coiling their rope on the rim, beer in hand . . . if all goes as planned.

Both sides of the Black Canyon have good long routes, though the greatest concentration is on North Chasm View, opposite the more touristed and developed South Chasm View. Whichever wall you choose, it helps a lot to view your prospective route from across the way. Few big walls offer such an opportunity for a straight-on view. Yet with no bridge spanning the gap, it's a hundred-mile drive to the opposite edge. The view from the south rim is dominated by the Painted Wall, the highest cliff in Colorado. The squiggly pink lines are pegmatite dikes, intruded into the vertical joints of the cliff. The wall was first climbed over eight days by Bill Forrest and Kris Walker, the first Grade VI outside of Yosemite. Its fearsome reputation remains today, and though routes here are gradually being free-climbed, virtually no one jumps on one of these Painted Wall routes without an apprenticeship elsewhere in the canyon. The north side holds only a

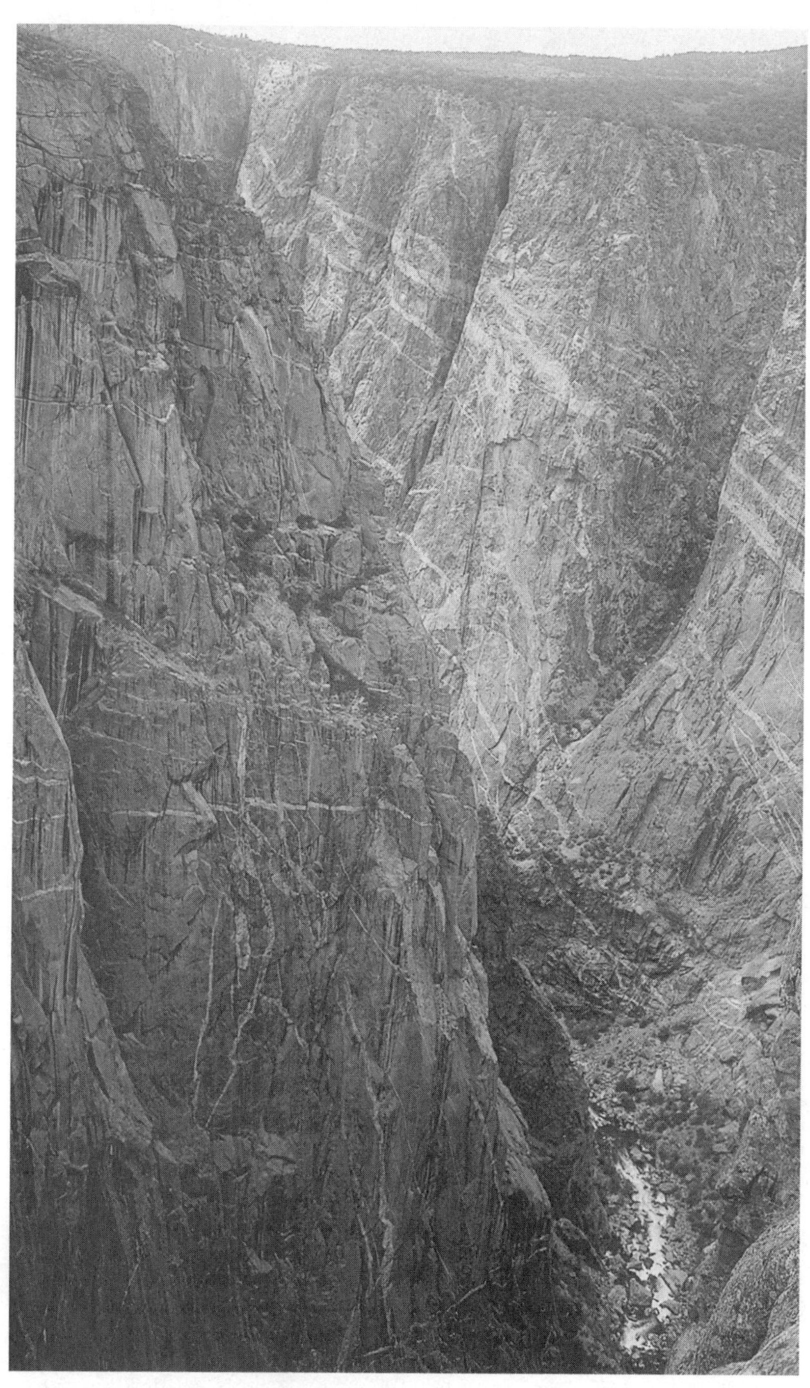

Black Canyon of the Gunnison

rough camping area and a railing at the brink, a good place to look across at *Astrodog* (V 5.11d), the best route on the south wall.

With the exception of the Grade VI climbs on the Painted Wall, climbs in the Black are best done in a day to avoid the problems of hauling, made especially undesirable by the long descent, the indirect climbing lines, and the loose rock to be knocked off by the swinging bag. The single-day approach, however, creates an odd race; at other climbing areas, if time is short, you simply begin a series of rappels back to the base or the safety of your camp. At the Black, however, you might be only 200 agonizing feet from your car. You are even close enough to converse with those fortunate souls standing on the rim. Yet your car and those friendly voices at the railing might as well be in another state. The team that backs off faces multiple rappels, with no fixed anchors to aid the process, usually a bivouac by the river, followed by the demoralizing slog back up the gully the next day, made worse only by having to explain the affair to descending climbers and anglers.

Every route in the Black Canyon has at least one serving of that special treat called pegmatite, pink bands of terrifying crystalline rock. If you haven't stood on the large glassy crystals and wished you were somewhere else, then you haven't really climbed at the Black. Seen from afar, they seem like horizontal layers swirling across the face. Yet the jointing in the hard rack is vertical, not horizontal as in sandstone, and so the squiggly pink lines are more a veneer than a layer. No matter to the climber. Instead, he's contemplating the nasty raking he'll get on huge interlocking crystals of feldspar, quartz, and mica, some as big as three feet across. Climbing on pegmatite is nerve-racking. Holds are loose, protection nonexistent. Life is beautiful when you're finally back on hard granite.

The Black Canyon is for competent, seasoned climbers only. There are too many decisions about route finding, too many committing moves away from protection, too much loose rock. There's no guidebook at the moment, so the best one can do is to get a rough topo of the route. Climbers need to be light enough for speed, but equipped for a shivering night on a ledge. They need to be quick in switching leads, skilled in setting up multiple rappels, and willing to sacrifice some gear should retreat be necessary. Novices and sport-climbing specialists can expect cruel treatment at the Black.

Which route to do? The *Scenic Cruise* gets the most press; it's a superb and challenging climb that has gotten a surprising amount of traffic in the last few years. Trade route status or not, it's fifteen pitches of challenging climbing with a devious traverse up high. To its right is *Journey Home,* slightly less committing (at least above the run-out first pitch). Left of *Scenic Cruise* are some harder affairs, like the well-publicized *Nose Route* (5.12) or *Air Voyage* (5.11+) with its notorious 5.11 off-width, still considered one of the harder cracks in the land. The first-time visitor is well advised, however, to take on one of the shorter routes on the gully walls, routes like *Debutante's Ball.* Even though it's 5.11, you can start at the bottom and walk off halfway, or walk in halfway and climb to the top. (You can even do the whole thing for a real Grade V.) Also good starter climbs are *Escape Artist* (5.10-) and *Comic Relief* (5.10).

From Canyons to Summits

Rock climbing, in its earliest days, evolved from the human desire to stand on a summit. It wasn't the route that mattered so much as the destination. Everest loomed large, and the short routes burgeoning in Britain and New England were little more than practice climbs. Once the summits were reached, harder routes were attempted and the focus gradually shifted from the summit to the route. Seen in the original context, climbing out of a canyon is the antithesis of gaining a lofty summit, more akin to caving than mountaineering.

However, there's a continuum of all kinds of climbing on the Colorado Plateau. On one end of the continuum is the narrow canyon. On the other is the narrow spire. From one we emerge out of the earth and on the other we stand high above it. In the narrowest gorges like the Black Canyon of the Gunnison, you start in a deep hole, the sky a crooked blue line above. When you finally crawl onto the rim, you haven't gotten up something, you've gotten out of something. There's your car and your campsite. And from a few yards back from the crest, there's nothing that would indicate a great canyon nearby—nothing but a thinly forested, rolling plateau. You haven't been mountain climbing; you've just been probing a giant wound on the land.

The Black Canyon is the tightest of the canyons of the Colorado drainage. Farther downstream, things widen steadily as the river runs into the sandstone layers. Even though the walls here might be miles apart, it's still canyon climbing. At places like Wall Street near Moab or Indian Creek, you look across at the corresponding cliff bands and you are reminded that you are in a gorge, not on a mountain face. Perhaps the route attains the flat tableland above; maybe it just ends at a two-bolt anchor and chain. Either way, it's obvious that the route itself was your project. There was no destination at its end, save for the satisfaction of having gotten it done.

As the canyon widens, summits appear as stranded islands of the upland plateau. Some are broad mesas, and unless you hike all the way across the top, you have little sense of being up high. Others, however, are the fragile remnants of an earth level of the past, needles stabbing the blue sky, summits so small there's room for only one at a time, so precarious you suspect they might topple under your weight. It's just as easy to think of Monument Valley as a collection of spires as it is to perceive it as a widened canyon maze.

Perhaps because most every known summit has been attained, and because, given the time and technology, no place on earth is inaccessible, most climbers have turned their attention to routes, not summits. The sport-climber, especially, knows that when half his rope is paid out, there'll be chain sprouting from the rock. All along the high limestone cliffs of Rifle, Colorado, are short, gymnastic sport climbs. Very few routes continue to the rim of the gorge. On a busy day at Red Rocks, Nevada, there'll be crowds hanging from the tiny cliffs around the Gallery, while climbers on the twenty-pitch *Resolution Arête* on Mount Wilson in the background are all alone. Even Himalayan climbing has felt this shift in attention, with routes claimed and publicized simply because they cover new ground. No need to grovel over easier terrain to the top. It's a shift in mindset made even stronger by the proliferation of chains at every belay anchor on popular climbs. The climbers can take things a pitch at a time, instead of committing to the top when they leave the ground. Climbing has disintegrated into just so many disconnected pieces.

Yet there's still something about summit climbing, and therein lies the principal appeal of the Colorado Plateau. Consider this: Castleton Tower is a slender 400-foot spire with a base not much wider than its summit. Its circumference can't be more than 300 feet.

Yet it has ten full-length routes. Since its first ascent by Layton Kor and Huntley Ingalls in 1961, and the coronation of their route as one of North America's fifty classic climbs in the Roper-Steck book, the tower has gotten more traffic than any other major formation. There's often a queue at the base of Castleton routes and, more disturbingly, on top lining up for the rappel route. The congestion is frightening when the skies darken and rumble. Just as a spire attracts people, it also draws electricity. The feeling of euphoria one experiences on top is quickly replaced by one of sickening vulnerability when lightning crackles over nearby spires. From Castleton's top, one can see endless miles of the same layer of rock, the same vertically fractured band of excellent Wingate sandstone. Were this same concentration of established climbs found on Castleton to extend across all the rest of the solid layer, climbing routes would number in the millions. There's that much potential. And so why the density of routes on Castleton? Simply because it's a tower, not a wall. There's a destination more enticing than a canyon rim or a chain anchor. To stand alone on an island in the sky is to defy something deep within us. It makes us giddy.

Rivers enter the Colorado drainage from many directions, and canyons grow deeper south and west. To the traveler entering the region from the east via Interstate 70, Colorado National Monument is the first real canyon-type rock encountered. Just outside the town of Fruita is the park entrance to Rim Rock Drive, which runs the crest of the main cliff band. The road was built during the Depression by more than three hundred men in the Civilian Conservation Corps, inspired by John Otto, one of desert history's most eccentric characters. Otto moved to Fruita in 1906, and immediately fell in love with the wild canyons just south of town: "I came here and found these canyons, and they felt like the heart of the world to me. I'm going to stay . . . and promote this place because it should be a national park." His campaign was successful, and to celebrate the creation of the national monument in 1911, Otto made an outrageous ascent of Independence Monument by installing pipe rungs and chopping bucket-sized steps. The *Otto Route* remains the most popular climb in the park, a seven-pitch classic, 5.8 now that the pipes are gone.

Rim Rock Drive is the access to most of the climbing. It rises in switchbacks from the west entrance gate up toward the rim and the visitors center, skirting high walls of dark red sandstone before snaking through two tunnels and emerging onto the rim itself. From here, most routes are reached by rappel. If the climb is to be up one of the many detached spires, then a rope and ascenders must be left at the rappel point for the return trip to the car.

Even with the easy access and rich legacy of climbing, the Colorado National Monument isn't mobbed with climbers. It's an alternative to the congestion in the better-publicized areas in the canyon country of Utah, combining easy access with good climbing. And though it lacks the drama of the higher routes in Utah, it's a good place to get a feel for the soft-rock climbing of the desert. If you are looking for a scene, however, continue on to Moab. Lowly Fruita lacks the scrape-kneed, tanned athleticism of this legendary desert sports Mecca.

MOAB

The spiritual center (though not the geographical center) of canyon climbing is Moab, Utah, a bustling town of about five thousand residents that sprawls across a flat basin. All around are the high walls of sandstone left exposed when the floor of the valley collapsed as ancient salt deposits dissolved below the surface. Moab has undergone several incarnations since its founding by Mormon settlers in the 1870s and naming for the biblical kingdom at the edge of Zion. For a while, it would be a rough frontier settlement, home of lowlifes, moral outcasts, and saloons. The Cold War and the atomic arms race changed that in a big way when uranium mining brought a boom much like California's gold rush of a hundred years earlier. A few fortunes were made, but the boom was short-lived, and quiet returned to the valley.

Americans know Moab mainly from the writing of Edward Abbey, cult father of the desert. His *Desert Solitaire* describes life at Arches National Monument (now a national park), where Abbey put in two six-month stints as seasonal ranger. The sad irony about the book is that, though it agonized about the encroachment of people on such sacred landscapes, the depiction of desert living was so romantically appealing that it brought an invasion of visitors. *The Monkey Wrench Gang* is a different book altogether, an irreverent, hilarious, inspira-

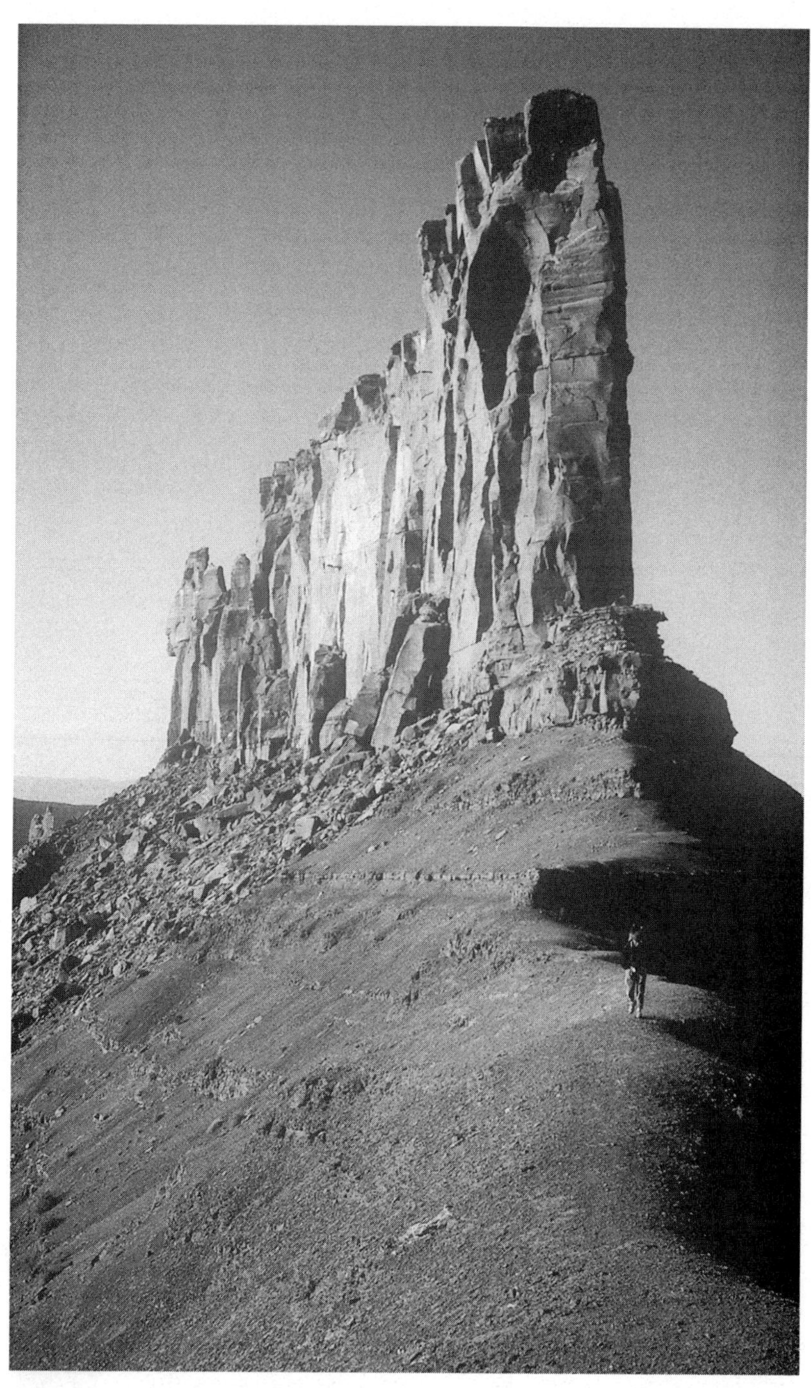

The Rectory, Moab, Utah

tional novel about a group of saboteurs bent on stopping the rape of the desert by tossing a monkey wrench in the gears of the Machine. In the finest traditions of sabotage (from *sabot,* the wooden shoes tossed into early factory machinery), they pull up survey stakes, disable bulldozers, and burn billboards as part of neighborhood beautification. "With a five-gallon can of gasoline he sloshed about the legs and support members of the selected target, then applied a match. Everyone should have a hobby." It's fitting that Abbey's master's thesis was titled "Anarchism and the Morality of Violence." Even in his last days Abbey resisted the Machine. Faced with a prolonged sickness aided by tubes and technology, he is said to have been spared by the actions of a friend and allowed to die naturally.

The main target of the Monkey Wrench Gang was Glen Canyon Dam, which created Lake Powell, the second-largest man-made lake in the world. The lake inundated some of the most spectacular canyon scenery in the region and allowed easy water access to the world's largest natural rock span, Rainbow Bridge. Before the lake, Rainbow Bridge was a remote prize open only to those willing to trek. Americans claim to love the wilderness; most even consider themselves environmentally conscious. Yet few stop to consider the irony that Lake Powell receives more visitors each year than either Yellowstone or the Grand Canyon. The comforts of houseboat living—the thrill of a Jet Ski. Ah, the great outdoors.

The desert of Edward Abbey is a place for quiet reflection. But if quiet reflection is your quest, move beyond Moab. A visit to Moab today is hardly a game of desert solitaire. More than a million people visit nearby Arches National Park each year, and many more skip the park and head directly for the trail. Most visitors today aren't so much in search of solitude as they are of adventure, and Moab has become a locus of outdoor recreation. Commercial operations on the main street offer Jeep excursions, rock-hounding and photography trips, rafting on the Colorado, and the king of outdoor pursuits: mountain biking. The biking here is as good as it gets, with the best routes traversing the slickrock. It's unique in the world of mountain biking, routes skipping along smooth rock layers on canyon rims and down dusty washes to levels below. Moab is a strip of cheap motels, endless eateries, and trendy brew pubs. Every vehicle on the strip is equipped either with big fat tires, designed for maximum purchase and impact, or roof racks stowing bikes and kayaks. These people have come to Moab to play. The climber in Moab is harder to spot, identified only by the Access Fund sticker in the car window, the festering sores on the back of hands badly taped, and the dazed expression that comes from multiple rappels off bolts drilled into mud.

Treading Gently

For the hard-rock climber, canyon country climbing takes some adjustment. Just getting to some of the places can be epic. Desert climbers must be desert drivers, part engineer, part artist, and eternal optimist. The desert driver can sniff out the best line down a rubbly wash, memorizing the details for the even more daunting trip back up. He knows the undercarriage of his vehicle intimately, its clearance, where the muffler hangs. He knows the sound of metal scraping sandstone, can discern from the noise whether it's axle grinding or whether it's just some nonessential tinny part that is being torn off. He carries a shovel, and he knows when to deflate his tire just a bit for better purchase in the sand. Upscale desert visitors do their wanderings in forty-thousand-dollar vehicles that ride high on big knobby tires. A seasoned desert climber gets the job done in a rusty Toyota.

He keeps the car, however, on established roads, protecting the cryptobiotic soil, the thin organic crust that covers much of the sand, protecting the life within and keeping the sand in place during high winds. It's a layer that has taken hundreds of years to develop but can also be damaged by a single careless step and ruined by a heedless driver. The desert is fragile and every visit leaves a mark. White chalk remains for years in a land where it hardly rains. An orange peel doesn't biodegrade here; it just dries up. Human waste remains intact, even if it's buried according to standard wilderness practice elsewhere. In the wet forests of the Northeast and the Northwest, things are thick and damp. Green is everywhere, and the remains of a campsite or footpath disappear soon after it is abandoned. The woods close in on people, obscuring them in the trees. Two groups camped a hundred yards apart might never know of the presence of the other. It's an up-close wilderness. The western desert, on the other hand, is wide open and dry. From on high, colorful tents are obvious, talk carries for long distances, foot trails leave lines easily visible and long lasting.

Locals are accustomed to treading lightly. Newcomers must be more mindful, until kind behavior becomes habit.

Many cliff sides in the canyon country are also valuable archaeological sites. The best known of these is Newspaper Rock, near Indian Creek. The rock art dates back as far as 1,500 years. Climbing on or near any archaeological site is unconscionable, not just from the obvious damage wrought by bolts and boot rubber. Even the oily residue of a fingerprint will speed deterioration of the rock surface.

Every visitor to canyon country must know the fragility of the place, and most seem to behave accordingly. But the actions of a few remain obvious in such a climate. Right near *Supercrack,* perhaps the most famous crack route in the world, newcomers have etched their names and even drawn little horses, facsimiles of the images at Newspaper Rock and elsewhere. Don't buy the argument that graffiti in 1990 is just as valid as graffiti written a millennium earlier. The new "art" is no more than vandalism. It demeans the originals, degrades the site, and risks sanctions levied against climbers as a group.

One archaeologist told of finding climbers gathered near some petroglyphs. (Petroglyphs are images etched into the surface of the rock; pictographs are paintings and drawings.) He didn't look official, dressed more like a tourist than a park ranger, and so one climber continued to boulder right on the rock art. When questioned, the young climber said something like, "Yeah it's really cool climbing on this stuff. It's kind of a zen thing." Later, the researcher was told that an area climbing gym had painted rock art on the artificial wall to bring the "zen" indoors. The climbers obviously respected the site, but they didn't think hard enough about their own role in its demise.

SHIFTING SANDS

The adjustment that visitors must make isn't just for the preservation of the place; it's for their own preservation as well. The sandstone of the Colorado Plateau runs from the relatively solid rock of Indian Creek to a variety of incarnations of sand. None of it is hard like granite, but occasionally that wired Stopper might actually hold. To the uninitiated, soft-rock climbing is fairly spooky. A moving belay rope will carve a deep groove into a ledge. Tiny grains of sand sometimes trickle from the hole of a bolt as it is weighted. People have even used ice tools on desert aid routes, some saying it's like climbing a vertical beach. Canyon country climbers know well the nuances of these different layers of rock, each with a character all its own. It's not just sandstone to such a climber. It's either Entrada or Navajo or Cutler or, best of all, Wingate.

Entrada is the remnant of giant sand dunes that swept across the region about 150 million years ago. It weathers into rounded shapes instead of splitting vertically like the Wingate. Entrada is the main layer of Arches National Park, hard enough to climb, but soft enough for the wind to carve tunnels and arches (more than two hundred of them). People climb at Arches not because of the quality of the rock, but because the features are so bizarre and alluring. The shapes have inspired fitting names for the formations: the Three Penguins at the park gate look ready to waddle away. The Three Gossips speak in hushed tones, but if you listen closely you might catch a bit of the news. Only Owl Rock seems ill named. The bird-shaped stone that adorned its top has since fallen away. One look and you'll know it's best not to rename the 90-foot spire today, what with the recent attention to family values and all.

The Entrada layer sits on top of the Navajo layer, high above the town of Moab. It is a similarly crackless rock, also made of petrified dunes. Many of the river-level climbing areas around town are on the Navajo. At Wall Street, the climbing is really good, the main problem being the proximity to the road. This is literally belay-from-your-car climbing. Watch kids and dogs. Two steps back from the cliff and they're right in the path of a line of fat-tired four-wheelers screaming out of town for another assault on solitude on the high desert. The canine carnage here has been disturbing. If you can manage to keep your companions and your rope from being run over, you'll find numerous bolt-protected sporty sport climbs, a rarity in the region, and a welcome relief from the eternal parallel-sided cracks of the region. So close to town, however, it's obviously going to attract a crowd.

Cutler is the stuff of Fisher Towers, the first big features seen when entering Moab from the north on Route 128. Fisher Towers is a collection of the fluted ridges and pillars composed of the weirdest rock in desert climbing, rock dribbled from the hand of a giant child at the beach or sculpted by a drunken Gaudi. Lacy curtains of brown mud hang draped over hollows, paper-thin deposits from the last rain. One climber told of urinating from a ledge and watching the water melt away part of the cliff, roll down for a few feet before hardening up again to become part of the wall. After the first ascent of Standing Rock in Monument Basin, another notorious exposure of Cutler sandstone, Steve Komito described the rock as alternating layers of Ry-Krisp and kitty litter.

Because of the rounded nature of the disintegrating surface of the Fisher Towers, much of the climbing here is artificial: creative aid while standing in slings. Dressed in goggles, gloves, and sneakers, ingenious climbers have used ice axes, lassoed horns of crumbling rock, chopped steps in vertical curtains of mud, and pounded ice hooks into ledges of dirt, just to stand on some of the most unlikely spots anywhere. Perhaps because it's tough to get a partner, or maybe because the odd rock brings out odd tendencies in odd climbers, a tradition of solo climbing has emerged at the Fishers. The most noteworthy solo routes have been done by Jim Beyer. On the east face of the Cottontail Tower, he climbed *Intifada* over nine lonely days. The result was a wildly difficult 900-foot route, one he considered rating A6 in a scale that grades aid difficulty from A0 to A5. The last pitch had thirty-eight hook moves, yet Beyer did the climb without a single bolt, not even for belay anchors.

Newcomers to Fisher will probably walk the base trail loop, take lots of pictures, and come up with a hundred reasons not to climb. Others might decide the best introduction is *Ancient Art* (5.11 or 5.9), a moderate route that leads to the bizarre and corkscrew summit and the mandatory hero shot. ("You go out there. I'll stay here and take the picture.") It's a feature so precarious it might well be gone by press time. Wiser still is to climb Lizard Rock. Even at 60 feet, it's an official Fisher Tower, and with the camera positioned just so, the summit shot might fool your friends.

WINGATE

The best rock by far is the Wingate Formation, the other end of the hardness scale from the Cutler. Wingate is the stuff, the mother lode of sandstone climbing. This is the rock that runs for endless miles of darkened red, parallel-sided cracks and geometric vertical corners, the

A lifetime of vertical cracks at Indian Creek, Utah

rock that, Siren-like, tempted climbers for many years but remained relatively unclimbed until the invention of Friends. To many climbers, Wingate is the only rock worth climbing, distinctive in its verticality, its smoothness, and especially its cracks. All along the formation, cracks shoot up every twenty feet or so, striking and parallel-sided, cracks by the thousands, any one of which would be famous if it were somewhere else where it could distinguish itself. Much of the Wingate layer is coated with desert varnish, an oxidized surface a bit harder than the lighter-colored rock underneath. The varnish makes a good medium for rock art; chipping away the surface leaves the lighter image highlighted in dark rock.

If ever there comes a time when all the routes are done, all the climbing areas on earth explored, climbed, and documented, Indian Creek will probably still top the list as crack-climbing Mecca to the world. Wingate sandstone, mile after mile of it, runs along the river valley from Newspaper Rock toward Canyonlands. The number of crack lines defies imagination.

So does the purity of the cracks. Few places on earth have such parallel-sided, featureless cracks. There's just no cheating, no searching around inside for a ripple that will compensate for crack-climbing weakness, no foothold destinations in sight. Instead, there's just jamming and laybacking at their most elemental. Such starkness will surprise the granite crack climber who is accustomed to a more featured surface of the rock. Competent Yosemite crack climbers have been humbled here.

This is a place where climbing would be unthinkable without camming gear. Earl Wiggins' 1976 ascent of *Supercrack* (5.10) predated Friends, a feat inconceivable to most climbers armed with a half-dozen number 2 and 3 Camalots (and still whining about the run-out). Yet it wasn't blind reliance on spring-loaded technology that got Wiggins up *Supercrack* but a secure faith in the ability to jam. With such an ability, a good hand feels like a moving belay. It's the same feeling of security that lures ice climbers into soloing. Years after *Supercrack*'s first ascent, one young buck, taped, chalked, and buffed, soloed the route, dragging a rope for descent. Back on the ground, his strut was a little much for fifty-three-year-old Hermann Gollner nearby. Barefoot, chalkless, and leaving his rope behind, Gollner climbed the route to the anchor, and then down-climbed back to his pack. Didn't need to say a word to the young hero standing mouth agape.

When the cracks of Indian Creek are the right size, they can be amazingly secure. Most people fit the *Incredible Handcrack* pretty well. Sure, it's 5.10, but if your hands are the right size, they lock like Friends in the crack. Vary the crack size as little as a half inch, however, and the whole world changes. In granite, you can usually grope a little higher to find a wider or narrower spot into which you can set your hand. At Indian Creek, if it doesn't fit, it doesn't fit. No need to search. No use in whining.

Indian Creek is a schoolroom for crack-climbing training; every conceivable size is somewhere near, just waiting to draw blood. Some warnings, however. First, you need more gear, not just doubles of a size, but as many as ten. To amass that many pieces, you need a lucky lottery ticket or lots of friends with Friends. Larger pieces are commonly "walked" up the crack in order to save gear, but in doing so, there grows an awful distance to the next good piece. Nor can you be sure the piece will hold. Leonard Coyne ripped three Friends in a fall, one of which broke his glasses and injured his eye. Ken Sims finished the project known as *Coyne Crack.* Some climbers dispute that camming gear tracks under load, leaving grooves on the interior walls of the crack. Others claim they've seen it happen, and some manufacturers are coming out with fat-cammed desert gear specifically for this problem.

Southwest of Moab is Canyonlands National Park, a vast area where one can find the solitude missing from Castle Valley and Indian Creek. Though most of the climbing is on the same Wingate layer, the climbs are much more committing because the rock isn't as consistently good and the routes are generally longer. Central to Canyonlands climbing is the broad mesa called Island in the Sky, where the Green River meets the Colorado. From here, the layering is especially distinct. The Island is Wingate, and from its crest, walls and splintered remnants of the good rock are scattered in all directions. Moses, with its well-known 5.11+ *Primrose Dihedrals,* stands next to Zeus down in Taylor Canyon. There's good climbing on Monster Tower and Washerwoman and countless other smaller formations surrounding Island in the Sky.

Adapting

It's impossible to overstate the impact that spring-loaded camming devices have had on canyon-country climbing. Right from the start, the rock was ill suited to regular pitons or chocks. In fact, it was on the first ascent of Shiprock that David Brower placed America's first drilled bolt anchor. Even though Shiprock is volcanic, not the soft sandstone for which the region is known today, Brower's bolt was the first of many efforts to find safe anchor points on desert rock. In the 1950s, Harvey T. Carter introduced to Colorado's Garden of the Gods the drilled angle, a bolt-piton hybrid, where a short angle piton is pounded into a drilled hole. The compressibility of the angle iron and the softness of the rock combined to make for a pretty sound anchor. Today, drilled angles are common in desert sandstone.

Among the first to feel the draw of these isolated platforms in the sky were Yosemite climbers Jerry Gallwas, Mark Powell, Don Wilson, and Bill Feuerer, who climbed the slender Totem Pole in 1956. In the early 1960s, Layton Kor and Huntley Ingalls climbed Castleton

Tower and the nearby Priest, and then, with George Hurley joining the team, ascended the tallest of the Fisher group, the Titan. From those early days, a small group, including Carter, Fred Beckey, and guidebook author Eric Bjornstad, continued to find creative ways to the tops of the slender desert spires. Still, outside of these circles, most climbers looked upon the sandstone climbing as little more than a dangerous stunt.

The 1970s, even prior to the advent of Friends, saw a surge of new-route exploration, and a host of new characters emerged as "desert rats." Jimmy Dunn, Ed Webster, Jeff Achey, Earl Wiggins, Ken Trout, and Bryan Becker were leaders in mastering the unique challenges presented by the soft rock. When *Mountain* magazine published Webster's account of the 1976 first ascent of Indian Creek's *Supercrack,* replete with a center-spread color photo of the route, the world came to know the potential of crack climbing on Utah sandstone. Nonetheless, there weren't too many climbers ready to match Wiggins' feat of doing such a route with chocks for protection.

Ray Jardine's ascent the year following of *Phoenix* in Yosemite, relying on the revolutionary Friends, was like the opening of a door in canyon country. At first, one would consider oneself lucky to own a full-size run of the pricey new gear; the first obstacle of a Utah crack climb was simply borrowing enough of the same-size piece to cover a long parallel-sided crack. Hard Wingate cracks can require as many as ten camming units of the same size. Across America, the same ritual has emerged: tell your friends that you are headed to Utah and, knowing your rack to be too meager for the task, they'll offer to lend you their cams.

ZION

In the southwest corner of Utah, Zion National Park is another soft-rock center where the cliffs are enormous and where an aspiring big-wall climber can learn the spartan existence of days standing in slings and nights stretched out on a portaledge. Zion is where big-wall climbing meets sandstone. It's a tight-walled, civilized park, no place for beginning climbers and no place for acrophobia. First-time visitors need to arrive with a soft-rock background; there are few introductory routes at Zion. Instead, the vertical walls offer hard free routes of a dozen pitches and aid routes only a bit less committing than Yosemite's, making it the country's number-two destination for big-wall climbing.

Zion leaves one with two impressions. First is the overwhelming tightness of the canyon, especially upstream toward Angel's Landing. The red and white walls loom right over the winding road. Everything seems so close, so closed in. The second impression is how ironically tamed the valley floor is. It's not a canyon where you can hide a Winnebago. The road is crowded, people are all around, and you never feel too far from the entrance gate or to the small town of Springdale. Even from the walls you can hear and see the commotion below. Most approaches are short; the classic *Touchstone Wall* seems to climb right out of the road and shoots vertically for eight airy pitches. There are, of course, some tedious uphill trudges, but the most popular routes in the canyon are fairly accessible.

To someone having just spent time in Canyonlands or around Moab, Zion will seem lush and green. It's much wetter than the areas to the north. Walls in places are draped with hanging gardens and masses of dripping moss. The easterner will feel right at home on some of the slimier sections of Zion. So much desert is barren rock and stark sky. Zion adds green to the mix, trees on ledges, thick bushes in the gullies, lichens of all colors. The Virgin River wanders along the base of the valley having emerged from the fantastic Narrows (don't miss this short tour, and don't leave your camera behind). Most of the year it's a demure river, one that doesn't seem capable of carving such a trench.

Zion's long free climbs are some of the best on sandstone. There's the *Northeast Buttress of Angel's Landing*, a ten-pitch 5.11 that generally follows the left ridge of the wall from the Landing view parking area. Unlike the other summits, this one has a popular trail. On top you'll have to explain how long it took, how all those clips and gadgets work. At least the descent is easy: instead of facing a series of rappels, with the loose rock and rope-jamming so common on soft-rock routes, you have a two-and-a-half-mile paved path and a lot of company back to the base.

Downstream across the road, there's *Iron Messiah* (5.10), another ten-pitch route that follows a left-facing corner system for most of its length, only a few spots exceeding 5.8. And up toward the Zion–

Mount Carmel Tunnel is *The Headache,* a shorter route with crack pitches, finger- to fist-size, its 5.10 crux coming up high. Routes like these and so many others are good for competent parties, but reminders that neophytes need to work out the kinks elsewhere, and even experienced climbers unaccustomed to long routes need to keep an eye on the clock.

Aside from Fisher Towers, there isn't a lot of aid climbing in the desert. And so the high walls of Zion attract the odd breed who finds in soft rock a challenge and allure unlike that of granite. Aid climbing has a different impact on sandstone as well. Pitons carve their way easily into the soft rock, leaving a nasty scar when removed. In response, a culture of clean aid emerged at Zion, where the routes might be graded C2 or C3 (instead of A2 or A3, the C standing for clean). Led by the prolific desert wall climber Ron Olevsky, the goal was to create hammerless routes that could see multiple ascents without wearing out. If future parties will need a bolt or a piton, first-ascent teams ought to leave them in place, according to the Zion motto HAFWEN—Hammered Anchors Fixed Wherever Necessary. Also accepted was "creative" placement and removal of pins so as to leave a scar that would accept chocks in the future. Controversial, to be sure, but a solution that, in the long run, would lead to the least damage to the rock. Camming devices came along just in time at Zion, especially in the thin TCU range for the classic fingertips routes like *Moonlight Buttress,* 5.13 for some but an introductory aid route for most.

Zion's antithesis is an hour down the road at Saint George, the largest town in southern Utah. It's a tidy Mormon town, founded at the request of Brigham Young on cotton, and so called Utah's Dixie. For some it's a cragging respite from the towering walls of Zion. For others it's a destination unto itself. An extraordinary variety of rock is found in and around Saint George: limestone at Virgin River Gorge and Welcome Springs, sandstone at Snow Creek Canyon and countless smaller crags around town, and basalt at Black Rocks and Crawdad Canyon. This latter "full-service climbing resort" will go down in history as one of the pioneer climbing centers, a private, commercial sport-climbing area, replete with restaurant, pool, volleyball courts, and a rule unthinkable in climbing just a few years back: "No trad climbing." The bolt-protected routes, installed at the request of the landowner and under the supervision of guidebook author Todd Goss, begin at belay chairs and brass plaques with route name and first-ascent information. Stick clips required if the first bolt is painted yellow. Yes, Saint George is the antithesis of the high, wild, and decidedly traditional climbing at Zion National Park. The Virgin River that flows out of Zion and through Saint George cuts a steep gorge through the limestone mountains in the northwest corner of Arizona and continues across the flats to Lake Mead, just outside Las Vegas.

The red towers and steep canyons of the Southwest are symbols of America. They speak of open space and our will to explore. They are witness to the earth's great processes. They know the human story. The high canyon walls have seen bands of nomadic hunters traversing the region fifteen thousand years ago, witnessed the appearance and disappearance of the Anasazi with their cliff dwellings, and drawn the Navajo and Apache down from Canada. In these canyons Coronado sought Cibola, the Seven Cities of Gold, and Brigham Young sent his Mormon followers in search of Zion. To the same canyons come climbers, not just in search of routes but to immerse themselves in the place.

7 ESCAPE TO THE DESERT

Tucson's climbing gem, Mount Lemmon

The American Southwest is an odd place to settle down. It is a stark landscape baked by a pernicious sun. It is black-topped cities sprawling without boundary. It's naked yellow rock, and it's wide blue sky. It's alluring, but it's hostile. There's hardly any water. Agriculture exists only where it's forced upon an unwilling landscape. The plants and animals that dwell there are all horns and spines and poison. The Southwest is a place defined by the heat, where summer high temperatures average well above 100 degrees and routinely soar into the 120s. Yet even with so inhospitable a climate, it seems as though the United States is an inclined plane, tilted toward Phoenix, as an aging population migrates inexorably to escape the cruelty of northern winters.

Outsiders might dwell on the oversimplified images of today's desert Southwest: its nouveau-Spanish adobe homes, the requisite giant saguaro cactus out on the front lawn, homes built fast in expanding rings of plywood and roofers, around a downtown of tall glass towers. They hold vivid pictures of the Southwest's choked highways and the odd green splotches of its irrigated golf courses, when things all around are in need of a drink. It seems as if the only people who would live in such a place are either aging eastern transplants who spend most of their time in the artificial chill of homes, cars, and shopping malls, scurrying like scorpions on the burning sands as they dart outside from the sanctity of one air-conditioned place to another, or discontented Natives herded into the least-valued parcels, shaking their heads in disbelief at the irreverence of white invaders.

But it wasn't always so. Before air-conditioning and the explosive growth of big cities like Albuquerque and Phoenix, America saw the Southwest as raw and renegade, the province of outlaw towns of drunks and whores and silver mining, where shootouts were ritual. In 1882, things got so bad in Tombstone, Arizona, that President Arthur threatened to send in federal troops just to restore the peace. It was here in Tombstone just the year before that Wyatt Earp and "Doc" Holliday had shot it out with the Clanton gang at the OK Corral, adding to the grim newspaper column called "Death's Doings," listing the month's casualties. And it was just a few miles north of Tombstone where the U.S. Cavalry sought futilely to capture one of the region's heroes, Cochise, Apache chief. During the late 1800s, Cochise and four other chiefs had been accused of rustling cattle and abducting a white child. As they were being interrogated, one of the chiefs was shot, and the other three were hanged. Cochise, bleeding from bullet wounds, escaped. With two hundred warriors, he holed up in the Dragoon Mountains and for several years raided towns, farms, and stage lines with impunity. Those days in Tombstone they say you could get a drink more than one hundred different joints. Today, at the Crystal Palace Saloon, climbers still collect to knit back together their frayed nerves after a day linking lines of granite chickenheads and chasing Apache ghosts up in the Dragoons.

Today, no single image captures the American Southwest. Instead, it's a collage of color and cultures, of wilderness and cities, of old and new. The region is all things to rock climbers as well. It offers almost every kind of climbing experience and embraces almost every ethos in a blend that's as rich as the region itself. Just look at Arizona. Up in the northwest corner is the towering limestone of Virgin River Gorge, where the country's top climbers shut out the noise of Interstate 15 as they crimp hard 5.14s on a wall they call Blasphemy. In the northeast corner is Monument Valley, mostly Navajo land, with slender and fragile red sandstone towers like the sacred Totem Pole. South, along the state's border with Mexico, are the Dragoon Mountains, tall spires and domes of yellow granite; to their west are Baboquivari Peak, where wall routes soar in relative obscurity. And in the middle of Arizona are the high white bastion of hard grades and traditional climbing at Granite Mountain and the low yellow limestone walls of Jack's Canyon, where grades are soft and so is the rock under a route creator's drill. Up near Flagstaff are the hard parallel cracks of Paradise Forks basalt and the crumbling red towers around Sedona, and right on the urban edges of the state's two biggest cities are popular climbing destinations like the Superstition Mountains of Phoenix and the Santa Catalinas of Tucson.

Traditional Roots

Especially as sport climbing bloomed in the desert, so did climbers elsewhere begin to acknowledge that the Southwest is one of America's richest climbing resources, holding so much more than long, cactus-choked approach gullies and long run-outs on wild outback granite. Instead of being a place to get away from, the region fast became a place to come together. First was the famous Beanfest. Then came the big annual Phoenix Bouldering Contest, an event with more than five hundred competitors, making it the largest organized climbing competition in the nation. Northern climbers have little reason to invest thousands of dollars in ice tools when they can divert those funds into a van and a Coleman stove and climb year-round.

The Beanfest has been a southwestern Thanksgiving, a collection of climbers who travel huge distances to see old faces, to embellish old stories, to boulder till there's no skin left on the tips of their fingers, to walk balanced on a line of glass Pepsi bottles, to howl at the Arizona moon. It's a celebration, held once or twice a year, depending on the ambition of the year's Beanmaster, who makes the plans, picks the site, and sends out the invitations. The Beanfest was born of two such revels. In the south it was Tucson's Climarama, held annually at Cochise Stronghold in the Dragoons, featuring lots of climbing and a roasted goat. Up north in Prescott, it was the annual Banquet of the Syndicato Granitica, one of the most colorful and independent groups in American climbing history. The current site has drifted north and south, but any time it's held at the Stronghold, there's a climactic mob assault on "the boulder," where dozens of lubricated climbers, having formed a human ladder and knitted themselves into a writhing drunken mass on top, try annually to break the record. The Beanfest is also a time to smoke a peace pipe, in a figurative sense, of course, as Arizona isn't so much a homogenized state as a collection of insular fiefdoms.

The Banquet was a reflection of the boys of Granite Mountain—Scott Baxter, David Lovejoy, Karl Karlstrom, Lee Dexter, and Tom Taber, and mentored by Rhodesian legend Rusty Baillie, who scoured the white granite castle looming above Prescott for new routes, producing some of the best pure granite crack and face climbing anywhere, creating what's been called one of the ten best crags in America.

Regionalism in climbing is reflected especially in an area's grading systems. Any place that got a relatively early start, that is to say, pre-'70s, before the magazines spread the word and the stars took to the road and wrote about their adventures, and any place whose climbs were being established by an isolated group, learning as they go, has a tendency to be conservative in its grades. Such is the case at Granite

Mountain, where the independent Syndicato began with *Chim Chimney* in 1966, and kept at it until all the main crack lines had been climbed. Perhaps because they didn't travel much, or maybe because they refused to acknowledge just how much stronger they'd become as they worked over Granite Mountain, they consistently undergraded their routes. *Classic,* at 5.7, has been compared in difficulty to the country's first 5.9, the *Open Book* at Tahquitz in southern California, literally just a couple hundred miles away but figuratively across a gap as deep and desolate as the Mojave Desert. The grades at Granite Mountain are at least as stiff as those at the eastern bastion of traditionalism, Seneca Rocks.

Like Seneca Rocks, Granite Mountain is no longer on the hard man's tick list because there's not a lot of room for new routes and because there aren't too many clip-ups. The routes there might have regional acclaim, but not national status. And with so-called "harder" climbs being done at the newer sport-climbing areas, places like Granite Mountain draw the next tier of climbers, those looking more for adventure than acclaim. Exacerbating this decline is the stringent half-year closure of the mountain for peregrine falcon nesting. Even though the bird has recently been taken from the endangered species list, and even though officials at other nesting sites around the nation deem a much shorter closure period necessary to ensure successful breeding, the Granite Mountain closures are long and complete.

Too bad. Because otherwise, Granite Mountain is in many ways the ideal climbing area, at least for anyone of the traditional persuasion. Prescott is a very livable town with a population of 26,000 and an elevation just about a mile above sea level. It's the rare southwestern city that enjoys a four-season climate. Its heritage is as colorful as that of any outlaw Arizona town: Montezuma Street still goes by the informal name of Whiskey Row for the forty-plus saloons of its heyday. Nearby, Prescott College offers one of the country's best outdoor-based educations, lauded for their trash cleanup of El Cap's *Nose* route, but lambasted for teaching safe bolting at nearby Granite Dells as part of a credited course. David Lovejoy and Rusty Baillie, central to the Syndicato, still serve full-time on the faculty of Prescott College.

In 1973, two years after Scott Baxter returned from his tour as helicopter gunner in Vietnam, the Prescott team of Lovejoy, Baillie,

Baxter, and Karlstrom traveled north to the Painted Wall of the Black Canyon of the Gunnison in Colorado to establish the *Dragon Route.* It was a world-class big-wall climb, proof that the isolated band of Arizonans were as powerful as the big-name guys of Colorado and California. The *Dragon Route,* free-climbed in 1999 by Jeff Achey and Kennan Harvey, remains a standard of long, hard rock climbing.

It's impossible to overstate Baxter's legacy in Arizona's climbing history. Not only was he a driving force at Granite Mountain, but he was also the "discoverer" of Paradise Forks, near Flagstaff, transporting the old-school traditions that marked Granite Mountain. By 1979, when Scott Baxter began exploring Paradise Forks, the new route explosion at Granite Mountain had subsided, but the attitude thrived. For the next few years, the vertical cracks defining symmetrical columns in the hundred-foot-thick basalt layer would become Arizona's next generation of stiff, undergraded, traditionally protected routes. Even today, it has only a handful of bolts, and a visitor brandishing a drill would find it hard not to listen to the traditions that waft from the narrow canyon walls.

Paradise Forks is a small, concentrated collection of crack climbs, few more than a half-rope in length, on the walls of a narrow gash in the country's largest forest of ponderosa pine. Driving west from Flagstaff, you don't see much topography that would suggest rock climbing, just a rolling volcanic landscape of tall and well-spaced trees. At 7,000 feet in elevation, it is cool, green, and parklike, so different from the parched expanses just to the south. It's a place with a real winter, though with exposures facing in all directions, it's usually possible to find a spot warmed for a few hours by a sun slung low in the winter sky. That is, so long as the roads are passable.

Paradise Forks is a Y-shaped, tight-walled canyon. On both sides are the distinctive columns of dark basalt, much like those at Smith Rock's Crooked River or along Washington State's Columbia River. It's a crack-climber's crag: countless parallel cracks and flaring stem boxes, but not much in the way of face holds. Seen from across the canyon, they look the scale of practice rocks, the kind you top-rope in training for real climbs somewhere else. But to the lead climber, the parallel-sided fissures snake upward for a short eternity, cruelly stretching the groin and the imagination. Somehow, a rest must be found. But the walls offer nothing and the crack is the wrong size.

Paradise Forks, Arizona

Twist this way and that. Make a chimney out of the two flaring walls, and experiment with those funky finger stacks you've read about in the "techniques" sections of the climbing magazines. Grunt and groan, and finally swear out loud. You thought you could crack climb, but under the duress of Paradise Forks, you reluctantly confess that your jamming victories at home were really built on hidden face holds and bottleneck slots, not on any mastery of the nuances of real jamming. It's the kind of confession you might have already made if you've been to Indian Creek in Utah.

In its grand scale, the sandstone of Utah's canyon country is nothing like basalt. It's sedimentary and soft. The lava flow at Paradise Forks, on the other hand, is the essence of igneous rock. Look from afar and you can readily imagine the molten stuff flowing onto the surface and cooling solid. It's ten times harder than the canyon-country sandstone, too. But up close, when there's nothing to do but jam and stem, nothing on the walls but blank expanses for your boot soles and palms to ooze across, the routes of Paradise Forks share a lot with those at Indian Creek. Jams, when they're good, are so solid you feel as though you could belay from the sunken hand. When they're the wrong size, they're really the wrong size, and it won't help much to search for a widening or a narrowing for better fit. Instead, you've got to accept the discomfort that accompanies creative finger-stacking and off-sized hand twisting. But neither place is greasy, and chalking up is more a therapeutic ritual than a necessity, part of the reason that, even in the 1980s, Paradise Forks was considered by many to be a chalk-free zone.

A local climbing ethic—that is, the accepted methods used to develop new routes—usually grows from two roots: the values brought in by the crag's pioneers and the special characteristics of the rock itself. We see this all over America. At Smith Rock, out of the climbing mainstream and thus free from hardened tradition, Alan Watts and company adjusted to the blank and crumbling volcanic rock by removing loose rock and drilling bolts while hanging on rappel. The practices that made Smith Rock one of the country's best climbing areas were transported easily to other cliffs of welded tuff and crackless limestone. All across the Southwest, cliffs are being developed in that model. In Yosemite, on the other hand, the rock is solid and clean, and the cracks accepted pitons in the early days and then chocks and later camming devices. With a deep and rich heritage and with rock like that, route development in Yosemite Valley was much different from that at Smith Rock.

It's fitting, then, that Paradise Forks would become and remain a model of old-school, ground-up climbing values. What good would it be to try a new route on a top rope? Why stoop to protecting routes from above, when Hexes were good, the newly invented Friends even better, and Wired Bliss, maker of the extraordinary Three Cam Unit (or TCU) had just moved to Flagstaff? Right from the beginning with Baxter's *Born Under a Bad Sine,* routes were established without inspection, without hanging on the rope after a fall, and without chalk. The white stuff crept in soon thereafter (some say from Phoenix), but the invasion of bolts was kept at bay. One climb that did get some bolts was a doubled-edged 5.12 arête called *Americans at Arapiles.* It was promptly chopped, of course, then rebolted in the same kind of worn-out ideological warfare that was waged at most every other cliff in the land. Climbers at the Forks today know that top-down bolted routes can be found in increasing proliferation elsewhere. No need to desecrate such a crack-climbing museum as Paradise Forks.

Two Cities in Arizona

Phoenix became the first hub city of southwestern climbing in the 1940s when Ray Garner mentored a Boy Scout group, bringing with him modern alpine skills from his days as a Teton guide. All around the city they found exposed rock, first on the odd but very familiar Phoenix landmark Camelback, right in town, and then at Pinnacle Peak, and on the granite of the McDowell Mountains. Garner's group, the Kachinas, dispersed after about a decade, and the next incarnation of organized climbing was the Arizona Mountain Club, which thrives today. One of its founders, Bill Forrest, then a student at Arizona State University, would go on to leave a mark on many of the big walls in the West, most notably the Diamond of Longs Peak and the Black Canyon of the Gunnison, both in Colorado. His Forrest Mountaineering equipment pioneered in the development of ice tools and clean protection, including a short-lived plastic chock and the simple but effective T-ton chock. Back in Arizona, it was Forrest and George Hurley who climbed the state's first Grade VI, the *Spring Route* on Baboquivari Peak over four hard days in 1968.

Phoenix is a case study in the encroachment of civilization into wilderness climbing areas. Worst was the envelopment of the ironically named Carefree Rockpile, once one of the most popular crags in Phoenix. As urban sprawl swept like a wave emanating from the central city, the Rockpile was lost to the Boulders Resort and golf course. Many of the remaining rocks in and around Phoenix have faced the same threat, with the bulldozer and the golf course as twin symbols of a city growing too fast and without enough planning. Lack of water alone will bring it all to a halt one day, but in the meantime, outdoor activists have gone from one battlefront to another trying to stem the tidal surge of development. And with some success: Pinnacle Peak was recently dedicated to the city of Scottsdale as part of the McDowell Mountain Regional Park, making it one of the best municipal climbing areas in the country. Surrounded by golf courses and private homes, the Pinnacle stands as a symbolic and defiant island in the sprawl.

Phoenix today has a hugely active climbing population, crawling all over the in-town crags, venturing out into the more remote Superstition Mountains for adventure on big, complicated volcanic spires, or pulling down hard on roadside welded tuff on almost a thousand routes at Queen Creek in the southeast corner of the Superstitions. The combination of the very urban cragging in the city, the adventure climbing in the Supes, and the first-rate sport climbing at Queen Creek makes Phoenix a true climber's town. If only it weren't the hottest city in America.

Surprisingly, Phoenix climbers can escape the heat by heading *south,* to Tucson, where a mountain road climbs more than 6,000 feet up Mount Lemmon. The road snakes steadily uphill, passing rocks in the sun and rocks in the shade, hot rocks among giant saguaro cactus near the base elevation of around 3,000 feet and cool rocks up high in the pine forests surrounding the 9,157-foot summit.

Much smaller than Phoenix, and very aware of the differences between the two cities, Tucson is also sprawling too fast and shallow: a grid of shopping centers interlaced with dry arroyos that flood furiously during the summer monsoons. Nonetheless, Tucson is ringed with mountains, from Mount Lemmon Highway and the Santa Catalinas to Table Mountain and Leviathan Dome, where even so close to town, the desert climbing is wild, with steep, nasty approaches and a malignant conspiracy of plants bearing long, angry needles.

Santa Catalina climbs can be big and committing. Leviathan Dome, for example, is a full 1,000 feet of climbing. The rugged two- to three-hour approach today is a whole lot easier than it used to be before the establishment of Catalina State Park. Still, these are not climbs on which to dawdle. Attempting a route like the ten-pitch *North Face* (5.10) is a singular mission; even fast parties need to start early, approach efficiently, and move fast. That means being tidy at belays, expedient in the changeover. Getting caught high up on the Leviathan during one of the notorious July or August thunderstorms is an unenviable experience. Friendlier (of course) is *User Friendly* to its left, a seven-pitch 5.9. Up behind the big Leviathan Dome is another huge piece of stone, Wilderness Dome, at more than 600 feet.

Visitors to Tucson will invariably, however, begin their explorations at Mount Lemmon, where the long, winding road begins just out of town in a forest of saguaro cactus. Blurry-eyed drivers awake with a start at the first sighting of these apparitions standing by the side of the road, arms raised like desperate hitchhikers. Perhaps their anthropomorphism makes people just want to take a whack at them. Arrows were found riddling such a cactus as early as 1854, and in the mid-1980s, a Phoenix man walked up to one with a shotgun, firing blast after blast into the thick trunk until it finally toppled over and killed him. To living Americans, the saguaro stands for all that is desert wilderness, so much so that cactuses are "kidnapped" and sold to landscape architects across the Southwest for transplanting in the yards of the fake adobe houses. In 1951, plaster casts of saguaros were painted up and propped in the background of the classic western *Broken Arrow,* filmed up in Sedona, far from any real saguaros. Like the red rocks of Monument Valley, the saguaro cactus has become the quintessential emblem of the Southwest.

Though Tucson is surrounded by climbing potential, most of it relatively undeveloped wilderness domes and spires scattered in all directions, the principal climbing area is Mount Lemmon Highway. There's an incredible amount of rock here, some right off the road and some requiring the lungs and legs of a mountaineer to approach. Some routes are as short as 20 feet, and others up to 600. Crack climbs and jug hauls aren't the essence here. Instead, it's the sharp-edged face climbing of the banded gneiss that distinguishes the climbs of Mount Lemmon. Anyone who has kept up with the magazines in the last decade knows the distinctive look of its horizontally banded yellows and grays.

American climbers first became aware of Mount Lemmon as the site of two of the country's hardest routes, the two versions of *Golden Beaver,* the left of which became the first 5.13 in the state when Japanese climber Hidataki Suzuki linked the moves on lead in 1986. For a while, bolts were installed and bolts were chopped. Remember, Arizona's clean traditions were as deep as anywhere in the nation. But at a place like Mount Lemmon Highway, where face holds are everywhere, approaches casual, and route possibilities endless, the rappel-placed bolt would triumph. Today, every incarnation of route style exists there, and with the backcountry potential so great, even the old-school locals have come to accept sport climbing as a legitimate identity for Mount Lemmon.

HIDING OUT

Some places in American climbing are so staggeringly beautiful that climbers' talk always seems to center on the scenery more than the routes. The Needles in the southern Sierra is one such place. So are Utah's canyon country and Wyoming's Wind River Range. Cochise Stronghold in the Dragoon Mountains of southern Arizona is another such area where visitors arrive mouth agape at the dazzling array of yellow towers piercing the hot sky of southern Arizona and are content just to wander around until they remember that they had come to climb.

Cochise Stronghold is a collection of granite spires and domes sailing the desert sea like ghost ships of stone. It's a complicated maze of spires and gullies, dead-end ravines and brush-covered hillsides. From its heights one can see deep into Mexico and east across the Chihuahuan Desert to New Mexico. To the north is the eerie mirage of Wilcox Playa, a dried alkaline lake bed, fifty square miles of shimmering flats where locals say they've seen strange illusions, from speeding trains to dancing girls in the silvery waves of heat. From these same heights the warriors of Chief Cochise kept vigil for federal troops and the Butterfield stage that ran to Tucson. The Butterfield line was a favored target for Cochise and his men: in one sixteen-month period, twenty-two drivers were killed in Apache raids. One trip into the canyons of the Stronghold and it's easy to see how safe Cochise was from capture. Rumors persist that he is buried somewhere in the Stronghold, in a spot only one white man knew, but now, so many years later, one that remains a secret of the rocks.

Mightiest of all the formations is the Rockfellow Dome formation. Colorado climbers will see a resemblance to Cynical Pinnacle in the South Platte; Californians might think Rockfellow was looted from the Needles of the southern Sierra. Rockfellow is exceedingly beautiful. Routes are long (up to five pitches), exposed, and sustained. *Abracadaver* at 5.11a is the centerpiece climb on the biggest tower; nearby End Pinnacle, the northernmost spire of the Rockfellow group, has the area's most photographed and, thus, most familiar route, *Days of Future Passed,* a deep, continuous slot that ends 200 feet short of the summit.

The Rockfellow formation is the largest and most central set of

Cochise Stronghold, Arizona

domes and towers at the Stronghold, but scattered in all directions are more rocks wanting to be climbed. Some, like the close-to-the-campground *Beeline* (5.9 fingers) are strikingly obvious; others are a bit more coy, like the amazing *What's My Line?* (5.6) on Cochise Dome. Climbers who have experienced this route call it one of the most distinctive climbing experiences they've had, even with its relatively modest difficulty. After a scramble well up the left side of the formation, the leader pendulums right off toward the blank unknown. But once out there, you're in a sea of chickenheads, an extraordinary romp up huge holds, some big enough to tie off for protection, so secure that they suffice for belay anchors. Clearly, the Dragoon experience is much more than just the physical climbing. It's noticing the rock itself, with its case-hardened plates and the tunnels, and its bizarre fields of chickenheads. It is admiring the color of the yellow towers against the dark blue desert sky. And it's getting to know the wildlife, the peregrine falcons and the coatimundis and the giant centipedes, odd as the region itself.

Another place to get high is Baboquivari Peak, Arizona's big wall, a "dark, bullet-shaped monolith" according to Karl Rickson. It's a huge piece of rock seventy miles southwest of Tucson, one of the few big southwestern summits with no easy trail to the top. Much of its 1,000-foot east face overhangs, and several of the routes here have earned the big-wall Grade VI, a rating reserved mainly for the multiday climbs of Yosemite or the longest, most committing routes on the Wind River Range's Mount Hooker, or the Painted Wall of the Black Canyon, or the Diamond. The big routes here, like the *Spring Route* (5.10) and the more recent *Universal Traveler* (5.10), remain relatively unknown. Perhaps, even in the mass-media days when every climber seems to know every place, the Arizonans still feel little need to pump the place to the masses. Best introductory route is the *Southeast Arête,* eight pitches of moderate climbing with huge exposure, fantastic views of the layered washes below, and a summit finish on the throne of what the Native tribe Tohono O'odham calls their God and creator, I'itoi.

SANDIA

Getting away can mean many things. Just because a line of crags sits in plain sight of a big city doesn't necessarily mean it's tamed and civilized. Climb on Sandia Peak above Albuquerque, New Mexico. As the sun dips behind the western hills and a million city lights flicker on below, you can't help but dwell on the unhappy paradox of being all alone in a crowd. True, you should have carried a headlamp. And yes, if you had headed down the right gully you would not have wasted that hour. But all that matters very little now as you settle in for a cold night on a dirty ledge by a scrawny little tree, watching cars race across a toylike grid, tracing the straight roads heading out of the city until the red taillights disappear into the wide desert floor.

Such a trap is the Sandia Range. A highway runs right to its 10,678-foot crest. So does the world's longest aerial tramway, a 2.7-mile, eighteen-minute ride. The access, at least to the top where you start your climb, couldn't be easier. You park your car and shoulder a pack along the flat crest bristling with electronic towers—MCI, weather monitors, the live-cam of the local TV news—and you scramble down a short limestone crag toward the gully of choice, which if chosen properly should deposit you quickly at the bottom of the day's climb. It all seems so simple, and from the wide aspen forest above the buttress of choice, you begin to think that your pack will be nothing but a drag as you climb. So you stop, put on your cragging shoes, fill your belly with as much water as it will hold, shoulder your rope and rack, and head happily downhill, leaving all that other gear behind. All seems rather naive now, from your little ledge, and you vow that next time your headlamp will have better things to do than keep your approach shoes company in a pack at the top of a climb.

Sandia means "watermelon" in Spanish. It's a commonplace but apt description of its open face of pink rock capped by a thin white rind of limestone and a thinner skin of deep green pines. The walls and towers of the Sandia Range are backdrop to the city of Albuquerque, a low-roofed, urban sprawl of 125 square miles on the banks of the Rio Grande. At about a mile in elevation, it's a bit cooler than other cities in the Southwest, and up on the mountain, it can be quite cold, even in the summer. The granite here isn't the gleaming white Yosemite granite. It's nondescript, rounded, loose in places. Routes take devious lines, hard to follow. Protection, even anchors, can be hard to arrange. The seriousness of Sandia climbing burst into the news in 1996, when three climbers were ripped from the very top of the seven-pitch *Warpy Moople* (5.10), considered to be one of the safer Sandia expeditions. Reconstructions of the accident surmise that the lead climber probably fell after having topped out and called "off belay"; the arrangement of the rope and the battered gear suggest that the huge fall was followed by a failed self-rescue attempt. So close to town. So far from help.

The Sandias play a huge role in the outdoor life of Albuquerque residents, who consider it a whole lot more than a simple climbing area. There's also alpine and cross-country skiing, a few minor ice climbs, hiking trails, archaeology, bird-watching, and mountain biking. Approached from above via one of the steep canyon hikes from its base, it's a quick escape from the hot city, and from its heights an opportunity to reflect upon all the goings-on below.

To the south, the mountain rib dips into the Plains, past the Trinity site where on July 16, 1945, the first atomic bomb turned sand to glass and changed the world, and on to the Organ Mountains

The Organ Mountains of southern New Mexico

in the southern part of New Mexico. The Organs form a striking backdrop to the university town of Las Cruces, a twenty-mile lineup of peaks, eerily steep, unexpectedly jagged, and reminiscent of California's Needles or Arizona's Dragoons.

The Spanish called the range Las Sierra de la Soledad, mountains of solitude, an appellation that fits as well today as it did in 1904, when the first major summit, Organ Needle, was climbed by two college students. Some locals and a few visitors developed a passion for that solitude (and its commensurate discomforts), most notably Dick Ingraham, whose climbing guides have compiled route descriptions since the 1960s. Even with printed information so readily available, with New Mexico State University so close, and with a tradition of mountain explorers that included German rocket scientists visiting White Sands and Yosemite legend Royal Robbins, stationed in the 1950s at nearby Fort Bliss, the Organs retain a wild flavor. It's a range that demands a lot.

It demands experience. This is not a beginner's place. It's difficult just to locate the start of many of the routes, and it gets more so once on the rock. Climbs wander, and myriad options lure inattentive leaders into sad dead ends. Quarter-inch bolts might mark the route, but don't expect them to hold a fall. Descents are complex, rap anchors few.

It demands a lot of gear. Lugging a heavy rack up the rock- and bush-choked washes between the towers, where fifth-class moves might be encountered just boulder-hopping up a dry streambed, isn't much fun. However, these decidedly trad routes need protection of all sizes, doubles on some routes. Water is heavy, but don't skimp. A helmet is cumbersome, but you'd best not leave it behind. The weather could change, so bring something warm, especially if an early-morning route-finding mistake has left you short on time. The lights of Las Cruces are no match for Albuquerque's, but they'll give you something to watch as you shiver the night away.

The Organ Mountains demand that you begin with your best attitude as well. A day wandering the complex maze of spires and cactus-clogged gullies is long and exhausting. There's uncertainty all the way, even on classic routes like everybody's favorite, *Tooth or Consequences* (III 5.10) and especially up on Sugarloaf, where a moderate route like the *North Face* (IV 5.6) can stretch out for a full fourteen pitches. Add the two- to three-hour approach and an equal time spent in retreat from the summit, and you know you aren't just craggin'. This is the desert version of alpine climbing, the kind that demands all-day focus, no ledge lounging, no foot dragging. The alarm rings at four in the morning, and from then on, a singular project must stay in the front of the mind until you are back to the cooler of cervesas stowed in the shade under your car.

Coming Together

Mountains like the Organs or Sandia are symbols of a duality in the Southwest, where the opportunities to wander off alone are balanced by an invitation to come together and share the experience. Born of a tradition that began with the Beanfest, the big coming together in the Southwest today is the annual Phoenix Bouldering Competition, the baby of Jim Waugh, master organizer and one of the most important Arizona climbers ever. The PBC draws climbers from all over the world, sponsors from all over the country, and lots of ink in the magazines. Yet for all the hubbub, egos are generally held in check. For a brief moment each year, the congregation exemplifies what's best about climbing: communion, encouragement, humor, and fun. Just as Jim Waugh had hoped when he kicked off the initial event back in 1982.

Not everyone shared his optimism, however. Many feared that the essence of rock climbing would be threatened by such organization and competition. But as Waugh explained almost twenty years later, with or without the Phoenix event, climbing has shifted from the fringe activity of eccentrics to a recreational pursuit whose chief objective is fun, not risk or status. There are a whole lot more climbers swarming over the well-bolted and close-to-the-road climbs of Queen Creek than out in the nearby Superstitions or outback Santa Catalinas. The mass gatherings at sport-climbing venues or bouldering competitions haven't affected the experience of those willing to trek to the wilderness.

Yet for all its growing popularity, the American Southwest still has those endless opportunities to wander. In fact, during the 1985 Harmonic Convergence, you could pay seventy-five dollars to sit atop Sedona's Bell Rock for a chance, literally, to leave this planet for the galaxy Andromeda. Most climbers, however, will find enough adventure to satisfy them right here on earth, so long as they carry enough water and don't mind plucking cactus spines from their legs after a day in the vast outback.

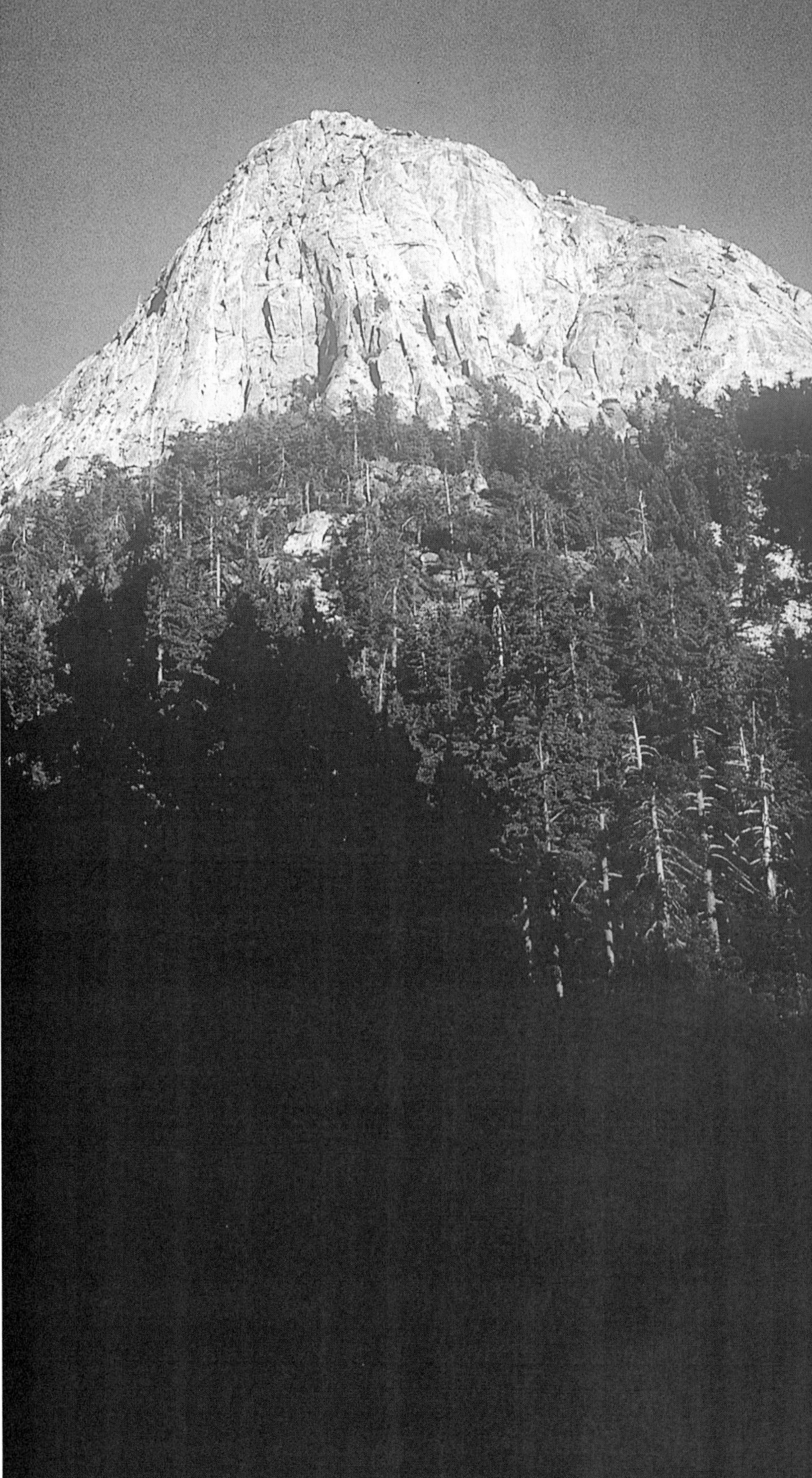

8

THE RANGE OF LIGHT

Historic Tahquitz Rock

It was March 1872, and John Muir was in his cabin under Sentinel Rock in Yosemite when the rumbling began. A giant earthquake, larger than the one that would flatten San Francisco in 1906, shook a wide area of California's Sierra Nevada. Fearing danger from falling rocks, Muir sought shelter behind a nearby yellow pine. Had the boulders indeed come his way, the tiny tree would have done little to save him; about a half mile up the valley he watched Eagle Rock come crashing down, "falling in thousands of the great boulders I had so long been studying, pouring to the valley floor in a free curve luminous from friction, making a terribly sublime spectacle—an arc of glowing, passionate fire fifteen hundred feet span, as true in form and as serene in beauty as a rainbow in the midst of the stupendous, roaring rock-storm."

The quake, centered on the eastern side of the Sierra near the town of Lone Pine, killed twenty-seven people and left only seven of the town's fifty-nine buildings still standing. During the initial jolt and the smaller rumblings to follow for the next month, Mount Whitney and the rest of the Sierra crest above Lone Pine would rise a full 13 feet higher relative to the flat Owens River Valley below. It was fitting that Muir, who had by then made a life studying and describing the dynamic earth, be present to witness such a growth spurt in the life of his beloved Sierra Nevada. It was he who was the principal advocate for the establishment of a national park, and it was he who first understood and described the role of glaciers in shaping the walls and valley of the Yosemite. To him, nature wasn't just a state, but a process. And humans weren't just visitors, but a part of the grand scheme. John Muir must have enjoyed the show.

Americans generally know two things about the Sierra Nevada of California: that its jewel and centerpiece is Yosemite Valley, and that its Mount Whitney is the country's highest peak outside of Alaska. But there's a whole lot more lofty rock than these two well-publicized places. The Sierra Nevada is one of America's great mountain ranges, long (more than four hundred miles), wide (fifty to eighty miles), and continuous (a full two hundred miles between Yosemite and Lake Isabella without a road traversing the range). It contains nine national forests and three national parks: Kings Canyon, Sequoia, and Yosemite. On its east flank is the greatest single relief found in the Lower 48 states, more than 10,000 vertical feet from Lone Pine to the nearby summit of Mount Whitney, and almost 15,000 feet between the peak and Death Valley, two hundred miles away. The range covers more area than the Swiss, French, and Italian Alps combined. Eleven of its summits reach above 14,000 feet. It is one of the country's most prized wilderness areas, yet its mountains are within a half-day's drive for more than 30 million people.

Something Higher

Nowhere is granite so stark and prevalent, and nowhere is the history and culture of rock climbing so rich. It was here on Sierra granite that a national wilderness movement gained momentum, and it was from here that we first heard the voices of some of that movement's most vital advocates. There was David Brower and Norman Clyde, mountaineers, explorers, and wilderness advocates both. There was Robert Underhill, who during a brief visit in 1931 introduced modern rope techniques to American rock climbers. There was the resilient voice of Royal Robbins, who spoke so passionately about the higher and deeper meanings of climbing. And there were the pioneers: John Salathé, who forged both hard steel pitons and the will to suffer the privations of multiple days on the wall; Warren Harding, who invested the better part of a year in making the audacious first ascent of El Capitan; and Yvon Chouinard, whose creative gear designs far improved the rough pitons of Salathé and the modified stove legs that allowed Harding to climb the wide cracks of El Cap. Most colorful of all was the emergence of a subculture in a squalid Yosemite campground, whose denizens became legends of the vertical.

But the quest for higher meaning in the tradition of John Muir was never lost, even though the sport of rock climbing evolved furiously and in a multitude of experimental and fragmented directions. Muir himself explained that "there is not a fragment in all of nature, for every relative fragment of one thing is a full harmonious unit in itself" and, further, that "when we try to pick out anything by itself, we find it hitched to everything else in the Universe." At first look, the story of Sierra climbing has three elements: the geologic, the cultural, and the athletic. To know Sierra climbing, one must know the rock and its history, the ideas generated and promulgated by the country's voices of wilderness philosophy, and the amazing deeds of some of the world's best and most innovative climbers on some of the world's sheerest and highest vertical landscapes. But each is "hitched" to the other. Those three elements—white glaciated granite, the thoughts and deeds of a group of vagabond mountain philosophers, and the audacity of American climbers to envision climbs where it seemed only a fly could stick—are inextricably woven together in the story of Sierra climbing.

Each, as well, is part of the journey to infuse richer and more universal definition into the games we play in the mountains. The Sierra story, starting here with the peaceful wanderings of Sierra vagabonds on through the multiday adventures on El Capitan, is an enormous pyramid, with each ascent either building upon or responding to events just taking place. In 1872 Muir found himself about halfway up Mount Ritter, a peak he called king of the mountains. No rope and no partner, Muir lost control for a moment, believing that a fatal fall was seconds away. His mind reeled in confusion, but then returned with heightened clarity. He made the moves with ease, as though he had "been borne aloft with wings." In 1993 Lynn Hill free-climbed Harding's original *Nose* route, unlocking the most difficult passages with creative moves like stemming over her head on the Great Roof and, according to her partner, Brooke Sandahl, doing stuff he'd never seen before to climb the smooth corner on the twenty-ninth pitch. Hill's free ascent of the *Nose* remains the finest achievement of modern American rock climbing. When she repeated it in a single day the next year, it seemed as though a circle begun a century earlier was complete. Lynn Hill reaffirmed that, even in a pursuit so laden with gadgets, what counted most in exploring the great world in front of us was the discovery of the surprising resources within.

ESSENTIAL GRANITE

In 1860 Thomas Starr King wrote, "Great is granite and Yosemite is its prophet." True. There and throughout the Sierra, granite reigns. In many ranges, the Tetons and Cascades, for example, one's eye is drawn to the form more than the substance of the mountain. The jagged shapes of the range make the greatest impressions on the viewer, far greater than the dark, nondescript rock, clothed in snow for much of the year. But in California's Sierra, the rock is so white, so geometric, so startlingly sheer that one's eye moves from the feature to the rock itself. The towering granite of Keeler Needle. The striped vertical acres of Half Dome. The bizarre fin of Matthes Crest. There's something different about granite, something noble.

Granite is the ultimate *plutonic* rock (so named for the god of the underworld). And the Sierra batholith is one of America's most extensive. Formed deep in the earth, it was pushed to the surface by the forces of plate tectonics and stripped by erosion of thousands of feet of softer rock that had overlain the granite. Once exposed to the surface, the rock's form was largely determined by joint patterns. Joints are parallel fractures that result mainly from the stress relief as weight is taken off from above. Up on the Whitney crest these joint planes are especially obvious: countless vertical cracks splinter the east face of Mount Muir, all along the Keeler Needle, Mount Whitney, and especially Mount Russell to the north. Seen from high above, joint patterns also delineate drainage patterns, with rivers and streams carving out valleys predetermined by the fracturing and faulting of the batholith.

On a smaller scale, the onionlike sheeting of exfoliation determines much of the vertical topography. This is especially obvious on Half Dome or on the Tuolumne Meadows domes like Fairview or on the bizarre green and yellow Needles of the southern end of the range. Almost every crack on these formations is somehow related to an exfoliation layer. Granite climbers are crack climbers, as most routes trace these lines of exfoliation sheets pasted to the wall. It's either a layback up the broken side of the sheet or a straight-in jam up a crack in the sheet. Up close, the rock seems solid enough, but from afar, it's apparent that the route lies on the temporary shell of a mountain shedding its skin.

It was ironic that John Muir would be there for that Lone Pine earthquake in 1872, because events like that were figuring importantly in the scientific debates of the day. It was equally ironic that Mount Whitney's namesake, Josiah Whitney, would be his staunchest adversary in that debate. Whitney, in charge of the California Geologic Survey, explained Yosemite Valley as the result of some "grand cataclysm." Surely nothing else could explain the boxlike design of the valley. The bottom must surely have simply dropped down from the valley walls. Muir had another explanation. Having looked not only at the overall shape of the valley from a distance, but also close up at the more subtle features, he knew that ice was responsible for the final shape of the valley. It was the inexorable grinding of dirt-laden ice under the incalculable weight of glaciers that gave the valley its U-shaped form, left its river valleys hanging hundreds of feet above the valley floor (look at all the waterfalls), rounded its hillsides, and polished its rock to a mirrorlike surface. To Whitney, "A more absurd theory was never advanced." Muir's ridiculous claim that ice could make such an impact on solid granite was an idea "based on ignorance of the whole subject." To argue it further would be just a waste of time. The debate about the valley's origin is generally considered settled, yet the ironies continue: the range's grandest peak was named after Whitney, while a lesser point on the crest was named after Muir.

From the lookout at Glacier Point, high above Yosemite Valley, all these major features of glacial geomorphology are of textbook proportion. Experienced up close, however, there's another leftover from the ice, this one of particular interest to the climber fifty feet out from the last quarter-inch bolt on a Tuolumne slab route. It's glacial polish. With the weight of thousands of feet of ice above and with a dirt-laden surface grinding against the bedrock, a glacier can buff stone into a surface like glass. Up in Tuolumne Meadows, the glacial polish is unreal. It reflects blindingly in the sunlight and offers almost no friction at all. A twenty-degree incline that on most rock would be insignificant is actually hard to walk when it has been polished by ice. Many face climbs in the Meadows link sections of rougher, weathered rock where the polish has worn off. Relative to the weathered sections, the polished areas stand out in slight relief. Climbing sometimes becomes an exercise in edging, since frictioning on the glassy surface is practically impossible.

Yosemite is the world's best classroom of granitic and glacial geology, and so it's easy to focus too much on Yosemite Valley in any examination of the Sierra and to dote on its superlatives—sheerest, steepest, smoothest. Yet the range is enormous, with a climbing history and potential to match. From the spectacular Needles south near Bakersfield, up the Sierra crest past its highest peaks, on past Yosemite to the deep blue waters and good white rock of Lake Tahoe, all the

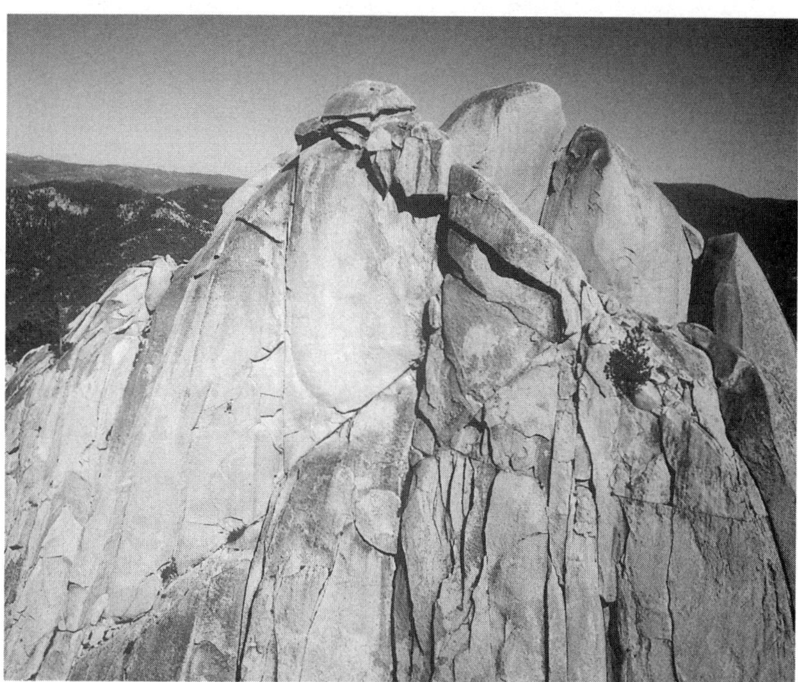

The Needles

way to Castle Crags in the shadow of Mount Shasta, where the Sierra granite dives under the more recent volcanic flows of the Cascades, it's all beauty and granite and tall trees, climbing for a hundred lifetimes.

Strictly speaking, the southern terminus of the Sierra Range is at the end of the Tehachapis, between Barstow and Bakersfield. Northward from there, the crest takes shape, initially for the rock climber in the Needles and the Dome Lands Wilderness, then on up the crest past the Whitney group toward Yosemite National Park. To the south, the range seems to disappear into the brown desert before rising up again at Tahquitz and Suicide Rocks. These historically vital climbing areas on the flanks of Mount San Jacinto Peak are technically part of Baja's Peninsula Range, separate from but closely related to the Sierra proper. But though geology might want to view them separately, the lore of climbing binds them tight together. It was at Tahquitz Rock that the core of Yosemite explorers learned their craft, and for many years thereafter, southern California's climbers would spend time up at Tahquitz in the spring, honing their skills before moving on to the Yosemite.

BEGINNINGS

Driving Route 243 from the town of Banning, near Palm Springs, up toward Tahquitz and the town of Idyllwild is like taking off in an airplane. The road tilts upward above arid flats, punctuated by patches of irrigated green. Upward it goes through a variety of life zones changing with altitude, from the desert to the high pine forest. Idyllwild sits at an elevation of a little over 5,000 feet, with Mount San Jacinto towering above. It's touristy quaint, with gift shops and real estate offices radiating from the commercial pine log building along a small but confusing matrix of roads.

From almost any vantage point in town, one can see Tahquitz towering white and impressive on the shoulder of 10,000-foot Mount San Jacinto. Under a clear mountain sky, it seems as if there are but three colors in the world, the dark green of the pines, the deep blue of the sky, and the bright white of the rock itself. The colors are especially rich when the sun glints off the angular features of the rock just right and individual classic routes can be discerned from miles away. Last to slip into afternoon shadow is *The Edge,* knife-sharp from so far away, a route that would play big in the lore of this most important American climbing area.

Many of the country's climbing areas are places that, even without a human history, would loom large in the public imagination. Devil's Tower, Canyonlands, the Teton Range—these have rich climbing histories to be sure, but for most climbers the grand rock drama far outweighs the relatively puny deeds of those who played there. Such compartmentalization, however, is nearly impossible at Tahquitz, where ghosts and legends loom as high as the rocks themselves. Tahquitz Rock played one of the most significant roles in the development of American rock climbing from the early days in the 1930s, when the rock climbing section of the southern California chapter of the Sierra Club discovered its potential and began the search for routes. The legends continued to grow, on through the era of Royal Robbins, arguably the most important voice in American climbing history, right to the emergence of the Stonemasters, self-proclaimed bad boys who disregarded limitations set by the establishment and put up routes into the then unbelievable range of 5.11 and 5.12. Tahquitz climbers even developed the rating system we use today. It's erroneously called YDS (Yosemite Decimal System), but it made its way to Yosemite only after it was given shape at Tahquitz.

Though it's a cliff of legends, Tahquitz today isn't an elite preserve of high-grade routes. In fact, it has some of the best long, intermediate climbs in the country, a rarity these days when so many newer areas seem to think that 5.10 is moderate and where 5.7s just don't exist. How is a climber supposed to learn crack technique at Indian Creek, where the purity of cracks might excite the expert, but where a neophyte will have a hard time getting both feet off the ground at the same time? What's a newcomer to do at the New River Gorge, where there are only twenty-five routes graded under 5.6 and more than five hundred over 5.10? Rivaled in this department by only the Shawangunks in New York, Tahquitz has a collection of long, intermediate routes where mortal climbers can get high off the deck to see the view and feel the commitment of a real rock climb.

It was this very characteristic—good, multipitch, intermediate climbing—that brought Tahquitz into the forefront of American climbing. Here was a place not so dauntingly smooth as Yosemite, but considerably higher than the sandstone boulders at Stoney Point near L.A. where so many of California's top climbers got their start. Since the 1930s Tahquitz has been a port of entry into the sport, a welcoming place, a bridge spanning the gap between mountaineering and modern technical rock climbing.

The roots of rock climbing at Tahquitz can be traced back again to the influence of Robert Underhill, who brought modern rope techniques to California during his training camp in the Sierra. The 1931 ascent of Whitney's east face by Underhill, Norman Clyde, Jules Eichorn, and Glen Dawson was the first of what would become a surge of new routes, climbs well into what modern climbers would deem fifth class. That surge would hit Tahquitz in 1935 when Sierra Club climbers discovered the rock, and in 1936 when the first route, *The Trough* (5.0), was done. Only a year later, Dick Jones led the *Mechanics Route* (5.8), unprotected, considered the hardest route in the country at the time.

There's no place at Tahquitz better than the base of the *Mechanics*

Route to think about the ghosts and stories that hover all around. To its left is the country's first 5.9, the *Open Book,* freed by the upstart Robbins in his second year of climbing. The elders of the Sierra Club had admonished newcomers to avoid unnecessary risk, but with the new nylon ropes that emerged with World War II, one could actually take a fall without worrying about the grim reaper. Robbins pushed the limits here, trusting the solid piton placements, his well-trained belayer Don Wilson, and a rope that would not fail.

Out to the right of the *Open Book* is the very obvious and appealing *Green Arch,* a 5.11 that would become a rite of passage for area climbers. In 1975 it was one of the country's hardest routes and would have been the crowning achievement that year were it not for an event that would take place out on the left edge of the *Open Book.* There, Tobin Sorenson should perhaps have taken the advice of the old Sierra Club members, because his ascent of *The Edge* (5.10) in 1975 certainly involved what most would describe as "unnecessary risk." Master storyteller and Tahquitz pioneer John Long wrote in a short tale called "The Edge" about Sorenson's position, forty feet out from protection, trying to drill a bolt. With every hammer blow, his feet would slide and he'd have to drop the hammer to slap back up the edge into position. Looking at a hundred-foot fall, Sorenson began sobbing as he slowly deepened the quarter-inch hole. Then the bit broke. Instead of sensibly quitting, he told his partner Eric Ericksson that he was just going to go for it. It took a while for Ericksson to convince him to try again to get something in. He finally succeeded in placing a bolt, and then launched into fifty feet of continuous 5.10 climbing to a ledge. The climb was only one of the many Tobin Sorenson legends that linger over the place, stories that include unroped solos and even a climb with the rope tied around his neck. He was one of the region's best when he died in 1980 on the North Face of Canada's Mount Alberta. All this history, and you haven't even moved from your spot below the 1937 *Mechanics Route.*

Simply Beautiful

Any climber who has followed the magazines for the past few years will recognize the yellow-green lichens of the Needles, the remote but increasingly popular series of towers in the southern Sierra. The climbs here are the most photographically alluring in America, as the rock rises in dramatic spires high over the rich green Sierra forest and as colorful lichens change shades with the seasons, browner some years when it's dry, and exploding with rich yellows and greens in the wet season.

Unlike Tahquitz, it isn't the legends or the stories that grip a first-time visitor to the Needles: it's the place. Walking for the first time in the supernatural landscape and gazing up at the Witch or the Sorcerer or the big, round-topped Warlock, one can't help but be gripped by the magic of the Needles. No climber returns without spewing superlatives not just for the climbs, but for the mysterious beauty of the spires.

The Needles are in the remote hills of the southern Sierra, right up the road from the trailer-park "town" of Johnsondale. The nearest real civilized outpost, though, is Kernville, sixty-five miles to the south. Nearer to the cliff is the Ponderosa Lodge, a roadhouse not to be missed for those wishing to find local color. A tattered guidebook hanging from a post confirms that it's a stop for climbers. The owner waves his hand at both the decorations and the stock on the shelves and says, "Everything's for sale," but you won't find much in the way of groceries here. Just beer and onions and odd assortments of camping gear. And gas? Sure, that's for sale too. Just bring your own gallon jug.

From the informal campsites at the end of the road, it's a quick and easy two-and-a-half-mile walk to the climbs on a well-graded trail that skirts the crest of a ridge, just far enough to scare away climbers looking for roadside cragging. Stately sequoias and far-reaching views northward toward Mount Whitney make the approach seem even shorter. First rock in the series is the Magician, strangely capped by a fire tower bolted to its summit. In this tiny, one-room, glass-sided box is a bed, a stove, lots of books, and a Forest Service employee who has lived there for twelve years, watching for ominous wisps of smoke and baking up cookies for climbers every Sunday afternoon. It's a life she's grown to love, recounting with passion the thirty or so direct lightning hits she's experienced, putting as much faith in those thin copper wires that ground the room as the rest of us do in a three-bolt anchor.

The rock here at the Needles is more featured than most Sierra granite, with routes following either straight-in cracks or cracks formed by exfoliation sheets. Some of these have a rather hollow feel to them: the first pitch of *Atlantis* (5.11c), for example, is a 90-foot, fully detached flake pasted against the wall. Dan Osman soloed this 5.10c layback and topped it off with a straight-armed flag maneuver from the top of the flake and immortality in the poster for No Fear. Prophetic indeed, for Osman's performance in the face of fear would soon cost him his life when his rope broke during a 1,000-foot stunt jump from Yosemite's Leaning Tower.

Every spire has routes memorable for a lifetime: the *Spook Book* (5.10), a shallow, five-pitch, very sustained left-facing corner that also goes by the fitting name *Welcome to the Needles; Igor Unchained* (5.9), a full pitch of less-than-vertical perfect handcrack with even better stuff above; *White Punks on Dope* (5.8), as much variety as possible in only six pitches; *Sirocco* (5.12), the most photographed arête in the land; and *Romantic Warrior,* nine pitches and a stiff 5.12c. And on and on. There are scores of climbs that would be the best route at so many other places, and yet visitors continue to talk about the place a whole lot more than the climbs.

Off below in the distance is Dome Rock, not quite in the ridgetop lineup of the Needles themselves, but with the entrance road leading right out onto its flat top, you might like the easier approach. Here is knob and chickenhead climbing at its committing best, with xenoliths decorating the wall like a natty sweater. Except for the *Tree Route,* Doug Robinson's choice for the "best 5.6 in the country," many of the climbs are in the hard 5.10 realm, launching boldly upward, with much of the protection limited to tied-off chickenheads and route finding very problematic. Odd sometimes how such a casual approach can so quickly put you in harm's way. And daunting, too, with the carcass of a motorcycle crumpled nearby and the memories of its rider, a hapless hunter, and at least a half-dozen dogs having taken to the air, all owing to the perversity of putting a parking area on top of the cliff instead of safely at the bottom where it belongs.

THE HIGH SIERRA

Of all Sierra peaks, none attracts more attention than Mount Whitney, mainly because it's the highest, but also because of the clas-

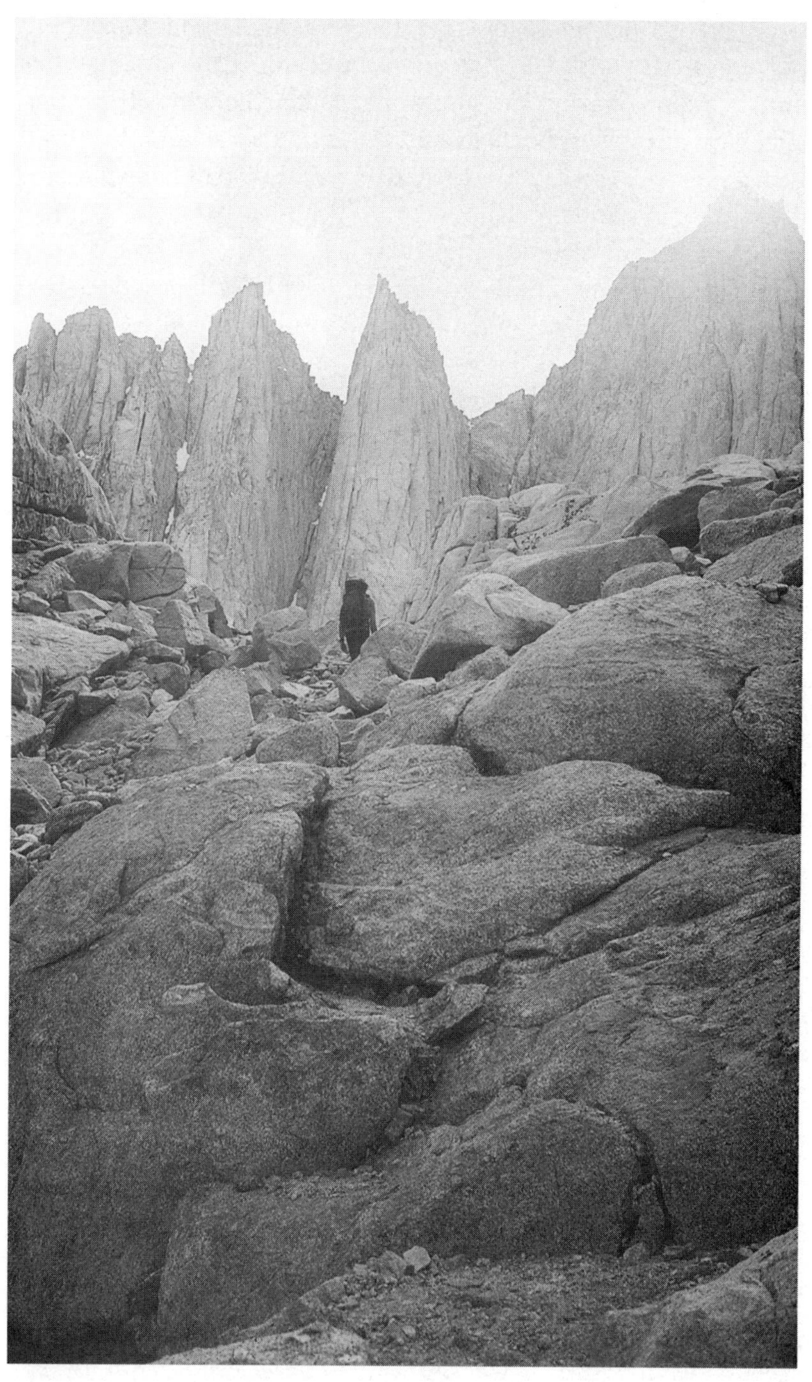

Approaching Mount Whitney from the east

sic Ansel Adams photograph of the mountain from Lone Pine. Visitors familiar with the photograph expect to see the mountain not in rusty yellow, but in black and white, its fluted granite crest towering above a tiny horse oblivious to the drama all around. Yet to get such a view it's necessary to step away from the strip of Lone Pine and get atop the Alabama Hills, away from the somewhat tacky strip that is the town's main street.

Any small town, one would think, would be well proud to sit at the base of such a notable mountain and would make such a location the centerpiece of its identity. Yet in a quick walk down the main street, a visitor finds a lot more John Wayne than John Muir. Lone Pine, close enough to Hollywood and classically western, has been the scene of more than 250 cowboy movies and TV shows. "GENE AUTRY SLEPT HERE," the motel sign will proclaim. Muir, one supposes, took his nights under the stars.

Above town—actually way above town—is Whitney Portal, opening to the Sierra Crest. Drive straight west through the rounded rocks of the Alabama Hills (there's some good bouldering here) and up the zigzagging road to the trailhead at 8,300 feet. Doing this first part of the climb by car is especially appreciated because the elevation difference between the town and the summit of the mountain is more than 10,000 feet. From the Portal parking and campground, the trail gets right to work, the informal climbers' path splitting off right from the main Mount Whitney Trail just a few minutes from the parking lot. It's a steep but easy walk up to the Boy Scout Lakes and up to Iceberg Lake, the ice-filled tarn at the base of Mount Whitney's East Face. Off to the left is Keeler Needle, where the *Harding Route* makes climbers grapple with a 5.10 off-width at 14,000 feet elevation. Hard to imagine.

The *East Face* of Whitney is one of the country's great and historic climbs, the route Robert Underhill picked out from below during his 1931 watershed visit. In pairs of two, Underhill with Glen Dawson and Norman Clyde with Jules Eichorn, the first-ascent teams obviously put those techniques to good use, climbing the *East Face* in only three and a half hours. To its right is the *East Buttress,* harder and more direct, with variations up to 5.8. Above and right of Iceberg Lake is Mount Russell, whose fractured *Fishhook Arête* (5.9) is as good as alpine rock climbing can get.

To continue northward, describing individual highlights of the grand Sierra Nevada would fill the rest of this book and several others. It's tough even to narrow down to some highlights. Some say the best is Temple Crag. Complex buttresses and airy blades of dark granite make up some of the longest technical routes outside Yosemite, with Grade IVs and even Vs that run up to twenty-five pitches. Temple Crag is a beautiful mountain, leading Norman Clyde to call it "the most striking crag mountain" in the Sierra and inspiring Don and Joan Jensen to name its features the Celestial Arêtes: Moon Goddess and Sun Ribbon and Venusian Blind, this last ridge named for Venus, which hovered over the mountain when Jensen made his first ascent in 1969. *Dark Star* (V 5.10c), the direct route of the buttress to the right of the Celestial Arêtes, might be the most classic climb of all, with featured rock similar to that of Middle Cathedral Rock in Yosemite, yet with a much more spectacular position out there on an alpine edge.

With a population of about four thousand, Bishop is the largest and busiest town on the east side of the range. It's home to guides and hot springs, cowboy bars and Wilson's Eastside Sports, the area's main climbing gear supplier and boot resoler. Nearby Buttermilk Boulders are among the best on the planet. The vast scattering of Joshua Tree-like granite rocks right near town has attracted quite a following. In the beginning was Smoke Blanchard's Rock Course, a technical maze of chimneys and summits. Sierra sage Doug Robinson described it as "a mountaineer's course," a bit different from the high-end bouldering that goes on there today. By the late 1990s, as bouldering surged in popularity, the Buttermilks and nearby boulderfields became destinations themselves, not just stopover training areas for visitors aiming for the bigger mountains just above.

And for anyone tiring of the uphill marches to the alpine rock climbs, there's Owens River Gorge. The gorge is a river-carved gash in the volcanic tableland that surrounds Bishop. At first, and especially in comparison to the scenery of the mountains just to the west, Owens is sort of ugly. On its rim is a huge pipeline and in its depths is a power plant, wires running in every direction over the gorge. Steep trails lead down the rubble to the Owens River, recently resurrected after having been diverted for a major water project. The rock here is welded tuff, the stuff that made Smith Rock famous, and the routes are generally repetitive face holds and pocket pulling on vertical and slightly overhanging faces. It's been called a good "intermediate" area because the bulk of its routes are within the 5.10 to low-end 5.12 range. (A lot of climbers, however, especially those from the old school, find this definition of *intermediate* a bit snooty.) Owing to the fact that there's good climbing on both sides of the crooked canyon, there's always shade to be found in summer. And owing to the climate of Bishop in the rain shadow of the range, there's always sun when it's cold. Although perennial snow can be seen just a short distance away up in the mountains, Bishop itself gets only six inches of snow and less than six inches of rain per year.

Excellent sport climbing and awesome bouldering. But with routes like the *North Buttress* of Mount Goode so near, most climbers visiting Bishop feel the magnetic pull of the magical high country above. North up the range from this classic route, peak after peak, route after route, line up toward Yosemite. There above Tuolumne Meadows are Mount Conness, Cathedral Peak, and the Matthes Crest, each with memorable and historic granite wall and ridge routes. Some of the best climbs in this neighborhood of the Sierra are traverses along these serrated ridges, like the *North Ridge* of Conness (5.6), a climb that could extend all the way to Tioga Pass, and the Cathedral Range Traverse, a remarkable alpine day that takes in fifteen summits along the way. Exhausting? Yes. Exhilarating? Absolutely. But at least your nerves, frayed from the slick Tuolumne run-outs and the agonizingly distant quarter-inch bolts, get a full day off on such a climb.

TUOLUMNE

Yosemite National Park, for the climber, is really two places: the Valley with its towering walls and crowded floor, and Tuolumne Meadows, a high and rolling expanse of lush forests punctuated by white and golden domes of rock. Tuolumne is an escape from the claustrophobic Valley. At an elevation of 8,500 feet, the air is cooler and the crowds are few. The climbing is especially distinct, and when climbers speak of "Tuolumne-like" climbing, others know well that they mean smooth expanses of white rock, inclined planes of granite glazed by glacial polish. Or where the polish has been worn away by time, they mean fields of feldspar knobs, frightful route finding, and high step-ups. They mean hideously long run-outs between bolts, rusting quarter-inch Rawl split-shaft bolts. They mean deeply traditional climbing, bold climbing, where inner calm means a whole lot more than physical strength. It's a realm unto itself.

The elevated atmosphere has a quieting effect, especially after having escaped from the Valley. Campsites at the Meadows campground are easier to get and very much tidier than those at Sunnyside, the climbers' tent ghetto in the Valley. The routes feel wide and spread out, instead of boxed in. The scene is more subtle. Climbers congregate around the Grill and the gas station/climbing school next door. Long-distance hikers with heavy packs stagger off the trail with that "I need a beer" look in their eyes. It's a place of tall trees and grassy meadows and rounded glacial domes. It's easy to imagine Tuolumne just a few thousand years ago, freshly emerged from the ice, a landscape like Baffin Island. Today, much of that rolling topography is clothed in gentle green as living things reclaim the land.

The Tuolumne story paralleled in some ways the story unfolding in the Valley below, though without the numbers or the public scrutiny. The largest rocks and the most obvious lines were the first to be climbed, and as a bold Tuolumne ethic evolved, one of the strongest demonstrations was made by Bob Kamps who, with Tom Higgins, retreated from high on Fairview Dome rather than resort to a few drilled aid points. So many climbers have admonished impatient youths to let a potential route wait until someone was up to the task rather than hammer it into submission just for a first-ascent credit. Higgins would indeed return, this time with Mike Irwin in 1973, and both this time were up to the task. *Fairest of All* (5.10c) was a powerful statement of how things ought to be done up on the domes of the Tuolumne.

No statements were louder, however, than those made by John Bachar on Mendlicott Dome. Bachar had already established a reputation for boldness and purity of style. His mission was to keep climbing as natural as possible, resisting the trend to resort to the drill whenever things got tough. He was a marvel of self-control, free-soloing routes as high and hard as the *Moratorium,* in Yosemite Valley, at 5.11b, then the hardest solo yet done in this country. First on Mendlicott came *You Asked for It,* a hard 5.10 with two bolts on the first pitch and only one on the second. Then, as if this hadn't reached the limit of human nerve, Bachar led Dave Yerian up an improbable, dark, water-streaked line of knobs to the left. The resulting four-pitch route has only seven protection bolts. This keeps most people away. Those who do venture up for a look usually fail, either after a frightening fall or, more commonly, after simply looking at the route up close, at the huge distances between bolts and the unrelenting difficulty between them. *Bachar-Yerian,* at 5.11c, is one of the country's lasting symbols of a climbing style.

As it has everywhere else, the missionary zeal of an area's leading climbers holds sway for a while but is ultimately challenged. If the challenge is by newcomers or outsiders, then the locals usually resist. But if the challenge is from respected climbers within, those who have already proven themselves with traditional styles, then the code begins to relax. Up in Tuolumne, the challenge was initiated by Ron Kauk and picked up by others, including Tom Herbert, all deeply respected climbers and each perfectly capable of bringing himself up to the level of the route rather than tearing the route down to meet his own weaknesses. But each also saw little future in Bachar's method. Even Bachar had resorted to hanging on a hook on knobs to place the bolts of *Bachar-Yerian.* Purity, thus, was a relative thing. British sensation Jerry Moffatt bolted nearby *Clash of the Titans* (5.13) while hanging on hooks—a practice distinctly American at the time—but later at Smith Rock in Oregon, it was Moffatt who encouraged Kauk to rehearse moves while hanging from protection bolts on *To Bolt or Not to Be,* the country's first 5.14. Kauk, once one of the most ardent proponents of ground-up, traditional style, saw the new techniques not as hangdogging, but as simple common sense. This more pragmatic view of climbing on the steep, crackless walls of the Tuolumne, like everywhere else, were initially criticized, then gradually gained acceptance. Yet a few rappel-bolted routes have not ruined the essential qualities of climbing at Tuolumne Meadows. And in the great Valley below the Meadows, bigger shifts than this were under way.

THE VALLEY

The Valley of the Yosemite is the most famous rock climbing area on earth, a magnet for climbers the world over. It has the biggest, smoothest walls in America and so, inevitably, it would also come to have the richest history and the deepest traditions. Yosemite climbing is the heart of American climbing. The evolution of rock climbing in Yosemite Valley, from George Anderson's bolt route up Half Dome to the amazing speed records being set almost weekly, ensued all within the context of the size of the cliffs, and the traditions that hover over the great valley are responses to the unique challenges such big rocks present to the climber. Salathé's multiday climbs of the '40s and '50s were big leaps forward in ambition and technique. Unless he was willing to spend nights out in the cold, suffer the awful privations of hunger and thirst, and develop pitons that could be reused again and again, Salathé could not have even considered big walls such as the Lost Arrow, Half Dome, or the Sentinel. Those who followed, too, would have to view climbing in new ways in order to adjust to the unique demands of Yosemite.

Any history of Yosemite climbing must be a distillation, for too much has gone on for too long by too many people to capture in one chapter of one book. Whole books have been written on the subject, including *The Vertical World of Yosemite,* edited by climber/photographer Galen Rowell, Steve Roper's *Camp 4: Recollections of a Yosemite Rockclimber,* and *Defying Gravity,* a thorough history of rock climbing in Yosemite written by Gary Arce. Even these rich accounts are only selections of the thousands of tales floating above the valley floor. Regardless of the need to condense, the Yosemite story is a story about personalities and strongly held beliefs. If we pick up the discussion after Salathé's revolutionary ascents, the two strongest personalities were those of Royal Robbins and Warren Harding. They emerged side by side, both pushing rock climbing into realms then unknown, and they came to represent two antithetical stances about how things ought to be done.

Robbins, having free-climbed Tahquitz's *Open Book* in 1952, came to Yosemite the following year intent on following Salathé and Allen Steck's route on the Sentinel, one of the biggest routes of the era. That completed, he linked up with Warren Harding, Jerry Gallwas, and Don Wilson, for a shot at the 2,000-foot Northwest Face of Half Dome, second only to El Capitan in size. Their 1955 attempt fell short, but Robbins would come back in 1957, this time with Gallwas and Michael Sherrick, and in five grueling days, including hard free climbing and a long pendulum, reached the top. The

Northwest Face of Half Dome represented a new level in the evolution of big-wall climbing.

Warren Harding was gracious about Robbins' success, even though he had been keen to do the climb himself. He even hiked to the top to congratulate Robbins and his team. But six days later, Harding was at work on the biggest cliff of all, El Cap, and he had chosen the most dramatic feature, the central rib they called the Nose. Warren Harding's ascent of El Capitan was a landmark in American climbing history, not only because the country's largest wall had been overcome, but also because it was here that two philosophies diverged and two charismatic leaders emerged to define them.

Harding accepted right from the start that the size of the walls in Yosemite presented a unique challenge and would require a unique approach. Robbins believed that the clean style of ascent that was the norm on the smaller crags could be carried higher, and that the solutions to the problems must be found within. He respected much about Harding's El Cap route but thought that the extensive use of fixed ropes connecting the team to the ground for supplies or escape reflected a lack of commitment. Later, Robbins was part of a team that made the second ascent of the *Nose,* but this time made the climb in one push as a self-contained unit with no ready bailout. Later Robbins would make two more such statements on El Cap, beginning with the 1961 first ascent of the long, complex *Salathé Wall,* with Tom Frost and Chuck Pratt. After cutting loose the fixed rope from the 1,000-foot level, they headed up into a series of overhangs with the route unsure and little chance for retreat. In 1968 Robbins soloed the *Muir Wall* over ten days, an achievement way ahead of what others were willing to attempt.

Harding, on the other hand, continued to forge his way up smooth rock with little overt regard to higher meaning or public acclaim. The same year that Robbins and company used only thirteen bolts on the *Salathé Wall,* Harding placed 110 on the much shorter Leaning Tower. In 1970 the divergence in styles became a rift and then an open wound on the Yosemite rock scene. Partnered by Dean Caldwell, Harding set off on the sheer wall right of the Nose, where the sun first hit each morning as it swung its way into the tight valley. The *Wall of the Early Morning Light* took an amazing twenty-seven continuous days spent on the wall, and each day the ire of those

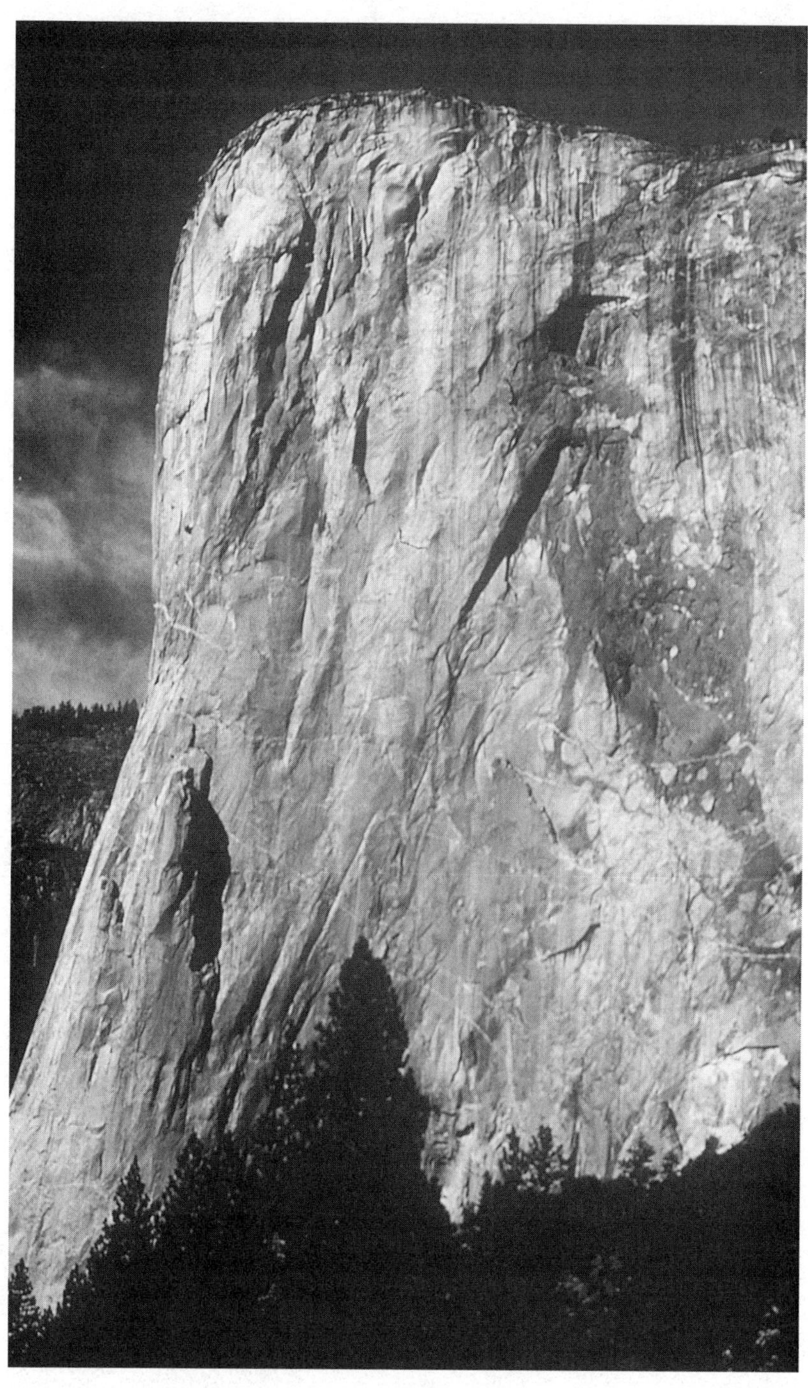

The Nose *route in profile on El Capitan*

below increased. First there was the drilling: from below it looked as if Harding was simply bolting his way up rock where no natural line existed. Second was the media hype: performing for the nightly news was hardly a noble reason to climb.

On top Harding was met by hordes of reporters. Down below, Robbins and others in Camp 4 feared the end of climbing as they knew it. It was time to make a stand. If a 330-bolt route was allowed to exist, then someone else would step onto the slippery slope and place 500. How long would it be before a thousand-bolt line made the Captain an easy climb for those unwilling to commit?

The next year Robbins, joined by Don Lauria, made the second ascent of the *Wall of the Early Morning Light.* Early on, Lauria and Robbins shared leads, with the second chopping the bolts. Higher on the route and far from the intensity of campfire debate, they began to see the route with new eyes. Yes, there were lots of bolts, but there was also excellent and difficult climbing as well. Harding hadn't simply bolted his way to the top; he had applied aid skills matched by few, and he'd found an elegant line on a blank piece of rock. Robbins and Lauria continued to the rim, leaving most of the route intact, and admitting, much as Kauk would do when he embraced sport climbing, that things aren't black and white. All climbing is contrived in a way, and simply because one had been a vocal advocate of one style doesn't mean he can't find new ways to look at the world of climbing, provided he's honest with himself and accepts Emerson's admonition that "a foolish consistency is the hobgoblin of little minds. . . . With consistency a great soul has simply nothing to do."

Throughout the history of Yosemite climbing, an idea would split and two systems of thought would travel parallel but separate from each other. Proponents of the systems would become adversaries, and their groups would stay distrustfully apart, huddled safe at campfires of the like-minded. The rift would have many faces. Sometimes it would involve actual erasure of a route. Often the antagonists would simply paint the other side with broad and denigrating strokes. "Valley Christians," Harding called the judgmental purists. "Vandals in the temple," Robbins described the sport-climbers knocking on the valley door. At their ugliest, the contentions would even lead to fights. John Bachar, for example, was slugged in the neck during an argument over a Ron Kauk route that would later be fittingly named *Punchline.*

Peace, too, would come in a variety of ways. Sometimes these parallel systems of thought would converge because the pugilists found it too enervating to keep their heels dug in so deeply. Sometimes cooperation came after each side found that the world was big enough for different styles of climbing to exist without threatening each other. Sometimes minds were broadened by travel. Sometimes it would take a person who just seemed bigger than the petty debates.

Perhaps the widest vision, and thus the greatest influence, of all Yosemite climbers came from Jim Bridwell. For more than a quarter century, Bridwell was the trendsetter, free-climbing the horrifically exposed stoveleg cracks on the Nose in 1968, and leading the charge for the first one-day ascent of the route in 1975. He was an aid-climbing master, not only putting up such hard routes as *Sea of Dreams* and *Zenyatta Mondatta,* both El Cap A5s (aid climbing's hardest rating), but also taking his craft abroad for the remarkable two-day ascent of Cerro Torre via Maestri's *Compressor Route,* a winter ascent of Alaska's Moose's Tooth, and numerous big climbs in the Alps. And it was Bridwell who placed the bolts next to the fragile *Wheat Thin* (5.10) layback crack way back in 1971. Bridwell reasoned that the wafer-thin flake would be destroyed by hammering in bong pitons, the only protection wide enough at the time to protect the climb, and so a few bolts would be the better alternative. In 1973, Bridwell wrote an article entitled "Brave New World" for the British publication *Mountain.* Already bigger than life in the eyes of those visiting and dwelling in the Valley, Bridwell, with his craggy face and ever-present cigarette, his long hair, and his penchant for hard climbing, had become the symbol around the world of the supremacy of American rock climbing.

In 1975 Bridwell teamed up with John Long and Billy Westbay to climb the *Nose* in a day. It was a heralded success, especially with the photograph of the trio after the climb, posing before the granite backdrop of El Capitan, decked out in colorful hippie garb and mock arrogance on their faces, a photo spoofing one they'd seen of a meticulously dressed climbing team posing boastfully in front of the Eiger North Face in Switzerland. The El Cap photo etched in the collective mind that American climbers were surly and irreverent, at a station confidently distinct from their European contemporaries.

Speed climbing in Yosemite Valley was nothing new. Right from the beginnings of the Camp 4 culture, climbers had valued record keeping and were willing to compare. Robbins and Joe Fitchen had made the first one-day ascent of a Grade V doing the *Steck-Salathé Route* on Sentinel in 1960. Steve Roper and Frank Sacherer beat their time the next year, and that same week, Robbins returned with Tom Frost to make the climb in three and a quarter hours.

The same goes for today. And the same will hold true tomorrow. One El Cap route in a day in 1975. An El Cap route *and* a Half Dome route in a day (Peter Croft and John Bachar, the *Nose* and the *Northwest Face* in 1986). Then two El Cap routes in a single day (Steve Schneider and Romain Volger, the *West Face* and the *Nose* in 1987). And three El Cap routes in a day (Schneider and Hans Florine, *Lurking Fear,* the *West Face,* and the *Nose* in 1994). And so on. Routes are blitzed, records set. The speed-climbing accomplishments going on in Yosemite are awesome and ongoing, but they represent only one side of this multifaceted jewel of the Sierra.

There is unroped soloing on big routes. In 1973 Henry Barber climbed the *Steck-Salathé Route* without a rope in what veterans called a visionary act. When John Bachar climbed the *Moratorium,* the praise was mixed with questions about his sanity. And when Peter Croft soloed *Astroman* (5.11c) it seemed as though there were no limits, that the soloists were neither insane nor visionary, but were just built of stuff mortals would never understand. Then British climber Derek Hersey was found dead at the base of the Sentinel. The *Steck-Salethé Route* was well within his limit; in fact, he'd already put together an astonishing record of soloing in Colorado: the *Naked Edge* (5.11), *Wunsch's Dihedral* (5.11d) and a triple crown on the Diamond on Longs Peak, doing the *Yellow Wall,* down-climbing the *Casual Route,* and finishing on *Pervertical Sanctuary* for twenty-two pitches in three and a half hours. Technically, the *Steck-Salathé* shouldn't have presented any problems. Who knows? Perhaps the route was wet. It was a sobering moment for a lot of climbers, but judging from recent trends, Hersey's demonstration of mortality hasn't stopped others from pushing out without a rope.

All the while that big dramas are unfolding on big rocks high above the valley floor, others are happening on modest white boulders scattered throughout the forests. Yosemite bouldering is among the best on granite in the world. Some visitors arrive each year from abroad and never rope up for even one climb. Instead, they spend their days slapping rounded edges, crashing onto dusty foam mats or into the arms of an army of spotters. No longer is Camp 4's *Midnight Lightning* Yosemite's hardest boulder problem. Pushed by British climbers Sean Myles, Ben Moon, and Jerry Moffatt, and swept up in a national reenergized interest in bouldering, the fragments of rock scattered in the cool pine forests have become every bit as alluring as the high walls from which the boulders have fallen.

Yosemite is big, and the games are many. Sport climbing, once deemed a plague to be kept locked outside the Valley, has grown some, mainly on more remote cliffs without infecting the traditional cracks or better-known walls. Long, moderate, traditional routes continue to be the focus of most visiting climbers, and these will probably remain forever as the real Yosemite experience for most people: ten or so pitches, rock a bit less than vertical, cracks of all sizes, some irritatingly wide, others a perfect match for hands and fingers. Not enough water, not enough time. Bushy ledges crawling with ants. A headlamp descent down the wrong gully. Friends back at camp getting ready to call in a search when you stagger in minutes after everything closes. The beer will have to wait, but memories of that quintessential Yosemite experience will last.

Experiencing Yosemite

Indeed, Yosemite is an experience as much as it is a place. Principally, it is a valley, not a mountain range. One's first response upon entering is often claustrophobia: a few hundred acres of flat woods and meadow, a drifting stream, and immense gray walls boxing it all in. It's really three worlds far apart. There's life for the tourist. There's life for the climber camping in the Valley. And there's life on the wall. Life in the Yosemite Valley for the tourist is little more than a scenic traffic jam. The one-way road that circles the central valley floor is choked during summer weekends with giant RVs, dwarfed only by the scale of the cliffs. The big rigs pull over onto the shoulder of the road at El Cap Meadows and the family gets out. Their eyes strain until someone points out a tiny white spot—a haul bag or a climber. It's impossible to tell. Then another and another. If they were to come back after dark, they'd see bivy lights all over the face. Life for the one- or two-day visitor includes photo stops below all the major waterfalls, a short hike, perhaps to Lower Yosemite Falls (sharing the path with up to four thousand others on a good summer day), and maybe a drive up to Glacier Point, where the views up to Half Dome and back down to the valley floor are superb and from which until the late 1960s a huge evening bonfire would be bulldozed over the brink, thrilling the tourists below with a thousand-foot streak of fire as the burning logs hurtled earthward.

Since then, park officials have concluded the natural show to be good enough, so there's no more tunneling roads through the trunks of ancient trees, no more flaming cascades to compete with the park's magnificent waterfalls. More than 4 million visitors annually provide enough circus atmosphere for most people's liking. Park rangers now complain that they spend more time in law enforcement than in environmental education. They worry about drug busts and murders, gangs from L.A. packing guns. One day it looked like terrorism had finally entered the big stone canyon as a cylindrical container was spotted by the side of the road in El Cap Meadows. Cops and rangers sprang into action, stopping traffic, cordoning off the area with yellow barrier tape. The bomb squad moved in, but instead of deadly explosives, the container was just a poop tube, a PVC pipe carried up the wall to avoid having to toss those nasty paper bags earthward, an odd tradition that lasted well into the 1980s.

Life for the climber isn't like life for the tourist. It centers around a cramped collection of campsites in the dust and boulders of Sunnyside Walk-In Campground, known in the climbing world as Camp 4. In the early days campgrounds were numbered. Camp 9 below Royal Arches was the original climbers' haunt, but since 1940, life for the climber has meant life in Camp 4, across from Sentinel Rock. Camp 4 has been home to almost all of the significant players in Yosemite climbing history. It is here that the great stories were first told. Maybe the best of these is the one about the dope-laden plane that nosed into frozen Upper Merced Lake in 1977. The pilot and passenger were dead when climbers arrived, and so they wouldn't miss their herbal cargo or the fat wad of cash that went along with it. A lot of climbers, it is said, were driving nice cars and eating regularly at the Ahwahnee for a lot of weeks thereafter.

Today Camp 4 is the same squalid, crowded, noisy place it was back in the years they call the Golden Age of Yosemite climbing. The chalk-marked lighting bolt on Columbia Boulder still points the way to the country's most famous boulder problem, *Midnight Lightning.* The bathroom sink remains clogged with Ramen noodles. Squirrels and bears still raid campsites with audacity and impunity. Barefoot kids run in the dust. Myriad languages rise over the whir of camp stoves. In the morning around eight, a lineup forms at the ranger's kiosk. Natty-haired and sleepy-eyed climbers in down jackets jockey in line to secure a three-dollar site for the next few days. A bulletin board offers "never-been-used" Sportivas for sixty-five dollars and begs a ride to Phoenix for "just me and my dog." The same scruffy groups at the same picnic tables, the same would-be Wallendas walking endlessly back and forth across a thirty-foot length of webbing strung banjo-tight between two trees, the same squirrels poking their heads out from their digs under the Columbia Boulder, and the same cheapskate sleeping 25 feet above, on top of the boulder, having climbed the tree on the back side in order to save three bucks.

Life at Camp 4 becomes a drug for many, inducing woeful apathy. Lots of bouldering. Lots of talk. Lots of plans. Not much action. For a few particularly parasitic residents, life in the Valley becomes a routine of hanging out at the cafeteria, weaseling free coffee refills by getting hold of a dirty cup left by a paying customer, working the Garden Terrace all-you-can-eat group-style (one pays, several slip in behind), targeting green cashiers at the market to claim the employees' 70 percent discount, grabbing the cookies left out for guests at the Ahwahnee. Like the bold, fat squirrels, these are a kind of park wildlife, relegated to a preserve at Sunnyside Walk-In Campground and inadvertently fed by the visitors.

Then there's life on the wall. Even the vagabond climber, once up on the big stone, acquires a purpose and a drive. This is necessarily so, for few experiences focus the attention like being high on a multiday wall, one's whole world packed in a haul bag or clipped to a tiny skyhook on a pencil-width flake.

Doin' a wall. That's what many climbers come to Yosemite for. Doin' a wall means spending a few days on high. It means wearing your palms raw from hauling gear, and wearing grooves into your arches from standing in slings. Pitches go by, oh, so slowly, while the belayer kicks back on a taut-skinned portaledge, feeding out rope every once in a while from a GriGri, listening to canned tunes or reading a mystery novel. Life on the wall blocks out everything else. It doesn't matter what day it is or whether work is piling up on your desk back at the office. You just want that bashed copperhead to hold until you can fire in a good pin above. Doin' a wall means uncertainty. It means thirst. It is the constant sky watch for killer Pacific storms, the not-quite-sleeping that they call a bivouac, and the endless hauling of the bag. It isn't like being in Patagonia, or Baffin Island, or even the Wind River Range, where the walls are big and remote. The Yosemite big-wall experience is a paradox of remoteness and proximity, miles away from the world but only hundreds of yards above the cars and lights of the valley floor.

Old trends continue and new ones begin. Some El Cap routes have been free-climbed, beginning with Paul Piana and Todd Skinner on the *Salathé Wall,* and on through Lynn Hill on the *Nose.* After repeating the *Salathé Wall* free, Germans Alex and Thomas Huber linked face-climbing variations on the North America Wall to create *El Niño.* After British teenager Leo Houlding repeated this 5.13 with relative ease, he added his own almost-free route, *Passage to Freedom,* bolting the hood ornament of an Alfa Romeo onto the cliff as a spinning handhold, one of the route's cruxes.

Things going on in the Valley today are irreverent and awesome, but this has long been the way. Steve Roper, Yosemite guidebook author and legendary route pioneer, wrote a reflective and illuminating piece for *Rock & Ice,* describing these upstarts as "unkempt kids fiddling with their earrings and listening mindlessly to what charitably might be called music. Wretched punks, I think. What do they know about climbing or life? Then I take a step back and reconsider. Yes, indeed, that kid sitting there is me, thirty years earlier."

Yosemite, the place where edges are probed, where accomplishments are scrutinized under a harsh light, where the craziness of one age becomes the standard of the next. Yosemite, even after all these years, still the heartbeat of the world's rock climbing.

NORTH TO TAHOE

But there's still more to the grand Sierra as it knifes northward. Up by Reno is the deep blue Lake Tahoe, a trendy resort straddling the

Lover's Leap

state line with Nevada. Shoreline access is locked up by wealthy property owners who circle the big lake in sport utility vehicles that seem to get bigger every year. It's an active, vital town, wrapped up in summer boating and winter skiing. It's also not a bad place to live for a climber who can afford the rent.

South of Tahoe is Lover's Leap, big and sheer, and horizontally laced with protruding dikes. The dikes aren't just part of the Lover's Leap experience; they *are* the Lover's Leap experience. Almost every route has them. Spaced about a body-length apart, and sticking out of the gray stone like elongated duck bills, they allow climbing up the steepest and most unlikely terrain. Two routes stand out: *Traveler's Buttress* and *The Line,* two of the best 5.9s in the universe. The inclusion of *Traveler's* in *Fifty Classic Climbs* ensured that it would be on every traveler's hit list. Deservedly so, with four pitches of memorable climbing, each so different from the last. The first pitch is wild, bucket-pulling up dikes so thin and sharp you well might be dismembered slamming into the wall if you fell. Above, there's a crux

5.9 off-width, avoidable by taking the "easier" 5.10 finger crack just left. The third pitch is way out there, following an exposed arête, once again possible only because of the generous dikes. Then it's child's play to the rim: an easy 200-foot dike ladder. Hard to tell whether *The Line* is named for its striking directness or from the inevitable queue at its base. Hard also to imagine a more climbable route: a 350-foot plumb-line crack on a near-vertical wall. It, too, takes good advantage of the dikes rippling across the face, but its essence is the thin crack. Two pitches up the finger-sized crack climax at an exposed 5.7 pull-over onto the rim.

On the north end of Lake Tahoe is Donner Summit, known also as the macabre site of cannibalism when the westbound Donner party was stranded by snows in the winter of 1846–47. Today, with the improved cuisine offered in town, travelers can concentrate instead on the fine granite outcrops that dot the pass, here near the northern end of the Range of Light. Donner is a worthwhile stop. The rock is excellent and easily accessible, though not as extensive as in the southern and central sections of the range. Even so, it holds an important place in the development of American rock climbing.

Mark Hudon and Max Jones, two pioneers who took free climbing to the high walls, spent a lot of time at Donner honing their crack-climbing skills. It was an effort that paid off in Yosemite when they took to the *Salathé Wall,* Mount Watkins, and Quarter Dome, audaciously free-climbing into the 5.12 range. They were among the first to envision the big-wall free climbing that is going on today. Also at Donner, Tony Yaniro climbed *Grand Illusion,* for a while the hardest climb in the world. Tahoe climbing continues today with the same energy. The scattering of granite cliffs high in the pass continues to draw crowds.

Down by the lake, quick-draws still hang all over the ceiling of Cave Rock, an odd hollow squeezed between the north- and southbound lanes of Highway 50, its access contested by Native Americans who know it to be a sacred place even though (or maybe because) it's been so hideously abused by the white man's intrusions. Deep in the cave, candles burn for Dan Osman, who established most of the routes, who would take joy in leaping from way above a bolt in celebration of the fun of climbing, who paved the floor with the blocks of debris left over from road building, even installing benches for more comfortable belaying, and who finally died up in Yosemite when a rope broke during one of his 1,000-foot dives from Leaning Tower. Cave Rock, perhaps more than any place in American climbing, brings to the surface the tension between the sacred and the temporal. The candles, the draws, the awful noise from the road below, the beauty of *tahoe,* Washoe Indian for the great and spiritual body of blue water—these beg us to speculate about ourselves, our games, and our place on earth. It is hard to do otherwise, standing in the mouth of the big cave.

True, California is a land of highways and fault lines, of sprawl and fashion. But it's also a place where climbing has deep meaning, where we can learn from the purity of Royal Robbins and John Bachar and the present-day activism of Chris McNamara, who by his early twenties had already done more than fifty routes on El Cap, but more importantly had initiated a selfless movement called the American Safe Climbing Association to clean up the litter of junk anchors on the walls of Yosemite.

John Muir first saw the Sierra in 1868 on a long walk to see the Valley of the Yosemite. Unsatisfied with the name Sierra Nevada, or "snowy range," he called it the Range of Light, "so gloriously colored and so radiant, it seemed not clothed with light but wholly composed of it, like the wall of some celestial city." Climbers who have trekked its passes, traversed its spired ridgelines, spent nights under its wide, starlit sky agree. It's a place of light and enlightenment, where the purity of the white rock is impressed upon those who go there.

Idaho's Silent City of Rocks

9 GRANITE IN SMALLER DOSES

In terms of size, Yosemite lords over the rest of America's granitic exposures. Even so, there are lots of humble outcrops elsewhere that have a passionate following. Four such places are collected here, four places that could well have been included in other chapters, but are separated from the pack because they have such striking and important identities. Each is a weird scattering of rock on a western plain, each with a personality shaped by the dual forces of the rock itself and the characters who climb there. Each draws a different kind of visitor because each offers such a different climbing experience. To the casual visitor, these rocks might look pretty much the same. But to the well-traveled climber, each stands for something distinct in the American rock climbing experience.

In the flat southeastern corner of Wyoming, the humble outcrop is called Vedauwoo, a word that means "land of the earthborn spirit" to Natives but to climbers means "home of the cruel off-width crack." West, near Idaho's border with Utah, is the Silent City of Rocks, where the white granite fortresses have grown a case-hardened skin, broken in places to form bizarre incuts, providing granite face climbing that is damn near perfection. Overnight it went from bolt-free obscurity to one of the nation's premier sport-climbing destinations. Out east a bit, in the unlikely climbing state of South Dakota, are the Needles, weirdest perhaps of any American rock. Here, behind the giant frowning faces of American presidents on Mount Rushmore, rise a series of spires that stand like bowling pins among the high evergreens of the Black Hills. And then there's Joshua Tree National Park, a fabulous collection of boulders and domes on the high California desert. It's a short drive from sprawling Los Angeles, yet its vastness absorbs the multitudes and offers solitude for anyone willing to hike a bit.

Land of the Earthborn Spirit

At some places, the myths rise bigger and more imposing than the rocks themselves. So it is at Vedauwoo, a cluster of rounded outcrops just over the Wyoming line north of Colorado's Front Range. The boys from Wyoming see the place as a Maginot Line of sorts, a rampart against the creeping civilization from Colorado. This here is crack climbing, climbing you've got to dress for. Stay home, sport

Avoiding the cracks at Vedauwoo

climbers, or you might get a run in your tights. As tales of Vedauwoo's bad wide cracks and cheese-grater surfaces seeped out, the place took on a one-dimensional persona where climbing wasn't pretty, nor was it fun. It was battle.

In truth, it's the outsider's myth that Vedauwoo is all off-width climbing. The granite bulbs that sit right off Interstate 80, sixteen miles east of Laramie, have cracks of every size, from seams to fingers, tight hands to fists. Between the cracks are numerous crystalline face climbs of the modern sport-climbing genre. There's every kind of climbing here, even for newcomers. But even with such a good variety of crack sizes, it's the daunting off-sized cracks that define the place.

Laramie is home to the University of Wyoming, and right from the start, climbers from the university began pioneering the new routes. Engineering professors Ray Jacquot and Jerry Edwards climbed one of the most prominent lines, *Edwards Crack,* in 1955. In the years to follow, as pitons gave way to nuts and, later, sophisticated wide-crack camming gear, steeper, smoother, harder climbs were accomplished. Colorado climbers, especially from nearby Fort

Collins, regularly forayed up to Vedauwoo for its cracks and cool summer breezes, but Wyoming climbers still dominated. Bob Scarpelli earned a reputation for being the area's wide-crack master, while Todd Skinner from Lander and Paul Piana of Newcastle searched out the blank walls between cracks. But all the while routes were being explored and a reputation was growing, Vedauwoo only fleetingly held the limelight, usually only when a story would seep out about a perverse and nasty off-width crack. After Jay Anderson's 1991 article in *Rock & Ice*, everyone knew the bad reputation of one particularly difficult wide crack, a crack named *Lucille.*

"A girl like that just gotta be named Lucille," George Kennedy told Paul Newman in the '70s film *Cool Hand Luke.* Leaning over their shovels from a chain gang, they watched intently as an ample young woman seductively washed her car nearby, splashing as much soapy water on her dress as on the car itself. *Lucille* is as bad as wide-crack climbing can get. Jay Anderson's first squirm up into its overhanging darkness in 1979 was his first of many tries. He placed a bolt in 1980, and broke it off in his hand in '81. On his final success in 1988, he recalled placing a number 4 Camalot where in '84 he had jammed a big Friend, the same spot he'd stuck a number 11 Hex on his first go almost a decade earlier. Sure, it could have been top-roped, he wrote, but this was the Reagan-Thatcher era, a time when one did things more conservatively. And this was Vedauwoo, where one does not tread disrespectfully upon tradition. Hard-earned *Lucille* was thought to be the world's first 5.13 squeeze chimney. Craig Luebben, one of the country's best wide-crack climbers and inventor of the tube-shaped Big Bro protection for wide cracks, repeated *Lucille* a few years later, saying it was somewhere in the 5.12 range. Grades, so easy to apply to overhanging sport climbs, fail to adequately measure perseverance and suffering.

Vedauwoo sits at a windy 8,000 feet among prairie hills of grasses and widely spaced trees. Light green dominates. The rich smell of life is in the air. In the old days, dusty roads led around and among the rocks. Today, things are much more trim, as black-topped roads and paths link tidy picnic groves among the aspens and under rock overhangs. Oldsters arrive in big campers and congregate around picnic tables nearest the rest rooms. It's a pleasant respite for a bus tour, a cool and shady stopover to get out and stretch the legs, perhaps take a tuna sandwich among friends. They huddle in quiet conversation while nearby at another table sits a group of younger folk, their hands taped white, and their CD player competing with the breezes. The climbers have come to Vedauwoo not just for the bloodbath crack climbing, nor to add high numbers to their tick lists. They come to Vedauwoo to be far away from the swarming hot crags of the Colorado Front Range and to savor the whole spectrum of granite crack climbing. Cracks everywhere, and everywhere else so many miles away.

The Needles

Up to the northeast, in the Black Hills of South Dakota, a climber is halfway up the back side of the Thimble, and right about now, he would give anything to find a crack, any crack, just someplace to put in a piece of gear. But no. Too far from the ground to retreat, he's got no choice but to continue. He digs deep into his experience of 5.10 leading, chalks up, takes a deep breath, and launches into a delicate sequence of high stepping and crystal pinching on the country's most frightening 5.3, the Thimble. Welcome to the Needles.

The Black Hills is a land of contradictions. It's a place where slender fingers of rock pierce the sky, yet where some of the best adventures aren't up the rocks, but are dark excursions through and around them. It's a place that exudes age and refuses to catch up with the frenzy of the modern world. Climbers here passionately eschew rap-bolting, believing the Needles to be a holy land where we have no right to leave a mark. It's a sentiment in crazy juxtaposition with the nation's largest rock carving, nearby Mount Rushmore. On one side of the crumpled granite landscape around the state's highest point, Harney Peak, the climbing is as clean and wild as it gets, and on the other side is the country's largest cliffside excavation, a monument to Manifest Destiny.

Long before the encroachment of white settlers the Arapaho, Cheyenne, Kiowa, and Lakota peoples were coming to the Black Hills seeking visions and self-purification. In 1886 the U.S. government signed a treaty with the Sioux, recognizing their hold on the land for all time. But the discovery of gold made the treaty little more than a piece of paper. When General George Custer's expedition surged over what the Sioux called the "thieves' road," it was clear to all that the

United States wanted the land back. After Sitting Bull and Crazy Horse met in September 1875 with a governmental commission, the U.S. officials responded by requesting a Native "head count," demanding that all Sioux report to agency headquarters to be registered. It was an impossible demand because it required traveling—children and elderly included—in the dead of winter. That February, General Sheridan moved in to round up "hostile" Sioux who hadn't checked in. Custer's Last Stand in early summer was a fleeting victory for the Sioux, who finally acceded to the pressure and signed away the land.

In 1907 the Black Hills became a national forest, and just twenty years later, the blasting began in prideful gratitude to the great men who made this country what it was: George Washington, America's first president; Thomas Jefferson, craftsman of constitutional democracy; Abraham Lincoln, stern mender of a nation split across the middle; and Theodore Roosevelt, expansionist and visionary of the country's growing place in the world. South Dakota state historian Doane Robinson called the carving "a shrine to democracy." But when someone suggested that the Needles be incorporated into the monument as a host of supportive marching Indians, one critic responded, "Man makes statues, but God made the Needles."

Climbers think upon the place with equal passion. There's something different here. Maybe it's the rock, laid out in a spooky collection of walls and spires. The biggest are the Cathedral Spires, with exciting moderate routes up to 400 feet high, routes that wander in and around the maze of ridges and gullies before topping out on some pretty spectacular summits. Right off the road are the Ten Pins, well-named towers, no more than a pitch in length. And stopping most tourists is the Needle's Eye, a name that fully captures the odd window in the slender spire. These are the main areas, but all around Sylvan Lake are tunnels and passageways, outcrops and boulders.

Up close, the rock is equally distinct. It's as coarse and crystalline as granite can get. Routes require leather skin and steel nerves, for a scraping fall here would be unthinkable. At first the crystals seem too insecure to trust, and many visitors have sampled a route or two and left for safer rock elsewhere, never to return. After a while, preferably an apprenticeship with someone who knows the nuances of the place, one learns which crystals to trust, which to avoid. The run-outs seem less suicidal and the grades begin to make more sense. Even so, like Vedauwoo, this is not a place to pad your numbers list.

Certainly, the first climbers cared little about the YDS system. After Fritz Wiessner's 1937 visit, the first "locals" were Herb and Jan Conn from Washington, D.C. The Conns had already established routes at Seneca Rocks in nearby West Virginia. Up in New Hampshire, where they had summered as children, they returned in 1945 to put up a very direct 1,000-foot 5.8 in tennis shoes, a route that was way ahead of anything yet done in the region. When the Conns arrived in the Black Hills, they found a paradise of climbing, tunneling, and scrambling, where they put up more than two hundred first ascents and left a penny atop each tower. Theirs was a cave-dwelling, idyllic lifestyle, and even into their old age, they would delight visitors with "tours" under, around, and over the complex rock garden, blending rock climbing with spelunking and hiking.

Next to leave a historic mark was renowned boulderer John Gill. Gill was the master, the first top-level rock technician, one who would crank one-finger pull-ups and do routes that the best struggle to repeat even today. His 1961 ascent of the overhanging front side of the Thimble (no, not the 5.3 back side) was one of the most significant rock-climbing achievements in the country's history, even though it's only 30 feet tall. The very committing, very hard 5.11 moves are hard to imagine even now, with sticky rubber shoes and, more important, with the removal of the guardrail below that would have made a fall even more crippling.

By now a tradition was beginning to emerge, and it became increasingly impossible to climb there without hearing the voices of climbers past, echoing around the rocks. It was a tradition strengthened in the Ten Pin area by Pete Cleveland from Devil's Lake, Wisconsin. Cleveland's outrageous routes would have made him a name climber had the Needles only been nearer to the hot spots of the East, California, or Colorado. Most notable was *Super Pin,* 5.11, in 1967. The higher he got, the more obvious it became to his belayer that a fall would be fatal, and so instead of managing the rope, Cleveland's partner simply left to get his camera. At least he'd have some purpose if Cleveland fell. On nearby *Hairy Pin,* another belayer was so horrified that he threatened to tie the rope off to a tree if Pete didn't stop to drill.

Henry Barber, missionary traditionalist from Boston, hopped on *Super Pin* in 1971, taking a different line from the unrepeated Cleveland route. He placed a piton for the crux, then ran it out, Cleveland-style, to the top. Later, after some discussion, other climbers decided to place a bolt on the upper run-out section.

If you've ever stopped on a foothold to hand-drill hard rock, you know that inscrutable process by which a foothold shrinks and slopes steadily away under your weight. At first the hold seems ample and flat. Then, as the minutes of *tap-tap-tap* go by, the foot begins to ooze off the rock. Once, friends saved Mike Todd from the disappearing foothold syndrome by racing up the formations on either side of the *Super Pin* and wrapping him against the rock with a climbing rope.

The Needles inspire lots of clever rope work like this. Cleverest is getting off the routes without leaving an unsightly sling anchor. The leader sits atop the spire, straddling the top, braced against the rock for security. When the second arrives, he wraps the rope around the leader's back as though it were a tree. The leader hugs the summit tight as the second rappels, pinning the top climber in place. Once on the ground, the second ties one end to a tree while the leader tosses the remaining end off the other side and rappels single-strand. The rope can then be pulled or flicked off, and the summit stays clean.

Many of America's best, bravest, and most prolific climbers have left their mark on the Needles: Fritz Wiessner, John Gill, Fred Beckey, Royal Robbins, Henry Barber, Bob Kamps, Kevin Bein, and Steve Wunsch among them. These marks, however, are of the cultural kind, existing only in the memory, not in any real defacement of the rocks themselves. The tourist or hiker will find no clue that the unlikely summits have been scaled unless they get to watch the crazy act themselves. Otherwise, the eerie spires stay clean.

THE SILENT CITY

Funny how some people like to leave a mark on things. There's something almost innate in humankind to want to scribe something onto any blank surface. It is tough for an urban kid to resist that oh-so-natural urge to spray his name or tag onto a bridge abutment. It's a tradition that goes way back. During the gold rush years in the early 1850s, as many as fifty thousand people passed over the Mormon

Trail, many stopping over in Idaho's Silent City of Rocks, where they would write their names on the rocks in axle grease, often as a message to those behind that they were OK. The Silent City was so odd, so memorable, that it naturally drew people as a meeting place.

Spellbound by the fantastic stone shapes, migrants would expound upon the oddities of the place in their journals. One called it a "stone village" replete with "steeples and domes." Another (perhaps the forebear of a climber?) described towers "several hundred feet high and split from pinnacle to base by numerous perpendicular cracks or fissures. Some are domelike and cracks run at different angles breaking up the large mass into huge blocks, many of which hang tottering on their lofty pointed beds." Each visitor, it seemed, was struck by the villagelike layout of the place, one likening it to "a dismantled rock-built city of the stone age."

The Silent City of Rocks remained eerily untouched in the years spanning the western migration and the explosion of sport climbing on the American scene. For years, climbers would recount tales, often second- and third-hand, about the amazing City of Rocks in deep southern Idaho. It was off the beaten track for most climbers. Idaho certainly wasn't the climbers' destination resort, especially with its hush-hush attitude about its routes. The Sawtooths got very little press, even with Elephant's Perch being one of the most impressive pieces of big granite in America. Idaho climbers kept to themselves and were content.

The most prolific visitor was Greg Lowe of the famed Utah climbing clan. Lowe thinks he might have done as many as four hundred routes during his many visits to the City. One 1965 route, the *Crack of Doom* (5.11c), might well have been the hardest climbing in America. But he kept his records to himself, and so over the years, countless others have had the pleasure of doing their own "first ascents."

Trad heritage or not, sooner or later climbers would no longer be able to resist venturing out onto the unlikely steep faces so littered with good holds. It's a granite surface that couldn't be better, and many well-traveled visitors have since described the place as their favorite in all the land. It is a favorite because of this absolutely climbable surface, where a case-hardened skin has formed, leaving chickenheads, hollows, and iron-hard incuts all over the place. Every crackless arête is a potential route. No blank face can be discounted as unclimbable.

One name is inextricably woven into the instant metamorphosis of the City of Rocks from an obscure traditional area to a sport-climbing wonderland. It was Dave Bingham who saw the potential, did many of the new routes, and spread the word. Old-time climbers, those who relished the mystique and obscurity of the place, were aghast to read in Bingham's 1990 article in *Climbing* that the City "has been transformed, almost overnight, into an international sport-climbing Mecca" resulting from "progressive and ethically open attitudes," with roadside crags "literally pincushioned with bolts, creating one of the most 'user-friendly' climbing areas this side of Buoux" in France.

Attaching a single name to such a tectonic shift is oversimplifying the evolution of the climbing. Others involved in the rapid development of the City were the traveling Todd Skinner, the colorful Jay Goodwin, and Darius Azin, who would later make his mark at Smith Rock, and later Tony Yaniro, same of *Grand Illusion*, America's hardest route in the early '80s. His *Calypso* (5.13d) was one of the hardest and best-known routes at the City, but as Tony Calderone explains in his area guidebook, every route over 5.12d is either glued or chipped. Even those embracing the new methods disagreed on the limits they ought to impose on the "creation" of new routes. Calderone explains that what made the City different from other climbing areas was the lack of a real local climbing community. Climbers came from Salt Lake City, Boise, and the Tetons, and so there wasn't a local forum for discussion on ethics, short of the numerous letters that appeared in the national magazines.

The historic landmark of the Silent City of Rocks became City of Rocks National Reserve in 1988, "in order to preserve and protect the significant historical and cultural resources; to manage recreational use; to protect and maintain scenic quality; and to interpret the nationally significant values" of the area. As a result, there is a strict management plan that allows new bolting only after an application has been approved and only if the proposed route isn't deemed detrimental to the natural or historical values of the reserve.

Though new-route exploration is limited at the City proper, climbers scored a big victory when they were granted the right to climb on nearby Castle Crags. Castle had earlier been the site of a competition in the '80s, the remote spot chosen because no one would be familiar with the routes. In the enthusiasm to hold a big event, plastic and rock holds were bolted and glued on to create routes that would please and challenge big-name climbers. Even the promoters now believe they went too far, and though the event drew huge criticism from the climbing media, it did serve as a catalyst for discussion. Castle Crags today has greatly expanded the climbing potential around the City of Rocks—a good thing because their popularity continues to grow.

Most residents of nearby Almo and Burley understand the economic benefits of having so many climbers spending time and money in their neighborhood. In fact, there's a tradition of seeking innovative ways to improve local commerce, ranging from mining to movies to the World War II–era beauty contests at Bath Rock that drew thousands of wide-eyed spectators.

Sure, the City of Rocks could well have remained deeply traditional like the Needles. Perhaps if Greg Lowe and his Steinfell Club had sought and received more acclaim, then the traditions would have been etched more deeply in the local rock and newcomers might have been hesitant to tamper. Instead, the City today is well developed and a whole lot of fun. It's no surprise that once people experienced the gratifying pleasure of latching onto one of the solid plates, frictioning up the welcoming, fine-grained white granite, and looking out from the top of one of the stone castles, the Silent City of Rocks would attract a pilgrimage of climbers hoping to leave their own message in stone, much as in the gold rush days of old.

Joshua Tree

Traveling to places like Vedauwoo, the Needles, and the City of Rocks, we tend to categorize them, give them singular definition as we focus on their salient features. In this vein, most climbers in America think of Joshua Tree National Park in the high desert east of Los Angeles as the ideal wintering spot. It's an enormous territory of smooth domes, squat walls, and overgrown boulders, home to more than four thousand routes. It is a major climbing area, with a recent and rich reputation. The routes are generally short, seldom more than

The vast scattering of rock at Joshua Tree National Park

a pitch, but there are just so many things to do there and it's so conveniently close to the megalopolis of southern California that Joshua Tree is one of the most important climbing centers in the country. Three things distinguish the place: the rock, the people, and the odd-shaped yucca plants for which the park is named. Otherwise, however, Joshua Tree resists simple definition. It's too vast. There's too much variety.

Starting with the rock itself, it helps to scramble up on one of the countless formations for a look. Begin by imagining a broad, continuous plateau of granite, the scene of many millions of years ago. In the ensuing eons, cracks would form, generally in a rectangular pattern, and into the cracks would trickle a slightly acidic rainwater that would wear away the surface, rounding the sharp edges of the block. Liken the process to the melting of a block of ice left in the sun. As it disappears, the hard corners become rounded off, and in its late stages, the block is almost ball-shaped. From your perch, you are looking at this last stage in the melting away of the granite plateau.

The widely spaced, rounded outcrops are the stubborn final chunks of what was one a massive region of rock.

This weathering process is fundamental to the climbing at Joshua Tree. Unlike the recently glaciated granite of Yosemite, the rock here has had much more time to weather. The ancient rock reflects the ages in its subtle scoops and dishes, in the coarsely crystalline surface that frictions so well but at the same time is so rough on your skin and shoe rubber. The climbing is often subtle, rounded. There are very few examples of bucket pulling, and many of the cracks are flaring and abrasive. People who have made it home know the nuances of J-Tree climbing. Visitors are often put off by its lack of angular definition.

The other natural feature that distinguishes the vast park is the Joshua tree, so human in form that on a still night, one feels in the midst of a crazed mob, tottering forward, arms contorted in the air. It's impossible not to ascribe human characteristics to the desert yucca plant. They are everywhere. And it's easy to believe the conclusion drawn by Elisha Hunt's band of Mormon colonists in 1851 when a miracle cloud blocked out the burning sun as the group approached a forest of yucca. "Look brethren! The sky is no longer like brazen brass. God has sent the clouds. It is as if the sun stood still—as Joshua commanded. These green trees are lifting their arms to heaven in supplication. We shall call them Joshua trees!" This odd cross between a bush and a tree is home to countless desert animals and thus an integral part of high-desert ecology. Some specimens are thought to be eight hundred years old.

It's a younger species, however, that dominates a spring weekend at J-Tree. They cluster like Joshua trees, around boulders and the open backs of pickup-truck campers. They too flail their arms about in wild animation. It's usually one who holds court over the others. One hand is low, down near his waist. Then the other reaches high and slaps an imaginary edge in the air. The session ends usually with the others waving their hands down at the leader in disbelief or disapproval.

Lynn Hill, who began her legendary rock-climbing career nearby at Riverside's Big Rock, says without hesitation that Joshua Tree is her favorite area. She closes her eyes and describes the smells of dust and desert bloom. It's a land of flowers and breezes, of open spaces. But it is Hollywood, she explains, that gives the climbing culture in southern California its showy confidence. One New Englander on his first visit to J-Tree had a humble rack of homemade chocks lying out by his tent, when one of the big guys strode up and kicked the rack in disbelief. "What the hell are these?" he muttered before getting into his shiny car and roaring off.

Joshua Tree National Park is so vast—1,236 square miles—that it's easy to escape the swarm of sunglasses that hang around Hidden Valley Campground and to wander forever. Even in the relatively nearby Wonderland of Rocks you can find solitude in any season, even on weekends. The visitors guide warns hikers to turn around frequently and memorize landmarks for the return. It's easy to imagine never finding your way out of such a labyrinth. They say that you can't be a local until you've done a thousand routes at Joshua Tree. There's even an informal competition among some very local climbers to gather the most routes. Several have amassed more than three thousand. Wandering is, indeed, a big part of the Joshua Tree experience.

Even with so much climbing (or perhaps because its reputation has been so pumped), some visitors don't like the place as much as they expected to. The crack climbing can be downright nasty, and tape is essential on some climbs. There's a monotony to it, as so many routes wander so featurelessly. Maybe there's even something anticlimactic about being able to hog so much climbing all in one place. But stay there and get to know it. Work on becoming, someday, a local. Like Lynn Hill, who can smell the smells even many thousands of miles away, you might find the wide desert expanses and rust and yellow rocks infusing themselves into your soul.

High in the Tetons

10 HIGH AND WILD

Five o'clock in the morning. Dark. The only sounds are the rhythmic taps of ice ax to rock and the occasional groan of boulders rolling and shifting underfoot. The whole world is in a circle of yellow light that shines from your helmet and bobs in front of your feet. The day began with the beeping of a watch and the throbbing whir of a cookstove. Thick hot coffee, plain oatmeal, a pack checked and rechecked again, just to be sure. Stuff in a frighteningly abbreviated rack and an extra lightweight rope for long, fast rappels, rain parka and pile sweater, hat and gloves, water bottle and lunch bars, batteries and first-aid kit. More gear than you want to heft—not enough to make you feel secure. The pink line over the eastern Plains thickens and glows, and as you twist off the headlamp and your eyes adjust to the new light, a jagged ridge of rock takes shape against a backdrop of dark blue.

A thousand feet below is a blue dot—your tent—but even as the distance stretches downward from your boot to the boulder field where you slept and each step takes you farther into the sky above your campsite, you seem no closer to the top. Sharp granite edges and zigzagging cracks between blocks on a ridge crest. Soft, mushy snowfields and wet rock slabs. Ledges of fresh scree. Wisps of flat clouds race by, benign in the early morning cold, but by afternoon the warm air over the Plains will raise them, darken them, ignite them with angry electricity. Uncertainty is a physical place in your stomach.

The thick margin of safety you have lived by down in the lowland crags evaporates into the thin air of the high mountains. Step behind a boulder and throw on an unanchored hip belay. Mantel with your knees on that sloping ledge because, fifty feet out from protection, burdened by clunky boots and a twenty-five-pound pack, style just isn't an issue. Move fast together, partners linked by two hundred feet of rope and the deep trust that the other won't slip on unseen ice, won't pull off a loose hold and take to the air. Yet it's still taking too long, and the ridge of rock continues to knife into the burgeoning clouds.

It's one thing to dream about, to talk about, to plan these great climbs, to imagine oneself, from the comfort of home, out on the dark north face or racing up a ragged yellow edge against the black sky. It's quite another thing to do it. There's so much more involved, so much more work, so much discomfort, so much fear. So hard are the miles of uphill hiking, thin air sapping your strength, making you dizzy and breathless. So unsettling are the route-finding dilemmas. So sickening is the droning engine noise of rocks falling past, drilling into the air below at unreal speed. You love it and you hate it, this encounter with a route you want to have done but, right now, aren't so sure you want to do.

You knew from the start, at least intellectually, that alpine rock climbing was different from lowland cragging. You understood, in a superficial way, that 5.6 could be quite serious in the mountains, where the dangers are external and lurk all around. You admitted, even out loud to friends, that the climb would tax you perhaps more than you were prepared to be taxed. But only now, out there on the mountain, hands numbed and clock ticking, do you know this deeply and fully.

Together on top. Finally. A handshake and a few quick photos. A short time to savor, but those wisps of the morning have bloomed into tall cumulus clouds. Soon the first crackle of lightning will flicker across the lacy curtain of rain fluttering in your direction. The race is on. You scurry down loose gullies and trust your weight and fate to faded old rappel slings wrapped around teetering blocks. Time hovers over all else and safety continues to be a relative thing.

Back in camp you feel older, humbled, smarter, lucky to have returned. The fear subsides, making room in your chest for a growing satisfaction. Feet sore and the frayed ends of nerves gradually weaving themselves back together, you reflect on a climb that you know has etched itself into your soul, carved grooves into your memory so much deeper than any simple rock climb. And though for much of the time you just wanted to be done with it, you now understand that today you had climbing at its best: rough granite and green lichens, lofty views of ridges and plains beyond, and a partnership welded by a shared experience.

This is alpine rock climbing. To many climbers, it's just too hard, too uncertain, too dangerous. To others, it's the ultimate expression of the game. For them, all else is mere practice for the real climbing in the extensive high mountains of America, a land with limitless places to play this alpine game.

The bony spine of the Continental Divide runs from the hot and arid mountains of New Mexico, up into Colorado and Wyoming, before hooking west through Idaho and on into the wild Canadian Rockies. This series of ranges—collectively called the Rocky Mountains—are America's alps, with climbing possibilities to last a hundred lifetimes. America's Rockies can stand proud next to the European peaks in scale, drama, and climbing potential. The only thing lacking is the domestication, the submission. There are no summit cafés atop America's alps, no cable cars, no crucifixes adorning the high points, no *via feratta,* pipes and cables that shuttle lines of fifth-class hikers upward beyond their abilities, no rude guides stepping on your rope as they pass. America's western alps offer the best of high rock climbing in a wilderness setting, alpine climbing with a cowboy flair.

There is a steady continuum of all kinds of climbing up in the western mountains, beginning with easy hiking and then harder scrambling, and on to bona fide technical rock climbing. Integrated into this continuum are the snow and ice routes. And so any discussion of so-called alpine rock climbing needs to be a selection along the lines of this continuum, and an incomplete one at that.

Alpine rock climbing can be found in almost every western state (and even in the East on New Hampshire's Mount Washington and Maine's remote Katahdin). Two major alpine rock-climbing areas—California's Sierra and Colorado's Rocky Mountain National Park—are not included specifically in this section because they've been dealt with elsewhere in this book. In this chapter, we'll trace the rugged arc of mountains from the Tetons and Wind Rivers in Wyoming, through the jagged Sawtooths in Idaho, and on into the Cascades in Washington. There, in the snowcapped volcanoes of the Northwest, the continuum from rock climbing to snow climbing is complete.

THE COWBOY STATE

Wyoming has the fewest people and some of the finest climbing in America. Near its eastern border is Devil's Tower. In the southeastern corner is Vedauwoo, within sight of Colorado's Rocky Mountains. Near the central section of the state are the limestone sport cliffs of Sinks Canyon and Wild Iris, and not too far from those, the deep granite slot called Fremont Canyon.

But really, climbing in Wyoming is mountain climbing, and the two best places, the Tetons and the Wind River Range, are, even in their proximity, as different as two ranges can be. One is a national icon, familiar even to the nonclimbing public, looming right over a busy tourist destination. The other is spread out, hidden, and outside the climbing world; few Americans would recognize the name or profile of any of the peaks. At one, it seems every handhold has been touched and probably incorporated into a well-documented variation of an earlier route named after the climbers who did it first. At the other, there's a sense of exploration. The routes are named for features, not people; you climb in the shadow of big peaks, not big names.

Every American knows the Teton Range, its familiar jagged profile a national symbol. Is there any product marketed today—from cars to cigarettes to insurance policies—that hasn't used the image as backdrop in their advertising? Usually the lineup includes the ample Middle Teton on the left, the majestic tooth of the Grand Teton in the Middle, with the jagged Teewinot and Mount Owen next in the series. Maybe it includes Mount Moran, broadest of the group, off to the right. In the foreground is the Snake River, where a lone fisherman is too immersed in the task at hand to look back at the range.

The Tetons are a small, compact range, only forty miles long and fifteen miles wide, with just seven summits exceeding 12,000 feet in elevation. You see most of the range from any single location along the flat basin called Jackson Hole. It is what mountain ranges are supposed to look like, and the jaded tourist can gobble it up in one viewing. The compactness matters to the climber as well. The highly featured rock seems made for climbing. There are few blank stretches of featureless slabs, few crumbling flanks that would deter climbers. As such, routes are jammed one right next to the other. The Grand Teton itself has thirty-eight distinct documented routes and variations.

Most of the climbs can be traced from below as well, right from the shared starting elevation of about 6,700 feet where the floor of Jackson Hole abruptly meets the block-fault uplift of the mountain lineup. The routes generally start with an hour or two of switchbacks before weaving up a ridge or entering a rounded glacial canyon. Sitting back for a rest, the climber looks out at the flat plain of Jackson Hole. The town of Jackson is off to the south, mercifully hidden by the broad, flat Gros Ventre Butte. The braided Snake River is plain to see; so is the climber's car, lined up with so many others at one of the trailheads. It's an in-your-face elevation gain, from the flats to the summits. Mallory may have attempted Everest "because it is there." The Teton Range beckons climbers because "it is *right* there."

The north-south lineup of the range is punctuated by deep canyons and good climbing within: Death Canyon, with the excellent *Snaz* and *Caveat Emptor,* both 5.10 and both among the best rock climbs in the national park; Garnet Canyon, standard approach to the Grand Teton, a busy place with troops of climbers making their way to camps below the peak; Cascade Canyon, the wide, glacially carved trough that breaches the range. This one is best approached by boat across Jenny Lake.

A Teton visit begins in the town of Jackson, where the two central images of cowboys and climbers merge into one. It's a busy, touristed town, upscale around its fringe. There are golf courses and ski areas, and Lear jets swoop in and out of the nearby Jackson Hole airport. The climber, however, sees Jackson more as a place to buy supplies or perhaps drink some beers after a hard climb. His digs are closer to the peaks, at the American Alpine Club Climbers' Ranch. Six dollars a night, on a first-come, first-served basis, will buy a bunk and a shower, but more important, it will immerse you in a society of fellow climbers. Evenings, climbers are clustered around cookstoves on a line of covered picnic tables, all within clear view of the range. One group tells a story about the pounding they took the day before as afternoon storms moved in early and turned them back from Teewinot. At the next table, a seasoned climber describes the intricate Valhalla Traverse to a newcomer who is aiming for the Black Ice Couloir. As a gathering place for climbers, the ranch is matched only by Camp 4 in Yosemite.

In the main house is a small room with a chessboard and a trove of dusty books, stacks of climbing magazines, and usually a few readers escaping the mosquitoes and the chatter at the picnic tables. It's here in the library that Teton history is most vivid. Generations of America's best climbers have sat in those same chairs, fingered those same old books. An evening spent in the reading room infuses the climbs that follow with deeper meaning. The Tetons aren't just inanimate chunks of jagged stone; they are repositories of human experience.

A brief history of Teton climbing can begin with the first undisputed ascent of the Grand by a team of William Owen, Frank Peterson, John Shive, and Frank Spaulding in 1898. Their route climbed up onto the Lower Saddle, the obvious col between the Middle Teton and the Grand, then wrapped around toward the Idaho side, linking inobvious ledges up the back side to the summit. The *Owen-Spaulding Route* is still the easiest route on the mountain, though it's dark and cold and often icy.

Paul Petzoldt, who would later found the National Outdoor Leadership School, arrived from Idaho in the early 1920s, becoming the range's most prolific climber and first professional guide. From the East came Robert Underhill and Kenneth Henderson, who climbed the East Ridge, and then in 1931 came the bold first ascent of the most prominent line on the mountain by teenaged Glenn Exum. The *Exum Ridge* remains the best and most popular easy route on the mountain. Climbers today can choose from a more difficult direct start, or they can follow Exum's example and traverse out the wide, sloping Wall Street ledge and make a committing hand traverse (Exum leapt here) over the void and onto the golden rib. Over the years, many of the country's top climbers would leave their mark on the mountain and the rest of the range: Yvon Chouinard, known more for his achievements on Yosemite big walls, climbed extensively here. So did Fred Beckey, Jack Durrance, and, more recently, Jeff Lowe and Alex Lowe. Teton climbers would go on to make even more significant marks on mountain ranges worldwide.

The Tetons are a worked-over range, and with most of the obvious lines already completed, climbers there have developed a kind of cramming to enhance what has, for some, become a very familiar piece of real estate. Speed records are kept and continually challenged. Exum guides on a free day might be off on a trail run that circles the range. Long multipeak traverses also add to the adventure. Alex Lowe once linked all the major summits—Teewinot, Owen, the Grand, Middle, and South Tetons, Cloudveil Dome, and Nez Perce—for what is known as the Grand Traverse. More than 12,000 feet of elevation gain and more than thirteen miles of hiking and climbing, expedited by what he called "tanktop-and-running-shoe tactics." It wasn't the crux 5.7 *North Face* of the Grand, however, that took its bite out of Lowe. Instead it was a stumble on the summit of Middle Teton that landed Lowe on his butt on a sharp rock. He finished the marathon in eight hours and fifteen minutes, even as the blood poured down his leg and crusted on his shorts.

Alex Lowe was only one of the many top climbers who have lived and guided in the Tetons. The ever-present aura of veteran climbers is obvious to all who venture up the Garnet Canyon on their way to the Lower Saddle, as guided parties seem to be everywhere. Exum's guide service, located right down by Jenny Lake, is one of the nation's oldest and most respected, and it does a huge business. Beginners are taken to smaller crags at the foot of the range, where they learn the basics before heading out with relatively light packs to the shelters up on the Lower Saddle. Sleeping bags and stoves wait for them at camp.

The guided parties are usually well up near the summit before the regular folks arrive, so their presence doesn't clog things up too badly. But descent options from the Grand are few, and there can be an irritating traffic jam at the rappel station when groups converge. The normal rappel route is more than 100 feet, overhanging for most of the way. Guides will often let other parties share their ropes, and on a sunny day, it's not so bad to sit and rest and take a drink until the rappel slings are clear. When the clouds move in, however, it's a different scene altogether, as every one of the fifty or so people on the mountain knows he is sharing a spot on the state's biggest lightning rod. Guide Tim Toula recalls a day when he spied a tiny black cloud way out over the Idaho hills. He watched it zero in on the Grand, as if it had sinister intent. As it neared, climbers all over the mountain scrambled toward the few main rappel points, like ants back toward their hole at an approaching footstep.

This is a busy and well-chronicled mountain range. But on a clear day, one can look out over Jackson Hole toward a more extensive, wilder, lesser-known gem, the Wind River Range. Here, one doesn't simply drive in from town and park at the foot of the escarpment. The summits don't loom tight over the town or road. Just to get to the base of a climb can take an hour on a dirt road and a day of hiking. All around are broad, gray walls of granite, so different from the jagged relief of the Tetons.

The location and topography help to determine the essential character of the climbing experience at any mountain range. Summits beckon in the Tetons. Right from their foot the jagged points beg to be climbed. Routes are the draw in the Winds. Many of the peaks are broad on top, accessible to hikers. The summit of Haystack, for example, is almost a mile long and a half-mile from the top of a technical route. Domestic sheep graze the summits of Warbonnet and the Warriors, yet from a camp below their steep faces that rise above a glacial cirque, they seem as inaccessible as Patagonian towers.

Legends loom over the Tetons. The unknown prevails in the Winds. A list of route names says a lot: On the Grand alone you'll find the Beckey Couloir, the Underhill Ridge, the Owen-Spaulding Route, the Exum Ridge, the Petzoldt Ridge, the Durrance Ridge, the Stettner Couloir, the Buckingham Buttress, and so on. On Gannett Peak, the highest mountain in the Wind Rivers, the routes are called the East Face Left and the East Buttress Right, the Northeast Ridge and the North Face, the North Ridge and the North Shoulder, the West Face and the West Couloir. In the Tetons there's history; in the Winds there's adventure.

Joe Kelsey, in his guidebook *Hiking and Climbing in the Wind River Mountains,* sets the tone that this essence of the Wind River Range is "largely protected from climber and hiker abuse by not affording an individual the opportunity to gain riches or fame, or a stage on which to demonstrate gymnastic prowess or fashionable sportswear. There isn't much reason to make the effort to visit the Wind Rivers unless you believe in something—something encompassed, however imprecisely, by the term wilderness." Kelsey even relegates first-ascent data to the back of the book, "dispelling the notion that Wind River accomplishments lead to fame. A name in the first-ascent list is much like a name in a telephone directory," he writes. While Teton climbs are made in the shadows of legends, Wind River ascents are enjoyed in the shadows of deep valleys and broad walls of granite.

The Wind River Range is long, running down the Continental Divide for more than one hundred miles, from Route 26 near Dubois to South Pass south of Lander. In the northern end of the range is Gannett Peak, at 13,804 feet topping the Grand Teton as the state's highest by 34 feet. It's a broad, glacier-clad mountain, attracting more summit baggers than technical rock climbers, who generally aim for the drier rock in the southern end of the range. West is Squaretop, a massive, barrel-shaped monolith that dominates the view from the Green River Lakes trailhead. The range continues southeast along the

Divide: hundreds of lakes and hundreds of summits dotting a topography that is a study in glacial geomorphology.

The biggest wall in Wyoming is found on the north face of Mount Hooker. Here are real Grade VI climbs, multiday affairs that require all the Yosemite big-wall skills and gear, but in a darker, colder, lonelier environment. Hooker was first climbed in 1964 by Royal Robbins, Dick McCracken, and Charlie Raymond. It's a big, intimidating wall that gets more acclaim than other Wind River peaks but, given its difficulty, one that won't likely see too much traffic. The distinction of busiest place will probably remain the Cirque of the Towers, where the highest concentration of classic routes draws the highest concentration of climbers. Even though one can find a lot more solitude and adventure elsewhere in the range, it's hard to resist the familiar lineup of Pingora (included in *Fifty Classic Climbs):* Wolf's Head, Shark's Nose, and the Warriors.

Although there is little tradition in trumpeting the climbs of the Wind River Range, there is a growing pressure on the resource from an increasing number of hikers, horse packers, and sheep ranchers. Incredibly, while climbers tenting in the cirques below the peaks work conscientiously to reduce their impact, hundreds of dirty, bleating sheep mow the nearby alpine lawns to golf-course length. While careful hikers tread gently on rocks in an effort to stay off the vegetation, horse packers stomp trails into ankle-deep wallows of mud-and-manure soup. It's a scene incongruous with our idea of wilderness, but it's one well within the legal guidelines of the 1964 Wilderness Act, the legislation that questions a rappel sling but grants broad privilege to the mining, logging, and ranching industries. Such interests are especially attracted to the particular qualities of the Wind River Range. In the Tetons, the terrain is just too steep and the area too limited; in the Cascades of Washington, the valleys too choked with jungle or glaciers. Though relatively remote, the Winds still invite weeklong backpack trips, groups of schoolkids on summer trips. And the topography allows easy movement of ranch animals up the broad valleys and across the flatter passes. In fact, where else would one find such warnings on the hiking maps that a particular divide is "impassable to livestock"?

After driving twenty or more miles on dirt roads and hiking in another full day to get to camp, climbers aren't likely to scamper up

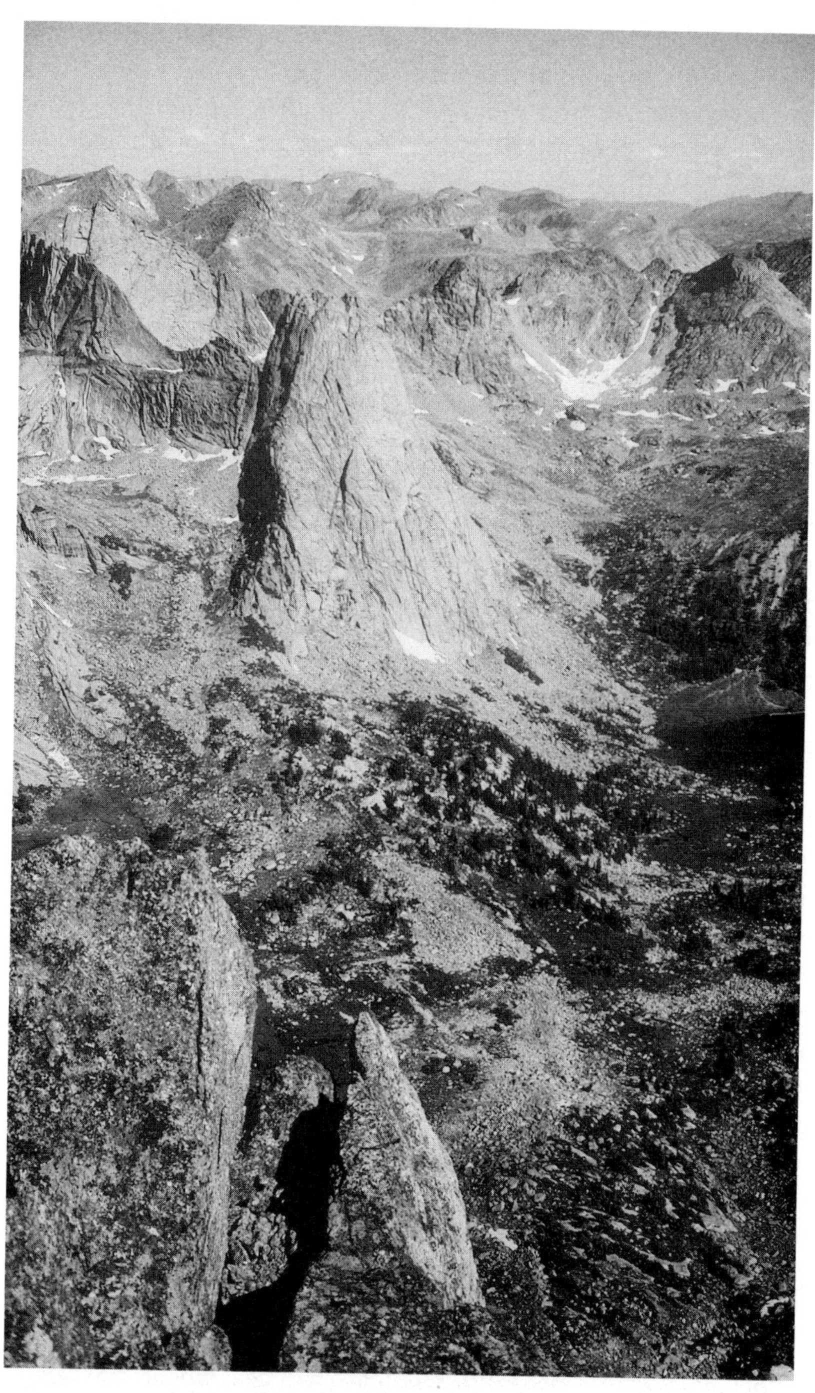

Endless exposures of granite in the Wind River Range

a single route and leave. No, they settle in, savoring the changing light and dropping temperatures of evenings, waking up when the sun turns the tips of the peaks pink and a warm cup of coffee tastes so good. One goes to the Tetons and climbs there. In contrast, one enters the Winds and lives there, if only for a few days. The climbing might be the best part of the Wind River experience, but still it's only a part of it. Kelsey worries that climbers today might be "less adventurous, seeking difficulties perhaps, but not surprises." Such climbers ought to avoid the Wind Rivers, a range cherished for its secrets.

More Secrets

The ranges of Wyoming dip and snake their way into Montana, another mysterious wilderness climbing region. Even with energized climbing communities, especially around the university towns of Bozeman and Missoula, little word seeps out about Montana rock. In fact, many will deny that there's much good rock climbing in the state. There's good alpine adventure down by the Wyoming border in the Beartooth Range, dominated by the state's highest summit, Granite Peak. And off to the west, the Bitterroots make up the rumpled line separating Montana from Idaho. There, on the steep granite buttresses of Blodgett Canyon, are Grade V rock climbs available to anyone willing to hike a few miles and slog an hour up a steep approach talus. Blodgett first gained national attention in John Harlin's *Climber's Guide to North America.* Harlin reasoned that because access was so convenient and route documentation so extensive, the inclusion wouldn't be giving away any secrets. This is true. And besides, Blodgett Canyon isn't the kind of place that is going to be overrun by top-ropers and camp groups. The biggest impact probably comes in the form of partying teenagers from nearby Hamilton or the awful forest fires of the summer of 2000.

Tight lips aren't limited to Montana. Idaho, too, has a lot more to offer than the potatoes and the City of Rocks, but you'd never know it talking to some of the coy veterans around Ketchum. At the Elephant's Perch climbing shop, you won't find a guidebook for the big chunk of rock of the same name. They've watched other places go public, they've witnessed the mess that often accompanies popularity. And they don't want it to happen here in Idaho. Route descriptions stay safe in a big notebook kept in the store. (Xerox copies? No, you can only have one at a time. Take this one and come back for another when you've gotten off the climb. Oh, you're a writer? Give it back.)

The climbing in the Sawtooth Range doesn't get much national publicity, but that's not to say there isn't a rich history in the region. The most prolific mountain rambler of the 1920s was "Two Gun" Bob Limbert, who built the Redfish Lake Lodge, today's starting point for many climbs. Then, in the next decade, two events ensured the Sawtooths' place as a climbing center. First was a visit by the traveling Underhills, who had heard tales of the jagged granite peaks, a bit like those they loved in Chamonix. The other big event in the opening of the region was the nation's first big ski resort, at Sun Valley, and the arrival of several guides from Europe. The most influential was Louis Stur, whose line up Mount Heyburn is one of the region's undisputed classics.

A climb of the *Stur Chimney* is a good way to grasp the essence of Sawtooth climbing. First, the mountains are not all that big. From below, Mount Heyburn might look huge and imposing. But in fact, the technical section of the route is less than 200 feet long. Compared to the big climbs in other American alpine areas, the Sawtooths are modest peaks. Second is the nature of the rock, the best and the worst of granite right next to each other. One section might be perfect, Sierra-like granite. Right next to it the rock will look more like packed gravel.

From Redfish Lake, where for a small fee climbers can ferry most of the four-mile approach to the "transfer camp," or better yet from a bivouac up in the Bench Lakes below Mount Heyburn, it's easy to understand why the Underhills focused as much on the wilderness as on the climbing itself. The forests are rich and green, the lakes blue. The topography is rugged; these are truly sawtooth mountains.

For pure, high-end rock climbing, the Elephant's Perch has no peer in Idaho. More than 1,000 feet high, steep and cleaved with long, hard crack systems, the Perch has long attracted some of the country's best climbers, and still does. There's only one climb for regular folks: the *Mountaineer's Route,* with seven pitches of moderate but exposed crack and face climbing up to 5.9. The big routes, however, aren't for those regular folks, climbs like *Astro-Elephant,* a ten-pitch 5.10 put up by Dave Hough and prolific Idaho climber Reid Dowdle, and the twelve-pitch *Beckey Route,* originally aided by Fred Beckey and now free at 5.11. Climbs on the Perch begin at Saddleback Lakes. One visit and it's easy to understand why Idaho climbers are so guarded about the place. The high orange granite wall reflects in the still waters of a tiny lake. Alpine flowers color the meadows. It's a fragile place, a place too close to the road to protect it. Visitors need to be gentle.

THE CASCADES

Way north and west of the Sawtooths and the Tetons and the Winds is the Cascade Range of Washington State. Here, the spectrum of alpine climbing in the Lower 48 merges into the snow and ice ascents of the big Pacific volcanoes. With an oceanic plate diving under the continental plate of North America, the region is alive with volcanic and seismic activity. Every American knows the profile of the mighty Rainier, just as most of the older ones remember May 18, 1980, when Mount St. Helens blew its top, killing fifty-seven people, devastating the landscape, and loosing a cloud of dust on cities like Yakima, where drivers had to keep their headlights on all day and home owners shoveled ash from their walks like so much fallen snow.

Reticent local climbers aren't necessary to protect the Cascades. The cause is taken up instead by a confederacy of mosquitoes, brush-choked gullies, crevasse-gridded glaciers, and weeklong deluges. Even with Seattle and its energetic climbing culture so near, and even with a steady reporting of routes, the backcountry of the Cascade Range is well girded against crowding and abuse.

Its position so far north and so close to the Pacific coast makes the Cascade Range unique in the country. Tree lines are low, and so even with modest elevations, the environment is decidedly alpine. Other than the volcanoes, no Cascade summit exceeds 9,600 feet above sea level. In Colorado, climbers *live* at those elevations. The main effect of its location, however, comes in the form of weather. Moist air riding inland off the Pacific rises over the first mountain barriers, cooling, then dumping huge amounts of rain and snow on the western flanks of the mountains. When the air masses drop over the range eastward, they warm up and dry up. It might be pouring rain at Index just east

Idaho's Stur Chimney

of Seattle, but two hours farther east, near the town of Vantage, climbers are stemming hot, dry basalt columns under a desert sun at Frenchman Coulee. This rain-shadow effect is the controlling weather phenomenon in all the West, but it is exaggerated in the Cascades where the western mountains are so high, the ocean so close, and the prevailing winds so steadily moving the wet air masses eastward.

Thus the Cascade region is known for its deep snows and deep forests, its glaciers and its jungled ravines. The approach is often the crux of alpine routes there, and it takes a certain kind of temperament to enjoy such an experience. Cascade climbers look south at Colorado, and say those guys don't have to work hard enough to get a route. Newcomers are welcomed with the wry prediction that "if you can last two seasons, you'll probably make it."

At first look, the Cascade region is a chaotic, crumpled landscape of deep green forest and slender fingers of rock. The only discernible pattern is the western lineup of volcanoes that starts in California at Lassen Peak and Mount Shasta and continues past Oregon's Crater Lake, Three Sisters, and Mount Hood and on into Washington, where St. Helens and Adams and Rainier and Glacier Peak and finally Baker lead into the Canadian Rockies to the north. Rainier is by far the biggest peak in the range and the number-one objective for many American peak baggers. At 14,410 feet, it's just shy of California's Mount Whitney, but while the latter is a low-angled stroll, Rainier is a mini-expedition, including route finding, glacier travel, and of course the whims of northwestern weather. One look at the peak, and it's obvious why Rainier climbers and guides have been America's most successful Himalayan climbers. There is no other place outside Alaska where American climbers can find so harsh a mountain environment.

North of Rainier is the extensive but lesser-known bulk of the Cascade Mountains. It is a huge wilderness area, breached east-west by only four highways. Though neither roads nor river valleys break up the area into true topographical entities, Fred Beckey's research into the range is so extensive that he needed to divide the areas into three separate volumes for his Cascade guide. The guidebooks are at odds with what climbers suppose this legendary Beckey to be. Fred Beckey is, without a doubt, the most prolific first-ascent climber in North American history. Over a career that began in the 1930s (and is still going strong), Beckey has ferreted out routes all over the Northwest, the desert Southwest, the Sierra, the Sawtooths, and the Tetons. The quintessential Beckey that climbers envision is a small man, standing in a phone booth (he knows everybody and has no trouble digging up a partner). In his hand is a black book—*the* black book—of routes he's done and routes to do.

Everybody has a Beckey story. Everest climber Geoff Tabin's is typical. They were at a bar, when Fred remarked that the partially clad dancer had one heck of a good body, would probably make one heck of a rock climber. Even in the face of stern rules that prohibited clients from speaking to the performers, he somehow summoned the girl to their table and made plans to pick her up the next day for a climb. The burly bouncer who tossed Beckey and Tabin out into the street didn't seem to understand Beckey's explanation that they were just making plans to go rock climbing.

Stories like this are hard to envision while reading Fred Beckey's guidebooks. Here, he avoids the trite puns and clever innuendo that is so common to guidebooks, a trait that Ed Webster attributes to the British. In contrast, Beckey's works are encyclopedic, scholarly, impressive textbooks on the natural and human history of the place. But in his *Cascade Alpine Guide* he explains that "in Britain there is an unusually high standard of accuracy in guidebooks, for it is usually feasible for an author to either climb a route or get a consensus view. In the Cascades, a wilderness range not yet fully explored, the standards of Britain (or even the Alps) are impossible to attain at this time." Between climbs, Beckey might be found in a library doing research, trying to fill those gaps. That is, if he's not in a phone booth.

Just north of Interstate 90 is the Stuart Range, in many minds the best of alpine Washington state. The sign on the highway calls Mount Stuart the greatest single mass of exposed granite in the United States. From Stuart (9,415 feet), the range knifes northeast past Dragontail and Colchuck and Prusik Peak (one of the most alluring alpine rock climbs in the country) and on to the Cashmere Crags, a vast collection of spires, all good scenic rock climbs. As good as the climbing is, maybe best of all is simply being up there on the Edward Plateau or at the Enchantment Lakes. Dotting the high meadows are glacial scoops filled with meltwater, a fabulous place. The Stuart Range is very close to Leavenworth and the popular cragging at Icicle Creek

Canyon but, typical of Cascade climbing, it doesn't loom right over town. Instead it hides a bit, shows itself only to those willing to beat it up one of the steep drainages above Icicle Creek. One approach from Icicle Creek leads under Snow Creek Wall, biggest crag by far in the valley. Here, mountain goats eye climbers aggressively, waiting to lick the salt from their urine.

To rain-soaked climbers in the Seattle area, a trip over Stevens Pass on Route 2 to Leavenworth offers a good chance of finding bluer skies. There, they might try Icicle Creek or Peshastin Pinnacles, or if this doesn't work, stay on the road all the way to Vantage, deep in the arid rain shadow of the big peaks. Leavenworth is, well, quite a place. In a concerted and relatively recent effort to give the town an edge in the tourist market, Leavenworth adapted the Bavarian theme, from the shop decor to the street-side accordion player in leather shorts. But even good things need to be served up in moderate doses. Mark Twain said that when he first got to Rome, he was sorry Michelangelo had died, but after a few months there, was sorry he didn't get to see him do it.

North of Leavenworth is another vast chunk of mountain wilderness that runs all the way to the North Cascades. Route 20, which links Mazama and the coast, splits North Cascades National Park into two sections, and since its opening in 1972 has given easy access to some of the most majestic rock in the country. This is Washington Pass, the best-known climbing destination outside the volcanoes, especially with the inclusion of *Liberty Crack* in Steck and Roper's *Fifty Classic Climbs.* When Fred and Helmy Beckey first visited the Early Winter Spires in the 1940s, they did so only after a sixteen-mile approach. Today, the incredible peaks line up right over the road. As such, their popularity is no surprise. The Early Winter Spire group offers a superb not-too-alpine, not-quite-big-wall climbing experience. Routes up to 1,200 feet long with grades as low as 5.6 snake their way up good solid granite, and unlike so much of the Cascade Range, the climbing here requires no glacier travel, no compass, and no overnight gear. In fact, many of the rappels are from trees. Washington Pass lies just above Mazama, a little mountain town where people have come to play, whether at the newly developed sport crags, on the nearby alpine rock routes, or on backcountry skis all around the Methow River Valley.

With the roads that now cut through the mountains and with the development of sport climbing in places like Frenchman Coulee, the Cascades are one of the most complete climbing areas in the country. Within a few hours' drive from Seattle, one can find Yosemite-like granite on the steep walls above Index, bolt-protected sport climbing at Vantage, and big-mountain glacier climbing on the volcanoes. But the real Cascades climbing experience combines almost all the elements of climbing. It is relying on a compass and being able to discern just which tiny circle on your map is the spire you seek and which subtle curved line is the correct drainage, and clawing your way for hours up a steep ravine through and on top of a conspiracy of slide alders and devil's club. Cascade climbing is keeping an eye on the weather, not so much for the electrical storms that drive Colorado climbers crazy, but instead for the inevitable downpour. It is glaciers and vegetation and the exhilaration of emerging onto a high tableland for that first look upon a granite tower.

Playing the Alpine Game

An old trad climber recently complained in an Internet chat that he had heard someone refer to a "rack of quick-draws." Wasn't this an oxymoron? he asked. For someone who has been trained in lowland crag climbing, taking to the higher mountains requires some big shifts in thinking. One eastern climber explained his first experience in the Tetons. "We did everything right," he said. "We roped up early, and we belayed all the hard sections." And they got stuck on top in a horrific lightning-and-snow storm at 2:30 in the afternoon while all the "careless" and faster parties were safe on the trail, nearing their cars.

The decisions about how to approach an alpine rock climb begin right from the initial preparation stage. The Tetons, the Wind Rivers, the Sawtooths, and the North Cascades—these are mountains, not crags, a reality both obvious and profound. For the rock jock, the transition to alpine rock climbing is huge. There's new thinking to be done about what to bring and how fast to move. Craggers who carry a big rack, overprotect every pitch, and set up textbook belays frequently spend nights out on the mountain. The approach alone demands more than many are willing to invest. Typically in most alpine settings, a climb is a two- or three-day affair. Day one holds the long hump in and the high bivouac; day two, the predawn start, the climb and the descent, the gathering of gear, and the exhausting knee-buckling, foot-flattening, shoulder-sagging return. Yes, in Washington Pass or even in the Tetons, there are alpine day trips. But remember, at the other end of the spectrum—the Picketts in the North Cascades, for example—a single climb could consume a week.

Because efficiency is so linked to safety, priorities rearrange themselves. Instead of working out the textbook equalized and redundant anchor, you might just stuff in a piece or two and shout "on belay," relying not so much on the gear as on the security of your position. Why, for instance, do you need any anchor at all when you can position yourself behind a good block on the opposite side of a ridge crest from your second? Alpine rock climbing is setting up anchors quickly, knowing when to simul-climb, and making transitions as fast as possible, never being idle at a belay. You can snack, pee, put on a jacket, loosen your shoes—all the while feeding out the rope. Just be ready to start climbing the moment you feel the tug of a belay from above.

And just as important as it is to move quickly uphill, so is it vital to be able to make a safe retreat. With an eye on the watch and the weather, the savvy alpine climber is making continuous calculations and, when the numbers no longer add up, this climber is quick to turn around and escape with a plan that's been in formulation since the first light of day.

One of the maxims about American climbers is that, when picking out a line on a steep mountain, those from the Northwest will find a ribbon of snow or ice while the rest will seek out a dry rock ridge. From the Rockies down in Colorado, where the summer climbing is actually high-altitude rock climbing, up through Wyoming and Idaho and Washington, where the routes involve more mixed climbing, combinations of snow and ice and rock, the nature of the game merges from gymnastic athleticism to big-boot mountaineering. Rather than choosing between the two, a lot of America's best climbers say that the best joy comes when there's one foot on rock and the other on ice.

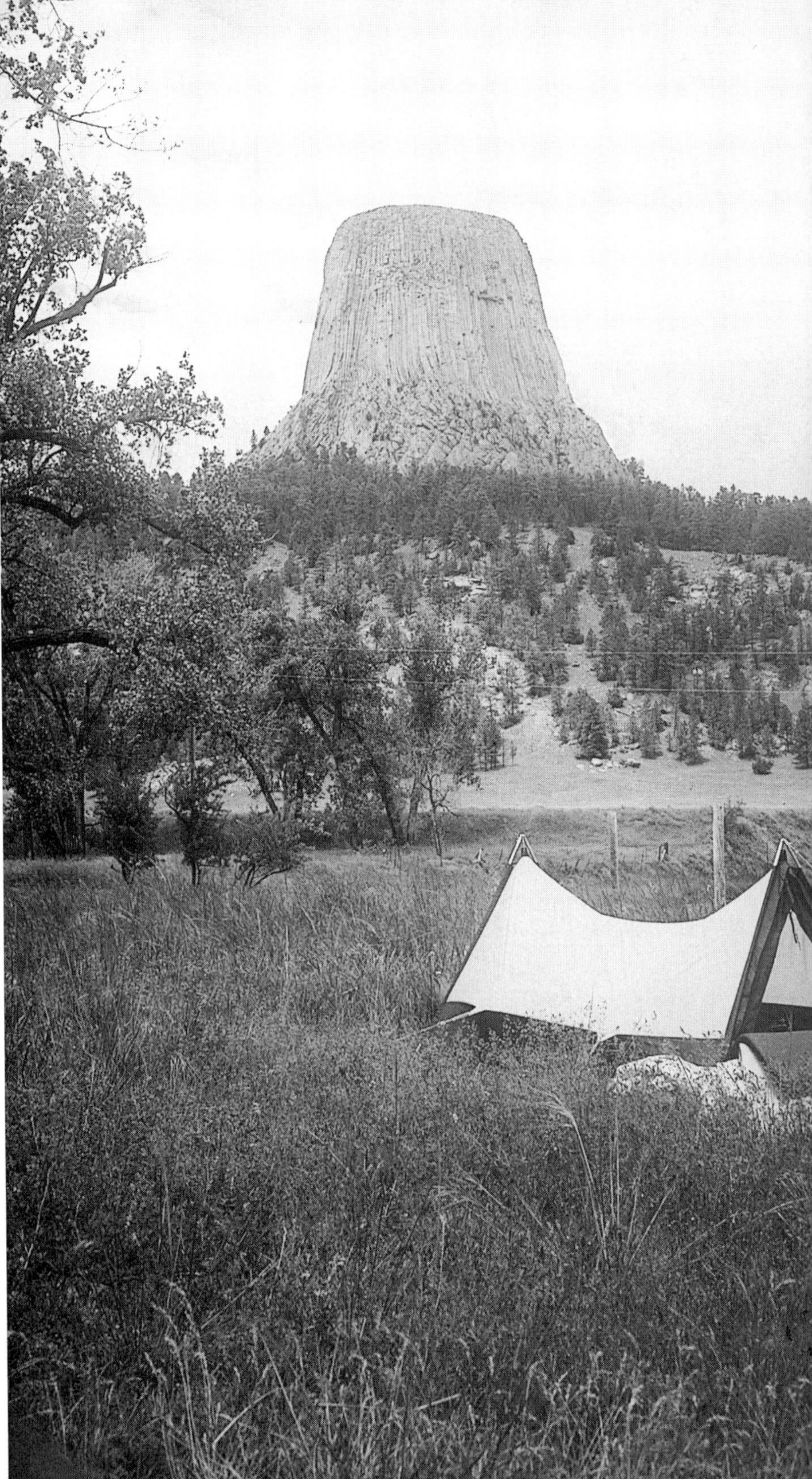

11 CHERISHING THE RESOURCE

Devil's Tower, a spiritual place

Yellowstone National Park was dedicated in 1872 "as a pleasuring ground for the benefit and enjoyment of the people." So began a distinctly American movement of setting aside wilderness areas from development, a movement that by the year 2000 had spread around the globe to include more than twelve hundred parks and preserves in more than one hundred countries. In 1916 Yellowstone was included in the broader National Park Service Act "to conserve the scenery and the natural and historic objects and the wild life therein for the enjoyment of the same in such a manner and by such means as will leave them unimpaired for the enjoyment of future generations." Consider such statements of mission carefully, for in the juxtaposition of the noble concepts of conserving land "unimpaired" and using land "for the enjoyment of the people" lies the roots of the struggle over access for climbers and other users of American wilderness.

American rock climbing faces a crisis like never before. As the number of wilderness users increases, so grows the pressure to save lands from the ravages of overuse. For climbers, the threat runs all the way from regulating fixed anchors in some areas to banning climbing altogether in others. The issue is real and its outcome vital to the future of American climbing. Though skirmishes are being fought on a state and local level, the war itself is being waged on federal lands, as three huge agencies, the National Park Service, the National Forest Service, and the Bureau of Land Management, each buffeted by political winds well beyond the scope and control of small-fry recreational users like rock climbers, work to establish policies designed to protect public lands from abuse. In the end, it's likely that the models set on the federal level will be those followed by state and city parks.

No one, save for the most ardent libertarian, disputes the need for governmental regulation of public lands. Free-for-all development would have exhausted the supply of recreational wilderness years ago had there not been strong environmental protections. Climbers support such laws. Yet every recreational user, from the angler to the rock climber to the motorist, degrades to some extent the very wilderness we all claim to cherish, and so there is an understandable ambivalence in climbers about the way they ought to use the land.

For a while, within the climbing community itself, there grew a philosophical rift between so-called sport-climbers, those who saw climbing as an athletic endeavor made possible by a proliferation of drilled anchors, and traditional climbers, those who sought cleaner ways to meet a mountain on its own terms. In retrospect, the Great Ethics Debate over bolting in the 1980s will be remembered as a spurious dichotomy, however. In fact, there really weren't deep divisions between these two groups; even the dyed-in-the-wool trad climber took good advantage of drilled anchors and left rappel slings for descent, and almost universally, sport-climbers showed a deep sense of environmental responsibility in the way they disguised or limited drilled anchors and vigorously eschewed any alterations to the rock. It's unfortunate that the two groups pitted themselves against each other while the real issue lurked unacknowledged just beyond, because it isn't the number of bolts or the manner in which they were installed that is at issue. No, it is the actual right to use public lands for climbing, for a sweeping prohibition of fixed anchors would be a de facto climbing ban. Big-wall climbing in Yosemite? A thing of the past. Routes that don't reach a summit descent trail, but end instead where the good rock degenerates into bad? Sorry. Either force your way to the top or stay off the climb. Classic traditional ascents of Devil's Tower, the Grand Teton, or any other peak involving a technical descent? Nope. You can climb, but you can't come down. And what about those times you're high on a route and either the weather looks threatening or you just don't feel right about continuing? Without the option of fixed anchors, you won't even get the latitude offered motorists on the interstate sign that says "no stopping except for emergencies." It's a misconception to describe the fixed-anchor ban as an effort to stem the grid-bolting at the roadside crag. No, in an awful irony, the anchor ban in wilderness areas targets traditional adventure climbers, a group deeply committed to the preservation of the planet.

Access issues are varied and complex. Some revolve around fears of legal liability on private or municipal properties. Others reflect the competing interests for limited space, like the cliff closures for raptor nesting or the ban on climbing near scenic trails. Sometimes archaeological or religious values outweigh the public's right to recreation.

Chief representative of the climbers is the Access Fund, born of the American Alpine Club's Access Committee in 1989. Since that time it has enlisted the backing of most of the outdoor industry, including retailers, climbing gyms, and major climbing publications, in addition to a growing membership of individual climbers. It's very effective, taking a two-track approach. First is raising the awareness of climbers to behave responsibly, to accept their stewardship of the lands they use. A big part of this they call minimum-impact climbing, limiting bolts, treading gently on carefully chosen paths around the crags, and working cooperatively with land managers and other interest groups. From this position of strength, the Access Fund can achieve its real mission, "Preserving America's Diverse Climbing Resources."

On the federal level, access really boils down to how we interpret a single act of Congress, the Wilderness Act of 1964. It is a historic piece of legislation designed to protect the country's vital wilderness areas, stating that "except as necessary to meet minimum management requirements for the administration of the area for the purpose of this Act (including measures required in emergencies involving the health and safety of persons within the area), there shall be no temporary road, no use of motorized vehicles, motorized equipment or motorboats, no landing of aircraft, no other form of mechanical transport, and no structure or installation within any such area." In its initial concept, the Wilderness Act of 1964 nobly ensures for future generations that wild places will exist and acknowledges the *idea* of wilderness as integral to American culture. But like all law, its interpretation and application are subject to debate.

Of particular interest to the climber is the phrase "structure or installation." If fixed anchors fall into this definition, then all bolting in wilderness areas is in direct violation of the law. It's unlikely that the crafters of the legislation had three-eighths-inch bolts, widely spaced and invisible to all but the users, in mind when they wrote those words. Nor is it likely that they feared a half-inch webbing sling draped over a horn on a remote mountain ridge. The law, however, in its strictest interpretation would make both the bolts and the sling a crime.

Although the original legislation failed to define "structure" or "installation" for the climber, it did allow for some noteworthy exceptions. Specific exceptions allowed trails, bridges, signs, and outhouses "for administrative and safety purposes and so . . . admissible under the Wilderness Act." There were even provisions for logging and grazing, all in keeping with Congress's goal to manage "the public lands and their various resource values so that they are utilized in the combination that will best meet the present and future needs of the

American people." These concessions probably made sense in the halls of Washington, D.C., but to the climber who reaches a summit ridge in the wild Wind River Range and is greeted by the stink and noise of hundreds of domestic sheep ravaging the alpine grasses at 11,000 feet, the logic of the law seems secondary to the reality that some interest groups have friends in high places and some don't.

Seen next to other users of wilderness, the rock climber's impact is hardly significant. Even in the climbing Mecca of Yosemite National Park, backpackers and climbers number only a tiny percentage of the total recreational users. And because chalk and bolts are nothing relative to the impact of highways, campgrounds, golf courses, and hotels, climbers need not berate themselves too harshly for their role in the plague. All the bolts at Rifle, Colorado, according to *Climbing* magazine's Michael Kennedy, wouldn't fill a five-gallon bucket. The real issues facing land managers are development, mining, grazing, logging, damming rivers, and building roadways into pristine areas; yet even so, there's a lens currently focused on the impact of rock climbers, and the way things play out in the next few years will have long-lasting impacts on the sport.

As bureaucrats argue about the meaning of "installation," so do all of us wrestle with the definition of "wilderness," a term so liberally applied, yet so relative in its meaning. Usually we describe areas as being wild not because they are untouched by man, but because relative to surrounding areas they encompass a nature closer to the way it was before man's arrival, a nature that exists more in our collective memory than in actuality. Most of the northeastern and northwestern woodlands described as wilderness are actually second- and third-growth forest reclaimed after logging or fire. Users of this forest know down deep that every acre has been explored, but it still feels good at least to call it wilderness and to imagine being the first one there.

Bill McKibben, in *The End of Nature,* argued that nature as we have classically defined it actually exists today only as a romantic memory. Nothing on the planet exists in a true natural state, as shifts in global temperature and alterations to oceanographic and atmospheric chemistry have rendered even the most remote regions of the world affected. According to McKibben, wilderness remains, however, a concept important to humanity far beyond its recreational or commercial potential. We preserve wild lands, not just because we

Below the sunlit wall of To Bolt or Not to Be, *America's first 5.14, this puzzling description of "clean climbing" describes installing bolts to "preserve" the rock. Wilderness philosophy is rife with such internal contradictions.*

wish to use them recreationally or hope to preserve an ecosystem for another creature, but also because we cherish the *idea* that such places exist. We might never visit the wilds of Alaska or see a peregrine falcon take flight, but our lives are richer knowing that the grizzly bear still reigns supreme in an unspoiled northern forest and that the hunter bird flies free.

The unique human history of America left its citizens the opportunity to think about wilderness in ways different from their European forebears. While the Europeans were packing their houses tightly and squeezing gardens into any available remaining space, white settlers in the New World were probing its vastness and defining themselves accordingly. Americans were individualists and explorers. Going it alone in nature wasn't just what they did so much as it defined who they were.

If wilderness is more an ideal than a reality, if natural wonders are selectively esteemed not for their intrinsic worth but because they stand for something of value to the human beholder, how are these places chosen? What is it in the natural world that we wish to save, even to worship? For surely there are things natural in this world in which we have little interest and that we have no desire to enshrine.

Many of our parks and preserves, obviously, are manifestations of a platonic ideal of nature as we think it should look. The Tetons of Wyoming, summits rising jagged and confident from the prairie, are embodiments of the ideal mountain range in our mind. Maybe we Americans make unconscious comparisons to the *real* mountains of Europe, with the Matterhorn being the perfect mountain, the shape against which all others are to be judged. Consider the numerous photographs of Nepal's Ama Dablam, much smaller than the big Himalayan peaks, but so much closer to the ideal than the more lofty but unfamiliar 28,208-foot Kanchenjunga, one of the world's biggest mountains, but too broad in shape, not pointed on top. For their perfect alpine symmetry, the Tetons are backdrop to probably more commercials and cowboy flicks, adorn more greeting cards and cheap calendars than any single piece of real estate in the nation. They have achieved their place in American reverence not because they actually represent the typical, but because they are precisely what we think the typical ought to be.

Conversely, many of our parks and preserves are created to protect things absolutely atypical, odd things, pieces of nature so unusual that they make us stop and wonder. Devil's Tower in northeastern Wyoming is one such place, where the columned stump rises 900 feet above the prairie. The Tower neither typifies the ideal nor is crucial to the existence of any particular species, nor does it serve some vital economic interest. We save it simply because it's so different. Same goes for Arches National Park, with its bizarre red stone bridges, and Yellowstone, with its geothermal geysers and pools, and of course the Grand Canyon. In their strangeness, places like these also give us the important reminder of the awful forces of nature and our relative place in things.

Standing on the rim of the Grand Canyon, we are ambivalent about wilderness; our attraction is born of fear. There's a visual aesthetic that draws us to the rim, but it is our uneasiness that leads us down into its depths. Had man no fear of animals or isolation, no discomfort from weather, no apprehension about great heights or vast distances, he would have little interest in subjecting himself to the discomforts necessarily part of a true wilderness encounter, little desire to backpack or mountain climb.

How many self-proclaimed outdoors people truly wish to encounter wilderness on its own terms, without the security of man-made things? Henry David Thoreau spent a stormy night high in the branches of a tall tree so that he could more intimately experience a storm. But the hardy outdoorsman today is more likely to gird himself in alternating layers of plastic underwear and Gore-Tex, arm himself with sophisticated technology—stoves, ropes, spring-loaded camming devices. At night before the climb, he lies awake absorbed in the fantasy, thinking not about the feel of rain on his bare skin, but about the sanctuary of his tent and the warmth of his sleeping bag. If we are not careful, ours might become an almost vicarious encounter with the elements. When we get swept into the materialism, there's more real pleasure to be had from shopping for and fondling the gear than actually suffering out its use. Standing at a trailhead, one old forest ranger watched a backpacker go by and remarked, "There goes another hundred pounds of lightweight gear."

The ambivalence about our encounters with nature show up everywhere as we rely on the "structures" and "installations" to help us find our way. How many Tucson climbers would enjoy Mount

Lemmon were it not for the highway? Yet how many of these same climbers would vote in favor of a referendum to carve a highway up Table Mountain? How many Yosemite purists complain about the cables route on Half Dome, yet how many opt for a more natural descent after climbing the Northwest Face? We love wilderness, but once the structures and installations are in place, we take their convenience for granted.

Given our confusion about wilderness and our dual desires to use it and to save it, there's little wonder that issues like climbing access will continue to be contentious. Aside from the many local struggles with climbing access (most resulting from fears of liability), the first closure with a national following occurred in Arizona's Superstition Mountains. Because the Supes are mainly odd towers of volcanic rock, much of the climbing is clearly bolt-dependent, not like so many other areas where clean removable protection is an option. As the issue heated up here and elsewhere, and as individual land managers began to make local and unpredictable rulings, climbers requested—and received—an official policy from the U.S. Forest Service. It wasn't the policy climbers had in mind. Instead, it stated a categorical adherence to the original Wilderness Act and defined officially that slings and bolts were, in fact, installations. Not only would a climber be in violation to install such an anchor, but simply using one would also be a crime. It was a policy that first surfaced up in Idaho's Sawtooth Mountain Wilderness, but is one that could well affect some of America's most cherished climbing destinations, like Yosemite, the Wind River Range, Joshua Tree, Tahquitz, and Linville Gorge, anyplace deemed a wilderness area.

The Forest Service was probably surprised at the breadth and volume of the opposition. Gear manufacturers and retailers, outdoor clubs, and even environmental groups like the Sierra Club howled that such categorical prohibition of climbing anchors would be the end of climbing and would unfairly target a single interest group while allowing many other, more destructive user groups to go on simply because they had deeper political connections. Congress felt the heat. At the 1999 Outdoor Retailer Trade Show in Salt Lake City, Undersecretary of the Interior Jim Lyons announced that the Forest Service plan had been temporarily rescinded and that the ultimate plan would involve more input from user groups. It was a sign of light. This book goes to print as climbers await a clarification. One likely and sensible outcome would be that local managers would be given wide latitude within the broader confines of the Wilderness Act to interpret policy according to the particular conditions of a place.

This ban on fixed anchors in designated federal wilderness areas is concerned with technical compliance with a regulation; it's not a battle between interest groups, like so many of the contests facing climbers. The wild lands of America mean different things to different groups, and when their interests collide, the search for compromise is difficult. Three such issues, case studies of sorts, have received lots of attention lately. Each is a struggle between competing interests, and in each case, no reasonable solution will be found unless all sides acknowledge their willingness to share the resource.

RAPTOR NESTING

The most common reason for cliff closure on public land is to protect nesting sites for peregrine falcons. Yes, there are countless other endangered plants and insects, but few are as visible and symbolic as the peregrine falcon. Even more than the bald eagle (which, after all, is a scavenger more than a hunter), the peregrine falcon embodies all we value about courage and strength. Soaring without restriction, diving at nearly two hundred miles per hour toward hapless prey, surveying the lowlands from perches hundreds of feet off the ground, the peregrine falcon is master of the high places.

Its role high on the food chain is also the bird's biggest liability, for the predator becomes final storage for any toxins ingested by the animals it eats. In the case of the peregrines and other large predatory birds, the killer was DDT, an insecticide that would weaken eggshells, causing them to break when parent birds sat upon the nest. Generation after generation would be lost, until by the late 1950s many of the historical nesting sites, principally in the East, were quiet.

When the culprit DDT was identified, it was banned, and an aggressive reintroduction program was launched. In New York, one such program brought Cornell University together with the State University at New Paltz to release western birds from the cliffs of the Shawangunks. Eggs were laid and hatched, then one by one, the young were picked off by great horned owls. Researchers later moved the release sites north to the Adirondacks, above the elevation where the owls were likely to hunt, while at the same time birds released earlier migrated south to New York City, establishing nests in the most unlikely places, like the Tappan Zee Bridge and downtown skyscrapers. Both suited the instinctive needs of the falcons just fine—elevated aeries with a steady food source of pigeons. The Adirondack program to the north was very successful, and by the year 2000, approximately fifteen nest sites were regularly bearing young. Success, however, demanded that climbers stay far from the cliff sites during a three- or four-month nesting period. Any disturbance early in the incubation process would cause the parents to leave the eggs untended and cold while they defended their nest. After the chicks had hatched, an intrusion might scare them into taking flight before they were ready.

All over the country, this cliff-dwelling bird vied for the same vertical real estate as the rock climber. Seasonal cliff closures became as ubiquitous to climbers as bad weather and loose rock. Cochise Stronghold, Granite Mountain, and Mount Lemmon Highway in Arizona; Joshua Tree, Yosemite, and Lover's Leap in California; Eldorado, the Black Canyon, and Lumpy Ridge in Colorado; Whitesides, Linville Gorge, and Looking Glass Rock in North Carolina; Cathedral Ledge, Cannon Cliff, and Rumney in New Hampshire—these and other of the country's top climbing areas saw partial closure to accommodate nesting peregrine falcons. In most cases, however, the climbers have not only respected the restrictions, but they have also actively supported the programs, identifying and monitoring nest sites, assisting with banding, and consulting with authorities over extent of the closures. Protecting the falcons has been an inconvenience, but in the bigger picture, sharing the resource with its original residents makes the climbing experience so much richer.

Sacred Tower

A second well-publicized contest of climbing rights occurred at Wyoming's Devil's Tower when Native Americans claimed the sacred rock was being desecrated by the presence and actions of climbers. Similar restrictions had already been in place in the Four Corners region of the Southwest, but these were on reservation, not public, lands.

The Tower sees about five thousand climbers annually, a number that has tapered off some from a high of almost seven thousand in 1991. Part of this decline is due to a voluntary closure as a gesture of respect for Native peoples who hold the Tower sacred. In fact, the name Devil's Tower was taken from an old Indian name, Bad Tower.

In 1996 the Mountain States Legal Foundation sued Secretary of the Interior Bruce Babbitt, the National Park Service, and the superintendent of Devil's Tower National Monument in an effort to overturn an official ruling closing the area each June out of respect for the beliefs of Native groups. Though the Tenth Circuit U.S. Court of Appeals upheld the policy, the Park Service has adopted a "voluntary closure," one monitored but not enforced. The response was embraced by the Access Fund, which agreed with the lawsuit in principle, but which at the same time wished to recognize the rights and plight of Native Americans. Here, and elsewhere, the Fund believed, some common ground must be found. Otherwise the two groups would be pitted against each other and both would lose.

Not all climbers agree with the Access Fund and the Park Service, however. In fact, Friends of Devil's Tower distributed a cartoon showing three people in bed together: one a Native American in ceremonial headdress, another wearing the Park Service's classic Smokey the Bear hat, and the third depicted as a representative of the Access Fund. The controversy over climbing at Devil's Tower has led to an unfortunate rift between interest groups, one of the most painful and publicized controversies in modern climbing. Led by outspoken guide Andy Petefish, Friends of Devil's Tower claims that the issue is a vital Constitutional one. The United States government simply cannot show deference toward any particular religious group at the expense of another. Petefish doesn't hold back in stating that climbing is his own spiritual quest, a belief no less valid than that held by anyone else. A few climbers have chosen to disregard the closure, but despite the announcement by Friends of Devil's Tower that "Devil's Tower is open in June," park officials estimate that there has been at least an 85 percent reduction in climbing during that month, with those exceptions being either uninformed visitors or guided parties who have consciously chosen to ignore the voluntary gesture.

A few years ago, the only thing that seemed to matter to climbers was the method by which bolts were placed. Traditionalists said the bolts needed to go in on a ground-up ascent. Sport-climbers didn't care how they were drilled, so long as they were safe and sensibly spaced. The two groups come together, however, when they contemplate the loss of an area to climbing. Although the debate of the 1980s was over the style of a climb, the issue at the turn of the twenty-first century will be the very right to climb. Devil's Tower is unique and precious. Climbers on both sides of the June closure are willing to fight for it. But if the groups get tangled among themselves, there won't be much of a united front in discussions with land managers who can shut the door at any time.

Free Hueco

"Have you ever been in your grandparents' house?" asks Alex Mares, park ranger and Native American, during a visitor's orientation. "There's an unwritten rule about the way you must behave there. There's a respect, an awe, for the generations who've gone before." The rocks of Hueco Tanks, he explains, have been home to hundreds of generations, where they've borne their young and buried their dead. It's been their grocery store and their post office, their meeting place, their shrine. Coronado's arrival in the Southwest began the clash of civilizations and the shedding of much blood, and though the ethnicities have mixed, the evidence of the cultural collision remains. Nowhere has it been more evident than at these outcrops in western Texas. To climbers, Hueco Tanks is ground zero, the battlefront where a 1998 ruling severely curtailed climbing. Since then, it's become a symbol of what could happen to climbing elsewhere if hostile bureaucrats get their wish. Seen through a different lens, however, Hueco could be a schoolroom and a model for climbers who acknowledge bigger values than raw athleticism.

Hueco Tanks State Historical Park is a collection of rocks twenty-five miles northeast of El Paso. Its three major formations are called mountains but in fact are little more than giant boulders, 200 to 300 feet high and covering a parcel of 860 acres. For eons, the syenitic porphyry (a kind of granite) has been exposed to harsh windblown sand, and wherever the hardened surface has been worn off, the softer rock underneath was hollowed out into fantastic shapes called *huecos,* some so deep that they serve as perennial water "tanks"; thus

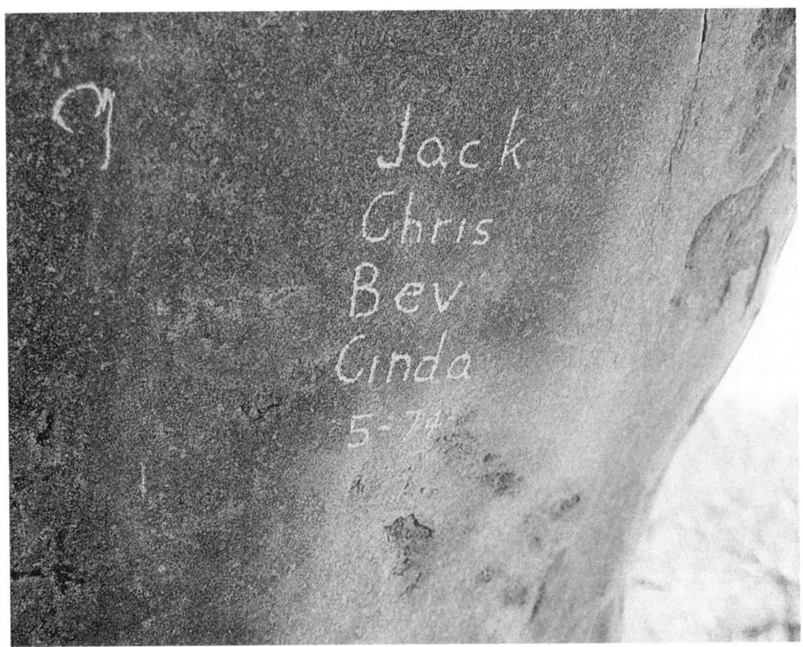

The pressure on Hueco Tanks began long before the arrival of climbers

the rocks were a vital stopover place for travelers. The rock surface is as good as it gets—it's absolutely climbable, with a proliferation of handholds, sharp solid edges, good friction. It's the perfect climbing environment.

The pioneer was Mike Head, who established the first series of bolt-protected routes in the late 1970s, often covertly to avoid arrest. Nighttime assaults were particularly productive. With the publication of his 1985 guidebook and a Todd Skinner cover shot on *Climbing* magazine the same year, the word had begun to spread, and the number of visitors steadily grew. In response to what they felt was irrevocable overuse, state park officials closed the cliffs to climbers in 1988. The next decade would see volleys lobbed back and forth between climbers and proponents of preservation, while the number of users grew and grew. For climbers, it was a decade of incredible activity at Hueco, the most energized scene outside Yosemite in American climbing history. The bouldering potential is especially good, and as this sport-within-a-sport exploded in popularity, Hueco became its Mecca.

Then in 1998, ten years after the initial closure, a comprehensive management plan went into effect. The reaction was swift and vocal. Ads appeared in climbing magazines showing well-known climbers, guns in hand, doing a little target practice. Not too subtle. The Access Fund howled in protest. Word around climbers' campfires all across the nation was that "they closed the place down, and it's time to fight." As in so many contentious struggles by special interest groups, sides scream so loudly that they fail to listen to the other. If quiet were to return, this is what they might hear from one side:

> *The Texas State Parks has no right to curtail a traditional use of a public land. Hueco is vital to climbers, every bit as important as it was to people who have gone before. It's simply the best bouldering in the world, birthplace of John Sherman's "V" system, magnet for international stars like Frederic Nicole, Jerry Moffatt, and Elie Chevieux. Hueco's boulder problems have been essential to the development of the sport. It's the perfect wintering area, and a climbing oasis in the southern heartland of the country. The ban targets the wrong crowd. It isn't climbers who have left their broken bottles and scratched their stupid graffiti into the rock. Climbers, more than any recreational user group, embody environmental sensitivity. It's counterproductive to alienate such a group.*

Blowing in the winds from the other direction:

> *Think about how long it took for huge woolly mammoths to rub the edges of boulders shiny smooth as they scratched their lice-infested hides against the rock. Imagine how many down-strokes are required to hollow out a rock basin for grinding grain? Now think about the tiny park overrun annually by 140,000 people, mostly climbers, as was the case in 1992. Imagine how quickly we'll lose the rock art, the tiny shrimp that come to life in the pools after a rain, how badly the ground will compact under so many irrever-*

> *ent feet. Imagine the hundred generations who have gone before, how gently they treated the place. Imagine this especially as you drive in from El Paso, past alternating acres of junk cars and fireworks stands, windblown, litter-strewn lots patrolled by packs of bony dogs. No, modern man can't be left on his own. The place needs rules.*

Climbing is still allowed but limited. North Mountain is open to fifty climbers per day; reservations help ensure a spot. Many places require a guide, available from the park, not to lead the climb but to make sure the visits don't compromise the historic treasures like the rock art. Newcomers are asked to take part in a short orientation that explains the sensitivity of many of the areas and reminds people that Hueco is decidedly a historical park, not a recreational one. Yes, most of the best bouldering is closed, and so the old scene will never return. The latest numbers indicated a 68 percent reduction in visitation after the regulations went into effect.

Many climbers will continue to see a bad situation here; they will take Scott Milton's advice in his 1999 *Rock & Ice* editorial to "wear the bureaucrats down" with letters. The El Paso Climbers Club is particularly energized over the issue. Climbers all over America are watching to see if this is a local anomaly or if restrictions will tighten like a noose around all places if agencies like Texas Parks and Wildlife wield an unnecessarily heavy hand.

But it's vital still that people both speak and listen. At one meeting, Alex Mares told the assembly, "Tonight those rocks are alone. No one is out there, just the plants and animals under the sky and the stars. No one owns the land. The land owns the people. The people come from the land, and the people will go back to the land. Someday the rock art will be gone, either through damage or natural erosion, but the rocks will endure long after the people are gone." Hueco Tanks is a different place with the 1999 regulations in place. No question. There are far fewer climbers. The soil is beginning to recover around the base of the cliffs. It's quiet. If you listen after a rain, you can hear the noise of tiny waterfalls all around, and as the hollows fill with water, tiny shrimp wriggle back to life.

AMERICANS DEEPLY RESENT REGULATION; it's an aversion old as the culture itself. But they also value wilderness, at least the idea of wilderness. They value private property and the right of landowners to decide the fate of their land. Americans also respect diversity and will usually defend the right of others to hold to whatever belief system they hold sacred. But vertical rock is limited and the number of climbers is growing. America used to be big. Its forests were endless, its borders mere hazy images far over an unimaginable horizon. The European settlers, rather than listening to the ways of the Natives already here, believed this to be a place without physical limit. Salmon, buffalo, trees, grazing lands—all could serve man's interests forever. It would take less than a hundred years for that horizon to take shape and the limits of the New World to be defined.

The romantic days of charging into the wilds and doing whatever you please are gone. Gone too is the idea that a single interest group can lock out another. Access to climbing areas in America, thus, depends on a deep respect for the place and a generous attitude toward those who see it in a different light.

EPILOGUE

I began *American Rock* with the idea that the distinctive experience one has at a climbing area is rooted in the larger culture. That culture is the aggregate of geography, weather, vegetation, and patterns of settlement. That the local climbers are made of this local stuff, and they practice their craft accordingly.

I started with a lot of anecdotal material that told me this was true: the cowboy strut of Todd Skinner and Paul Piana was elemental to the Wyoming climbing experience. They named their routes after rope tricks or knife fights. They carried guns on their way to put up new routes at Wild Iris in case they ran into bears. Sure, they were hamming it up, but still I always pictured Wyoming climbers wearing chaps, especially in the bad wide cracks of Vedauwoo.

Closer to home, my good friend Steve Larson was the embodiment of the New Englander: honest, positive, and willing to suffer. More than anyone else in my climbing career Steve pushed upon me the importance of traditional style, of climbing without cheating. He refused to go up on *Tourist Treat* (5.12) in his backyard cliff, Cathedral Ledge, because the crack had been deliberately overpitoned to create finger pockets. I remember being hit by a small avalanche on the Black Dike ice route, exactly the moment Steve had unzipped his woolen knickers to tuck in his shirt. When his pants filled with snow, he let out a laugh, "Isn't this great?" After he and I climbed El Cap together in 1976, I spent the next week and a half lying in the meadows looking up, striking up conversations with tourists, explaining to them how we "got the rope up there," what it was like to spend a night out in a nylon hammock. Steve didn't hang out with me to gloat. He got back to work, doing three six-day wall routes in a month.

I first met Kris Kline of North Carolina when he visited the Adirondacks about ten years ago. He was the first good climber I'd seen in a helmet. Like Steve up north, he didn't care what he looked like; he just loved to climb. Kris would visit regularly, pick out the hardest routes, regardless of protection ratings, and do them well. Last time I climbed with Kris was at Looking Glass. He led me up the crux pitch of a steep, eyebrowed route after I had backed off. Later, on the way back to his house in Asheville, he talked in serious tones about his allegiance to old-school, ground-up North Carolina climbing. It was important stuff to him, and when I climbed Whitesides, it seemed to me that the place was reserved for hard southern guys like Kline.

American climbing, to me, was a constellation of localities, each with its own styles and quirks and belief systems. In 1998, with this book in mind, I flew to Denver and rented a car, beginning a series of tours back to those old places to see if I was right.

I spoke to a lot of climbers along the way, and I explained to them what I was looking for. A lot of them agreed absolutely that the climbing experience in one place was different from that in another, but they couldn't put their finger on what those differences were, other than the obvious ones like rock type and weather. Isn't it the native influence? I would ask. Most would nod and say, "Sure, I guess so." But many thought I was reading too deeply into things.

Many of the climbers who did acknowledge the distinctiveness of individual climbing scenes were reluctant to connect the traits to the region. Black Diamond's Chris Harmston talked about the open, modest, positive scene in Salt Lake City, but said it has no connection with the city, the Mormonism, Black Diamond, or anything else in the region. It's simply a good scene and he's happy for it. Jimmy Surette, raised in New Hampshire and transplanted to the West, spoke derisively about the manufacturing of holds at the western sport-climbing areas, saying that he'd much prefer a good, natural line, preferably on granite. Asked if this preference wasn't evidence of his New England roots, he said, no, it's just that he likes granite and good lines.

Most climbers with whom I spoke thought that regionality was probably once important, but that the media and the travelers have blended the types together. *Rock & Ice* editor Dougald MacDonald thought it was probably more evident in older climbers. The young boulderers, he said, are the same everywhere you go. John Sherman said that because road tripping is so rampant, climbing everywhere is homogenized and the rules are becoming universal. In earlier times, he explained, there would be a local ethic, and peer pressure kept it intact. If there was a violation, there would be a response. Yet climbers today spend a lot of time outside their own community and aren't interested in local rules. To Sherman it's a basic sociological concept. Travel leads to homogenization. Regionality, he says, is a romantic myth.

As I look back, I see that *American Rock* began more as a mission than a report. I like the romantic myth, and I agreed when Doug Robinson wrote to me about resisting "the grinding forces of homogenization." The book, I think, evolved as I sifted the myths from the realities in my talks and travels.

Shortly before he left for Shishapangma, where he was killed in an avalanche, Alex Lowe was here in the Adirondacks. He shook his head at some of my thoughts about regional eccentricity. "Climbers are climbers," he said. What connects them is far more vital than what makes them different from each other.

On a recent trip to California, Nick Wakeman and I pulled into a campsite at the Needles. It was Thursday and the place was empty, save for a white VW camper and a guy named Josh who had strung a line of webbing, banjo-tight, between two big pines. He interrupted his tightrope walking exercise to give us some ideas about routes to do. With his friendly advice, we set off in the morning and had a really good day on really good granite. That evening, when we got back to camp, several more vehicles had pulled in. It was Friday, and the weekend had arrived. Men and women were standing about, sharing beers and talking excitedly about the routes they had had in mind and the climbs back home. Friendships were beginning.

Saturday, it didn't seem as though there were seven different parties at seven different campsites. Everyone had clustered around one red camper, the one with the biggest stove and the loudest music and the tacky candle-lanterns on sticks. Food and drink was communal.

There was lots of noise, and if you didn't join the family, you'd have a hard time sleeping. Sunday, after climbing, there were handshakes and the exchange of e-mail addresses with every intention of staying in touch.

How many times has this same scene unfolded, this coming together of strangers who share a passion for climbing? In the high desert campgrounds at Joshua Tree, along the muddy Colorado River outside Moab, below the T-Wall near Chattanooga, Camp 4, the Teton Climbers' Ranch. It's the same all across the land: sharing the wonder of America's incredible and diverse places with some of the best people you'll ever know.

ACKNOWLEDGMENTS

I suppose this book started in 1960. I was seven when my parents packed us five kids into a huge Chrysler station wagon and headed west to see the country. That trip left strong impressions on me about the importance of America's vastness and diversity, though with each trip as I got older, the country seemed more homogenized, the regions less quirky. Travels to Europe with my wife, Janet, gave me further opportunity to look from afar at our great land and to reflect on village life and the threat of encroaching modernization. Janet is an architect with a preservationist's bent, and she helped me think about the meaning of place in America.

The strongest influences on me when I started rock climbing in 1973 were the periodicals *Mountain, Summit,* and *Off Belay,* and more recently *Climbing* and *Rock & Ice.* Then there were the two thin manuals by Royal Robbins called *Basic Rockcraft* and *Advanced Rockcraft,* along with the 1972 Chouinard-Frost Equipment catalog, which ushered in the era of clean climbing. Outside influences rooted and grew, and my ideas about the meanings in American climbing evolved.

As *American Rock* took shape, I talked to a lot of climbers, including: Jeff Achey, Gary Allen, Henry Barber, Fred Beckey, John Bronaugh, Bruce Burgess, Tony Calderone, Russ Clune, Todd Eastman, Rick Fleming, Bob Gaines, Dennis Goode, Todd Goss, Chris Harmston, Jeremy Hass, Tom Herbert, Lynn Hill, Mark Ippolito, Porter Jarrard, Hans Johnston, Alan Jolley, Kris Kline, Fred Knapp, Colin Lantz, David Lovejoy, Alex Lowe, George Lowe, Jeff Lowe, Dougald MacDonald, Chris McNamara, Dan McQuade, Todd

Morgan, Bob Palais, Paul Piana, Patrick Purcell, Joe and Karen Quackenbush, Doug Reed, Doug Robinson, John Sherman, Harrison Shull, Geoff Tabin, Rick Thompson, Alex Van Steen, Alan Watts, Jim Waugh, Ed Webster, and Jesse Williams. Each conversation reminded me that one learns a lot more by climbing than by staying home trying to write about it.

Literary agent Susan Golomb named the book, encouraged me and The Countryman Press to get together, and, like my best belayers, freely told me to quit whining and get back to work whenever things got tough. Yet the most powerful words seeing me through the completion of *American Rock* came from my eight-year old daughter Elise, who kept saying "Daddy, when are you going to finish that stupid book so we can go do something together?"

INDEX

D

E

F

M

X

Y

Z

ABOUT THE AUTHOR

Don Mellor has been climbing, teaching climbing, and writing about climbing since the early seventies. He has climbed many of America's famous routes, including El Capitan, Half Dome, and the Diamond at Longs Peak, and has established more than 100 first ascents in the Adirondacks. He is Dean of Students at the Northwood School in Lake Placid, New York, and a guide at Rock and River Guide Service. Don is also the author of *Rock Climbing: A Trailside Guide* (W. W. Norton) and *Climbing in the Adirondacks* (Adirondack Mountain Club), and is the climbing expert on GORP.com.